THE NEW CLARENDON SHAKESPEARE

OTHELLO

Edited by

F. C. HORWOOD

Fellow and Tutor of
St. Catherine's College, Oxford

and

R. E. C. HOUGHTON

Emeritus Fellow of
St. Peter's College, Oxford

OXFORD UNIVERSITY PRESS

Oxford University Press, Walton Street, Oxford OX2 6DP

OXFORD NEW YORK TORONTO
DELHI BOMBAY CALCUTTA MADRAS KARACHI
PETALING JAYA SINGAPORE HONG KONG TOKYO
NAIROBI DAR ES SALAAM CAPE TOWN
MELBOURNE AUCKLAND

and associated companies in
BERLIN IBADAN

Oxford is a trade mark of Oxford University Press

First published 1968
Reprinted 1971, 1972, 1975, 1977, 1978, 1980, 1983, 1984, 1986,
1988, 1989

THE NEW CLARENDON SHAKESPEARE

Under the general editorship of R. E. C. HOUGHTON, M.A.

Printed in Hong Kong

CONTENTS

The text in this edition is printed
complete without expurgation

INTRODUCTION

AMONG Shakespeare's tragedies, *Othello* holds a place with *Antony and Cleopatra* for the beauty of its poetry, while far excelling it in beauty of structure. No other tragedy has its simplicity and swiftness of action: there is no sub-plot and no clownage of any space or significance. The play is tied fast to time: from the landings in Cyprus to Othello's suicide, the represented time, which appears to be continuous, occupies some thirty-three hours, from four o'clock on Saturday morning until the early hours of Monday morning. It is difficult to parallel its powers as 'theatre'. No character in the play is there simply as a function of the plot. Bradley speaks of it as the 'most painfully exciting and terrible' of the tragedies; and Johnson, who could not bear to reread *King Lear*, until he had to as editor, wrote in similar terms and for the same reason of the last scene of *Othello*: 'I am glad I have ended my revisal of this dreadful scene: it is not to be endured.'

The peculiar painfulness of the play arises from two main sources: from the especial hatefulness which destroys a world of uncommon beauty and splendour; and, more than this, from the fact that good itself is made the agent of evil in this destruction. No other hero of Shakespeare's dies such a lonely death as Othello, who has destroyed his own heaven, except Macbeth, who has made his own hell. The most powerful aspect of tragic mystery is that a man's very virtues, the qualities that the world values and needs, may bring him to ruin. Iago's opportunity lies, as he knows, in the goodness of Othello, who is of a 'free and open nature'. Only an Iago could see through an Iago. Shakespeare has taken special pains to show that Othello's trustfulness is not crass stupidity, for no one else in the play knows the real Iago, not even Roderigo. This is the reason why Iago is the most prolific soliloquist in Shakespeare, and only the audience look into the pit of his mind. Though much of the play deals with the ugly disease of jealousy, this is not self-induced; and Coleridge, with his usual moral insight, points out, when comparing Othello with Leontes (of *The Winter's Tale*), that Othello shows no signs of the *naturally* jealous man. His statement in his last moving speech, that he was 'not easily jealous', is strictly true. As we have been lately reminded, those who wonder at the speed of his collapse are thinking in terms of the novel, and not in terms of the time that the dramatist has at his disposal for the theatre.

Even so, Shakespeare more than once puts a strain on our sympathy with Othello. It is indeed painful to see a great man gulled, and to hear the change in his mode of speech that accompanies it. The scene when Othello sees but does not hear the conversation between Iago and Cassio, and, later, Bianca, is near to the burlesque. The instruction to Iago to put Emilia to spy on Desdemona is a vulgarity. The public striking of Desdemona is horrifying. The murder scene is agonizing. At such points, impatience and even anger with the hero are close to the surface; and no other Shakespearian hero, not even, oddly enough, Macbeth, runs more risks with the audience than Othello. It is perhaps for this reason that the character of Othello has been variously interpreted, not least in our own day. If Shakespeare sees with compassion, he also sees with severity, and we are not spared the final stages of Othello's degradation. In this respect Emilia acts as an important safety-valve when in the last scene she says that Desdemona 'was too fond of her most filthy bargain'.

Nevertheless, though still grievously deceived, the Othello of the last scene has regained the nobility he lost to Iago. The 'Iago-Othello' occurs even here from time to time; but the opening and closing speeches of the scene are pure examples of the 'Othello music'. The poetry of the play, which he dominates, as Iago dominates the prose, expresses a simple and a single character, but also one, as Bradley puts it, 'almost from wonderland', as he seems, indeed, to Desdemona. Thrilling rhythms and exotic references come naturally from him, so that a tale of marvels seems like 'a round unvarnished tale'. He is sometimes thought of as the most poetical of Shakespeare's heroes, by which is meant not that he is a poet, but that the medium which delineates him—the poetry—is of a particularly 'romantic' kind, expressive of his strange origin and career. The world he loves and has lived in is one of war, hardship, adventure, and travel; only the love of Desdemona persuades him to give up his 'unhoused free condition'. Thereafter, the two loves are one. Love in *Othello* is not seen as an isolated self-sufficing activity, but contains the whole of life, of honour, of action, and of glory. So it is that Othello's first great lament for his loss of faith in Desdemona is a farewell to the 'pride, pomp and circumstance of glorious war'. Where he has 'garnered up his heart' he must either 'live or bear no life'. Sylvester's fine line is true of him:

Not where I move, but where I love I live.

It is clear from the plays that Shakespeare had an obsessive hatred of deceitful appearance or false 'seeming' (cf. I. i. 60). Iago is the most concentrated and protracted expression of this in his works. He shifts from appearance to reality and back again like a chameleon, and could have made his fortune as an actor. He is the only example of studied personal revenge throughout the plays. Coleridge thought his soliloquies showed 'the motive-hunting of a motiveless malignity'. Iago, in fact, supplies himself with plenty of motives—too many; but his avowed motives are not necessarily those he believes in. Perhaps the most significant betrayal of what actuates him seems to be the half-involuntary and casually placed, as if it had been unconscious, tribute to Cassio:

> He hath a daily beauty in his life
> That makes me ugly.

Conversely, in his first soliloquy, he says simply 'I hate the Moor', and the 'motive' which follows is not causal but conjunctive, not 'for' but 'and':

> And it is thought abroad that 'twixt my sheets
> He has done my office.

The syntax makes this 'motive-hunting' with a vengeance.

Really, the only circumstantial motive he has is that of injured merit, which is put forward in the first scene (and only toyed with once again). He thinks he has been unfairly overlooked. The Signiory does not share his views of Cassio's efficiency when it appoints him to succeed Othello in Cyprus. When the play opens, Iago has no plot, only a desire to hurt and irritate. It has been said that he does not foresee all the consequences of what he starts, and that from III. iii. 360 onwards he is the victim of his own contrivings, and in personal danger unless he continues. This may be; but it is moonshine to suppose that he does not revel in what he now must do. Among his 'motives', no doubt, is a desire to add to the mean dossier of his life that he keeps, 'to have something more "on" them' (J. Bayley), i.e. on Desdemona, Othello, and Cassio. They have to be pinned in his book of behaviour, like museum butterflies. Therefore Cassio and Othello must cuckold him, he himself must lust for Desdemona, Desdemona must long for Cassio.

Only a masterly portrayal of Iago's kind of evil could

make the seduction of Othello tolerable for audience or reader. But we must not listen to talk of his 'supreme intellectual power', or Swinburne's absurd suggestion that his activities are those of a suppressed poet. He is shrewd but plebeian. His analysis of life, in the end, is worthless. He is very clever; he is a consummate actor; he knows how to manipulate good or weak men; he can improvise and be adroit. But he is much favoured by circumstances. The irregular nature of the marriage; Brabantio's grief, and his ominous words, as they come to seem; Othello's colour; Othello's ignorance of Venice; the nature of the very courtly Cassio and his innocent adoration of Desdemona; the obtuseness of Roderigo, and, in her own way, of Emilia; the unlucky handkerchief; above all, the characters of Desdemona and Othello, not merely good, but good in the way he can get at—all these are facts that he knows how to make the most of. He could not have succeeded without them; but a stupid man could not have succeeded with them. One of his triumphs is to involve Othello in his own world of generalizations. Neither Othello nor Desdemona makes a single generalization until they are caught by, or affected by, Iago. Once Othello picks up the 'generalizing trick' from Iago, he is lost: 'And, yet, how nature erring from itself'—he begins (III. iii. 227) and forgets from then on, except spasmodically ('If she be false, O! then heaven mocks itself!'), that, however nature itself may err, this particular Desdemona is true.

When all is said and done, Iago is an outsider, not just in a modern colloquial sense, but with a deeper meaning for the play and for the moral world at large. He is the only character in the play who is loveless. Even Roderigo, gull as he is, speaks some sort of language of love, and hears with incredulity Iago's views of Desdemona (II. i. 256 ff.); even poor Bianca shows her anxious care for Cassio. In Shakespeare's source, the Ensign at least has for motive his rejected love for Desdemona; the hint of this in our play (II. i. 303–6) is not a motive but an excuse. In the play he derives his excitement from manipulating other men's emotions, not in satisfying his own; and Bradley's perception of his peculiar 'deadness of feeling' is acute.

It is particularly horrible that so much malice should fall on the most loving of Shakespeare's heroines. The tale that Othello tells before the Signiory in Desdemona's absence gives the secret of their love. There, the appealing mingling of the domestic and the exotic, the familiar and the strange, of 'house-affairs' and of 'antres vast and deserts idle' sums up their relationship. It is not true to say that 'Desdemona's sense of Othello is more real to both of them, than is the sense of Desdemona to either'. They delight in each other's worlds and natures, though they speak differently about them. Othello delights in Desdemona's femininity, and she in his masculinity. When they meet on the quay at Cyprus after the dangerous voyage is over, there is a world of sex-difference in their speeches. Othello's splendid hyperboles touch hills of seas, hell, heaven, death, and Olympus before they reach the 'content so absolute' that Desdemona can give. She, who is not imaginative, speaks only of love and comfort as their 'days do grow'. It is through her that the domestic atmosphere as an important meaning of the play is expressed. Shakespeare wrote three tragedies of love, but this is the only one of marriage. In it 'the rapturous lark-and-nightingale rhapsodies' of Romeo and Juliet's wedding night are replaced by a maturer scene. As for Antony and Cleopatra, who could associate married life with either?

Brabantio, who does not know his daughter well, speaks of her as 'a maiden never bold', and can only suppose that magic arts have captured her. The daring of her elope-ment is all the greater when seen against her normal demeanour. She is fully conscious herself of her 'downright violence and storm of fortunes'. We must not underestimate Brabantio's shock, so great that it causes his death of a broken heart. If we do, we underestimate Desdemona's spirit, which is demonstrated not only in action but in her words before the Signiory. It is to be noted, however, that no other good character in the play makes anything of Othello's colour. Desdemona dismisses the matter with her memorable line 'I saw Othello's visage in his mind'; and thereafter it becomes material for Iago's plot. (And indeed Shakespeare is not concerned to show the particular jealousy of a Moor but of a man.)

She is a creature of extreme simplicity, a girl of natural goodness, always busy in acts of love, whether on behalf of Cassio, or in seeing to Othello's comfort. She shows a pretty, coaxing address in her intercessions for Cassio. That from Act III, Scene iv onwards she becomes progressively more bewildered with the change in the Othello she thought she knew, is natural enough. Good people are slow to suspect, and ready to blame themselves, or to find excuses ('Something sure of State . . . Hath puddled his clear spirit'). Hence her advocacy of Cassio at a dangerous time for both of them is not tactlessness but innocence. Her attempt to explain the puzzle by supposing that she had not allowed for the difference between courtship and marriage is deeply pathetic: we must not look, she says, 'for such observancy As fits the bridal'. She has been compared with Cordelia of *King Lear*, whose kind of constant love she shares, but not her uncompromising truth. Her 'foible of fibbing' produces only social lies, and anyone who attempts to make them more 'ought to be forbidden', as Raleigh says, 'to read Shakespeare'. It is true that Cordelia would not have begged for time before she was stifled ('But half an hour') and would have demanded reasons for her husband's lunatic behaviour. But then 'character is destiny', as the old saw says, and so long as we realize that this implies no moral guilt we are safe enough. Desdemona's last lie is sublime and ridiculous: 'Nobody: I myself'. She dies holding to her innocence, and trying to include Othello in it.

Othello expresses the sense of tragic incomprehensibility or mystery in its most poignant form. There is no attempt to account for the origin of evil, and no mitigation of the suffering of the innocent. Although Othello is a Christian, the play is insulated, like other Shakespearian tragedies, from religion, and no assurance comes from beyond the world that there is a meaning other than the secular in what happens. Othello's suicide is seen as the only possible *amende*. Nevertheless, in the world of the play there is brightness, splendour, heroism, and constant love, which are seen as supreme values. Dowden thought 'the spiritual motive that controls the tragedy' is that 'there is something more inimical to humanity than suffering—namely, an incapacity for noble pain . . . To die as Othello dies is indeed grievous. But to live as Iago lives, devouring the dust and stinging—this is more appalling.' We must not attempt to palliate Shakespearian tragedy; but the nobility and love which it portrays, even though these are crushed, are assertions which endure. Some commentators have seen in the tears that Othello's eyes let fall 'as fast as the Arabian trees Their med'cinable gums' tears of joy that Desdemona was true. It is good, at least, to think so.

THE DATE OF THE PLAY

Othello is first recorded as having been played on 1 November 1604 at Whitehall, by Shakespeare's company. This need not mean that *Othello* was a new play at this date; in the same record, other earlier plays of Shakespeare appear, including *The Comedy of Errors*, a play which belongs to the early nineties. It has also been claimed (by Greg) that a 'bad' (i.e. unauthorized) version of *Hamlet*, published in 1603, contains a few recollections from *Othello*, introduced by players who had previously acted in it. Some other supposed evidences of date, as, for example, an echo in *The Honest Whore* of 1604, are too vague to be of any use.

Although E. K. Chambers puts four plays between *Hamlet* and *Othello*, it is often thought that *Othello* was the next play written after *Hamlet* (1601). Bradley sees points of resemblance with *Hamlet* in style, diction, and versification which do not appear very convincing, while the substance of the two plays is quite dissimilar. The argument from imagery or atmosphere, namely that, as *Hamlet* deals with the corruption of a land and people by poisoning, so *Othello* deals with a particular instance of this, is far from persuasive. In short, any argument as to date which rests on any particular resemblances with *Hamlet* can get us nowhere. Tone, atmosphere, speech, situation, heroes, all are different.

On the other hand, in its own idiom and structure, *Othello* is at least as clearly a product of maturity as *Hamlet*. Othello is as clearly individualized in his speeches as Hamlet in his, different as their styles are; the bold and swift movement of *Othello* is at least as masterly as the digressive technique of *Hamlet*, and both suit their themes and characters.

In view of the vague nature of any evidence which tries to tie the play down too closely as to date, it seems best to rely on our one known fact, namely that *Othello* was first acted in late 1604. It could have been written any time between 1601 and then.

THE TEXT

Othello was first published in quarto size in 1622, the latest of the Shakespeare Quartos. It was followed within less than a year by the publication of the (First) Folio, the first collected edition of Shakespeare's plays, undertaken by his friends and fellow-actors, Heminge and Condell. *Othello* is unique in having a Quarto so close to a Folio publication, and speculation has been fertile as to the relation between the two texts, and on what sources they may respectively have been based.

There are about a thousand differences of reading between the two texts, of which a fairly large number can be regarded as misreadings, e.g. Quarto's 'returne' for Folio's 'relume' at v. ii. 13. But mistakes will not account for such differences as Q's 'utmost pleasure' and F's 'very quality', at I. iii. 253, or Q's 'Does bear all excellency' and F's 'Does tyre the Ingenieur' at I. ii. 65.

There are 160 more lines in F than in Q. Some of the matter found in F and not in Q may be due to a compositor's oversights; but the great bulk of it cannot be so regarded. Thus, in Q, a speech of Roderigo lacks 17 lines (I. i. 121–37), of Brabantio 6 lines (I. ii. 72–77), of the First Senator 7 lines (I. iii. 24–30), and of Emilia 18 lines (IV. iii. 89–106). Othello's Pontic sea simile (III. iii. 454–61) is not in Q; Desdemona's 'Here I kneel . . .' (IV. ii. 151–64), the Willow Song in IV. iii, and therefore Emilia's reference to it (v. ii. 244–7), are missing. These lines are undoubtedly Shakespearian, and justified on every dramaturgical and emotional ground. So, on dramatic grounds, the 17 lines in F which Roderigo does not speak in Q add immensely to the clarity of the exposition; or, on the second ground, who could now imagine IV. iii without the Willow Song? It has been suggested that the absence of these passages in Q is the result of stage-cuts to shorten the performance on some occasion. But, it has been pointed out, it takes only eight minutes to deliver a hundred and sixty lines of Shakespearian blank verse at a reasonable pace in a stage performance. No producer in his senses would sacrifice so much of value to gain eight minutes out of two hours and three quarters.

It seems to the present editor (following Coghill and other critics) that Q represents Shakespeare's first version of the play, and F his revision. He was a playwright, and saw, after performance, what could be strengthened dramatically; he was a poet, and saw what could be improved in style and psychology. Even such a curious variant as 'acerbe'/'bitter' (I. iii. 355) seems to be in favour of this theory. A leading actor might well have objected to Shakespeare that he disliked hissing like a snake ('as acerbe as'), particularly as he ran the danger of being unintelligible into the bargain. On the principle of *praestat difficilior lectio* (the more difficult reading is more likely to be the right one), to say nothing of the fact that the word is found in his source (in the super-lative, *acerbissimo*), it seems likely that 'acerbe' was the original Shakespearian word, congenial to his verbal acquisitiveness, but nevertheless altered by him after-wards.

The above discussion is summary, and does little justice to the complexity of the arguments deployed for the relationship of Q to F, or to their sources. Most modern editors follow F, but keep some Q readings (about 170). No good editor can afford to follow either through thick and thin, any more than in *King Lear*. (For an almost desperate attempt to stick to Q see the Commentary at v. ii. 362.) It is not the business of the present edition to produce a new or controversial text; its basis is the Oxford one-volume Shakespeare, edited by W. J. Craig, which is followed except for a number of mainly minor alterations. The more important of these changes are listed below:

I. i. 100 'bravery' (Q) for 'knavery' (F).

I. iii. 259 'rights' for 'rites' (Q, F).

I. 265–6

> Nor to comply with heat the young affects
> In my defunct and proper satisfaction (Q, F)

for Nor to comply with heat—the young effects
In me defunct—and proper satisfaction (an
emendation).

I. iii. 355 'acerbe' (Q) for 'bitter' (F).

III. iii. 123 'dilations' (F) for 'delations' (emendation).

III. iii. 448 'cell' (Q) for 'hell' (F).

IV. i. 21 'infections' (F) for 'infected' (Q).

IV. ii. 54 'Slow unmoving' (Q) for 'slow and moving' (F).

IV. ii. 108 'greatest abuse' (Q) for 'least misuse' (F).

THE PLAY ON THE ELIZABETHAN STAGE

Othello appears to have been acted first at Whitehall, that is, in the sumptuously appointed Banqueting House, before the Court. This, however, can scarcely be regarded as a typical Elizabethan stage, as far as such a type can be found. A simplified statement of the Elizabethan and Jacobean stage might perhaps be as follows:

1. It has a Front Stage, sometimes called the Platform, sometimes the Outer Stage, on three sides perhaps surrounded by audience, above as well as around. Bigger actions, and intimate confidences to the audience, would take place here—well forward, perhaps, for soliloquies.

2. It had an Inner Stage, sometimes called the Study or Rear Stage, usually reckoned to be about 7 or 8 feet in depth and 20 feet or more in width. This was used for 'interior' scenes and 'discoveries', e.g. in *The Tempest*, Act v, Scene i. These sometimes required properties such as tables, chairs, or beds.

3. It also had an Upper Stage or gallery, sometimes called the Chamber. This was used very many times in Shakespeare's plays as the walls of a town or castle, the

upper storey of a house, and for other miscellaneous elevated positions, places of observation, and so on.

Nearly all the scenes of *Othello* take place on the Front Stage, or in a combination of Front and Inner Stage. Thus all street scenes would be Front Stage; Act I, Scene iii, which, according to Q, discovers the 'Duke and Senators set at a Table with lights and attendants', would probably begin on the Inner Stage and move to the Front Stage as more actors came in—quite a crowd—at line 47. Act IV, Scene ii may perhaps begin on the Inner Stage, but it is not necessary that it should do so.

The most important use of the Inner Stage would probably be in Act V, Scene ii for the bed in which Desdemona sleeps. It both dominates and lies at the back of the whole scene, and is already mutely present in IV. iii. It is quite clear from l. 103 of v. ii ('let me the curtains draw') and ll. 363–4 ('the object poisons sight. Let it be hid') that curtains could be drawn over the bed and its load. Othello did the murder with his back to the audience, and presumably half-obscuring Desdemona; so that the visual horror of the act is subdued, as perhaps it was in the blinding of Gloucester in *Lear* (though this is not so certain).

As for the Upper Stage, *Othello* is one of the twenty plays of Shakespeare which require it, and one of the twelve which require it only once. This is when Brabantio appears 'at a window' at l. 81 of Act I. i.

'In his use of a gallery over the stage Shakespeare usually introduces a secondary action aloft in support of an original action upon the stage below' (R. Hosley). This is an ideal description of what happens in Act I, Scene i of *Othello*. It is directly parallel with Juliet's appearance on the balcony, where below Romeo awaits her (*Romeo and Juliet*, II. ii). It may also be taken as a general illustration of the use of the various parts of what we can gather was an Elizabethan stage. The use was fluid. Outer, Inner and Upper merged as dramatic wholes, and no scheme such as the above can be regarded as rigid.

THE PLOT OF THE PLAY

I. i. Brabantio, a Senator and father of Desdemona, is awakened in the night by Iago and Roderigo and told that his daughter has eloped with Othello. He sets off with a strong guard to arrest him.

I. ii. Iago warns Othello of Brabantio's anger. Cassio comes with an urgent summons from the Duke to his council. A clash with Brabantio and his followers seems imminent, but eventually the whole party goes off to the Duke's council.

I. iii. The Duke and the Senators are discussing the intentions of the Turks in respect of Cyprus. Brabantio's charge against Othello of using witchcraft or drugs to win Desdemona is refuted by both of them, and dismissed by the Duke. Othello is to go that night to Cyprus, and Desdemona is given permission to come after him in the care of Iago. Left alone with Roderigo, Iago persuades him to enlist and to go to Cyprus in disguise. Alone on the stage, Iago begins to reveal his true nature.

II. i. The scene changes to Cyprus during a terrifying storm, which disperses and destroys the Turkish fleet. Cassio arrives from sea, and is followed in a second vessel by Desdemona, Emilia, Iago, and Roderigo. Anxiety is felt for the fate of Othello, till he arrives in a third vessel.

Iago now sets in train the plot to ruin Cassio, having first pretended to Roderigo that Desdemona loves Cassio. Roderigo is to provoke Cassio into striking him that night when on guard duty. The scene ends with Iago's second major soliloquy.

II. ii. A celebration is proclaimed by a Herald to last

from five in the afternoon, the time of the proclamation, to eleven o'clock that night.

II. iii. On a pretence of good-fellowship, Iago persuades Cassio to drink. Cassio gets drunk, is provoked by Roderigo, and beats him. Montano is also wounded by Cassio. Iago sends Roderigo to ring the alarm-bell, which rouses the town and brings Othello and Desdemona on the scene. Othello cashiers Cassio.

Iago advises Cassio to ask Desdemona to intercede for him with Othello. When he is gone, Iago utters his third main soliloquy. The scene ends with the return of a disgruntled Roderigo, who is put off by Iago, and with a few more details of the plot, uttered in soliloquy by Iago.

III. i. Early the same morning, Cassio arrives before the Castle with some musicians to play wedding-music for the General, and also to ask Emilia to bring him where he can talk to Desdemona alone.

III. ii. Othello goes down to inspect the fortifications, and orders Iago to come after him.

III. iii. Desdemona promises Cassio her help in regaining his lieutenancy. As they are talking, they see Othello and Iago approaching, and Cassio, ill at ease, goes away. This gives Iago a change to begin the temptation of Othello, who, however, does not notice it. Desdemona begins her pleading for Cassio, but Othello is not yet ready for it, and desires to be left alone with Iago. Iago begins again, and makes much progress with the corruption of Othello. This is interrupted by the approach of Desdemona and Emilia. It is here that the fatal handkerchief is lost. It is picked up by Emilia and given to Iago, who, in a brief fourth soliloquy, speaks of his intention to leave it at Cassio's lodging.

A now almost convinced Othello returns, and the scene ends with their joint determination to kill Desdemona and Cassio.

III. iv. Desdemona, perturbed by the loss of the handkerchief, now has a painful encounter with Othello, enigmatic as far as she is concerned, in which he tells her of the magical properties of the handkerchief, and the disastrous consequences of its loss. She tells a white lie about this, but fatally proceeds to an intercession for Cassio. She becomes aware of a new and strange Othello, and later tells Cassio that the time is unpropitious for her to solicit Othello for him.

Cassio gives the handkerchief to Bianca for her to copy its embroidery.

IV. i. The corruption of Othello continues. Told that Cassio has confessed to lying with Desdemona, Othello falls in a trance. Iago arranges that he shall see but not hear him in conversation with Cassio, and believe it is Desdemona they are talking about, not Bianca. At the end of the conversation, Bianca appears by chance, bearing the handkerchief to throw back at Cassio because it is another woman's. When Cassio and Bianca have gone, Othello and Iago arrange that Desdemona shall be strangled in her bed that night by Othello, while Iago shall murder Cassio.

Letters of recall for Othello are brought by Lodovico, a kinsman of Brabantio. Cassio is to be placed in command of a Cyprus now at peace. Misconstruing the conversation of Desdemona with Lodovico, Othello strikes and further humiliates Desdemona.

IV. ii. Othello disbelieves Emilia's assertions of her mistress's chastity and treats both as inmates of a brothel.

Iago now has to deal with a very dissatisfied Roderigo. He does so by telling him the lie that Othello is to be sent to Mauritania, and that the best way to keep him in Cyprus with Desdemona is to knock out Cassio's brains.

IV. iii. This scene is concerned with Desdemona's

preparations for bed, her singing of the Willow Song, and a conversation with Emilia about marital infidelity.

v. i. Roderigo's attack on Cassio's life is unsuccessful, but both are wounded. Othello, believing Cassio to have been killed, leaves to dispatch Desdemona. Lodovico and Gratiano come in, which prevents the lurking Iago from ending Cassio, but allows him to finish off Roderigo. Cassio is taken off for treatment, and Emilia sent by Iago to tell Othello and Desdemona what has happened.

v. ii. Othello enters with a speech about his purpose and its motives. After an agonizing dialogue with Desdemona, he stifles her. Immediately on this, Emilia knocks for admission, and comes in to tell him that Cassio has killed Roderigo (as all believe). She discovers Desdemona's murder. She learns that her husband was responsible for Othello's belief in Desdemona's guilt, and calls for help. On the entry of Iago with Montano, Gratiano, and others, she reveals the truth about the handkerchief and about Iago. He stabs her and escapes. Othello is confined to the room, apparently without a sword, with Gratiano as guard outside. He entices Gratiano, who believes he is weaponless, into the room, and then produces his other sword, but not for offence.

Lodovico and Montano come in with Cassio in a chair, and Iago prisoner. Iago has partly confessed his villainy off-stage, but expresses his determination to say no more. His plot is, however, exposed from letters found in Roderigo's pocket, and by his own words on reviving, and by Cassio's account of his finding the handkerchief in his room. Lodovico takes command, puts Othello under guard, places Cassio in his stead, and condemns Iago to torture. Othello, after a moving speech, stabs himself. Lodovico leaves to report the dreadful facts to the Senate of Venice.

DRAMATIS PERSONAE

DUKE OF VENICE.

BRABANTIO, a Senator. Other Senators.

GRATIANO, Brother to Brabantio.

LODOVICO, Kinsman to Brabantio.

OTHELLO, a noble Moor; in the service of the Venetian State.

CASSIO, his Lieutenant.

IAGO, his Ancient.

RODERIGO, a Venetian Gentleman.

MONTANO, Othello's predecessor in the Government of Cyprus.

Clown, Servant to Othello.

DESDEMONA, Daughter to Brabantio, and Wife to Othello.

EMILIA, Wife to Iago.

BIANCA, Mistress to Cassio.

Sailors, Officers, Gentlemen, Messengers, Musicians, Heralds, Attendants.

SCENE.—*For the first Act, in Venice; during the rest of the Play, at a Sea-Port in Cyprus.*

OTHELLO
THE MOOR OF VENICE

ACT I

Scene I. VENICE. A STREET

Enter RODERIGO *and* IAGO.

Roderigo. Tush! Never tell me; I take it much unkindly
That thou, Iago, who hast had my purse
As if the strings were thine, shouldst know of this.

Iago. 'Sblood, but you will not hear me:
If ever I did dream of such a matter,   5
Abhor me.

Roderigo. Thou told'st me thou didst hold him in thy hate.

Iago. Despise me if I do not. Three great ones of the city,
In personal suit to make me his lieutenant,
Off-capp'd to him; and, by the faith of man,   10
I know my price, I am worth no worse a place;
But he, as loving his own pride and purposes,
Evades them, with a bombast circumstance
Horribly stuff'd with epithets of war;
And, in conclusion,   15
Nonsuits my mediators; for, 'Certes,' says he,

The letter [N] in the footnotes indicates that a *further* note on
that line will be found in the Commentary at the end.

1 **Never ... me :** phrase expressing incredulity [N].   2, 3 **who
... thine :** who have had complete control of my money.   3 **this :**
i.e. the elopement.   4 **'Sblood :** an oath (God's blood).   10 **Off-
capp'd :** took off their caps (as a mark of respect).   **by the faith
of man :** as surely as you can trust any man.   12 **loving ...
purposes :** conscious of his own position, and liking his own way.
13 **bombast circumstance :** inflated, detailed, and evasive
speeches [N].   14 **epithets :** terms [N].   16 **Nonsuits :** rejects
[N].   **mediators :** supporters.   **Certes :** certainly (a monosyllable
here).

'I have already chose my officer.'
And what was he?
Forsooth, a great arithmetician,
One Michael Cassio, a Florentine,   20
A fellow almost damn'd in a fair wife;
That never set a squadron in the field,
Nor the division of a battle knows
More than a spinster; unless the bookish theoric,
Wherein the toged consuls can propose   25
As masterly as he: mere prattle, without practice,
Is all his soldiership. But he, sir, had the election;
And I—of whom his eyes had seen the proof
At Rhodes, at Cyprus, and on other grounds
Christian and heathen—must be be-lee'd and calm'd   30
By debitor-and-creditor; this counter-caster,
He, in good time, must his lieutenant be,
And I—God bless the mark!—his Moorship's ancient.
 Roderigo. By heaven, I rather would have been his
 hangman.
 Iago. Why, there's no remedy: 'tis the curse of the
 service,   35
Preferment goes by letter and affection,
Not by the old gradation, where each second

19 **arithmetician**: theorist [*N*]. 21 **A fellow ... wife**:
(perhaps) a man so silly as to be about to marry [*N*]. 22 **set**:
arranged, manœuvred. **field**: battlefield. 23 **division**:
disposition. 24 **unless**: except for. **theoric**: theory. 25 **toged**
(disyllabic): wearing a toga, the dress of a civilian at Rome.
consuls: magistrates, rulers (cf. I. ii. 43). 27 **had the election**:
was chosen. 28 **proof**: test. 30 **be be-lee'd**: have the wind
taken out of my sails. **calm'd**: becalmed [*N*]. 31 **debitor-
and-creditor**: a mere clerk. **counter-caster**: accountant [*N*].
32 **in good time**: if you please! (scornful). 33 **God ... mark**:
expression of impatient scorn. **ancient**: ensign, i.e. standard-
bearer [*N*]. 35 **Why ... remedy**: well, there it is! 36 **Preferment**: promotion. **affection**: favouritism [*N*]. 37 **old
gradation**: promotion according to seniority.

Stood heir to the first. Now, sir, be judge yourself,
Whe'r I in any just term am affin'd
To love the Moor.

   Roderigo.   I would not follow him then.   **40**

   Iago. O! sir, content you;
I follow him to serve my turn upon him;
We cannot all be masters, nor all masters
Cannot be truly follow'd. You shall mark
Many a duteous and knee-crooking knave,   **45**
That, doting on his own obsequious bondage,
Wears out his time, much like his master's ass,
For nought but provender, and when he's old, cashier'd;
Whip me such honest knaves. Others there are
Who, trimm'd in forms and visages of duty,   **50**
Keep yet their hearts attending on themselves,
And, throwing but shows of service on their lords,
Do well thrive by them, and when they have lin'd their
   coats
Do themselves homage: these fellows have some soul;
And such a one do I profess myself. For, sir   **55**
It is as sure as you are Roderigo,
Were I the Moor, I would not be Iago:
In following him, I follow but myself;
Heaven is my judge, not I for love and duty,
But seeming so, for my peculiar end: **60**

---

   39 Whe'r: whether.   **in ... term**: in any way justly.   **affin'd**:
bound.   **41 content you**: don't worry about that.   **44 You
... mark**: you can see.   **45 knee-crooking**: subservient.
47 Wears out: spends.   **48 cashier'd**: (is) cast off.   **49 Whip
me**: may such simpletons be hanged [*N*].   **50 trimm'd ...
duty**: disguised or dressed up in the (outward) manners and looks of
an obedient servant.   **51 Keep ... themselves**: i.e. think first
of themselves.   **52 throwing ... on**: only appearing to serve.
53 their coats: i.e. their pockets.   **54 soul**: spirit.   **57 Were
... Iago**: i.e. I behave like this because I am a subordinate [*N*].
59 not I: I do not follow him.   **60 peculiar**: private, own.

For when my outward action doth demonstrate
The native act and figure of my heart
In compliment extern, 'tis not long after
But I will wear my heart upon my sleeve
For daws to peck at: I am not what I am.   65
   Roderigo. What a full fortune does the thick-lips owe,
If he can carry't thus!
   Iago.   Call up her father;
Rouse him, make after him, poison his delight,
Proclaim him in the streets, incense her kinsmen,
And, though he in a fertile climate dwell,   70
Plague him with flies; though that his joy be joy,
Yet throw such changes of vexation on't
As it may lose some colour.
   Roderigo. Here is her father's house; I'll call aloud.
   Iago. Do; with like timorous accent and dire yell   75
As when, by night and negligence, the fire
Is spied in populous cities.
   Roderigo. What, ho! Brabantio! Signior Brabantio, ho!
   Iago. Awake, what, ho! Brabantio! thieves! thieves!
    thieves!
Look to your house, your daughter, and your bags!   80
Thieves! thieves!

61 **demonstrate**: (accent on second syllable) [*N*].   62 **The native** . . . **heart**: the way in which my heart really works and its nature [*N*].   63 **In compliment extern**: in outward manners. 63–4 **'tis** . . . **But**: then it will not be long before.   65 **daws**: fools.   **I** . . . **am**: i.e. I don't show my real self [*N*].   66 **full**: splendid.   **owe**: possess [*N*].   67 **carry't thus**: get away with it in this fashion.   68–9 **him**: i.e. Othello, throughout. 69 **Proclaim**: denounce.   70–1 **And, though** . . . **flies**: though he lives in happiness, annoy him with petty irritations [*N*]. 72 **throw** . . . **colour**: vex it enough to detract from its character ('changes of vexation' = vexatious changes).   73 **As it**: so that it.   75 **timorous**: terrifying.   76 **by night and negligence**: i.e. because a night fire is caused by negligence before going to bed.   80 **bags**: money-bags.

Enter BRABANTIO, *above, at a window.*

Brabantio. What is the reason of this terrible summons?
What is the matter there?
  Roderigo. Signior, is all your family within?
  Iago. Are your doors lock'd?
  Brabantio.   Why? wherefore ask you this?   85
  Iago. 'Zounds! sir, you're robb'd; for shame, put on your
      gown;
Your heart is burst, you have lost half your soul;
Even now, now, very now, an old black ram
Is tupping your white ewe. Arise, arise!
Awake the snorting citizens with the bell,   90
Or else the devil will make a grandsire of you.
Arise, I say.
  Brabantio. What! have you lost your wits?
  Roderigo. Most reverend signior, do you know my voice?
  Brabantio. Not I, what are you?
  Roderigo. My name is Roderigo.
  Brabantio.   The worser welcome: 95
I have charg'd thee not to haunt about my doors:
In honest plainness thou hast heard me say
My daughter is not for thee; and now, in madness,
Being full of supper and distempering draughts,
Upon malicious bravery dost thou come   100
To start my quiet.
  Roderigo. Sir, sir, sir!
  Brabantio.   But thou must needs be sure
My spirit and my place have in them power
To make this bitter to thee.
  Roderigo.   Patience, good sir.

86 'Zounds: God's wounds (a common oath).   **87 is burst:**
(proleptic) will be broken.   **89 tupping:** copulating with.
90 snorting: snoring.   **96 haunt about:** hang about.   **99 dis-**
tempering draughts: intoxicating drinks.   **100 bravery:** bravado.
101 start: disturb.   **103 spirit:** disposition.   **place:** rank.

Brabantio. What tell'st thou me of robbing? this is
    Venice;   105
My house is not a grange.
    Roderigo.   Most grave Brabantio,
In simple and pure soul I come to you.

Iago. 'Zounds! sir, you are one of those that will not
serve God if the devil bid you. Because we come to
do you service and you think we are ruffians, you'll   110
have your daughter covered with a Barbary horse;
you'll have your nephews neigh to you; you'll have
coursers for cousins and gennets for germans.

Brabantio. What profane wretch art thou?   114
Iago. I am one, sir, that comes to tell you, your daughter
and the Moor are now making the beast with two backs.

Brabantio. Thou art a villain.
Iago.   You are—a senator.
Brabantio. This thou shalt answer; I know thee, Roderigo.
Roderigo. Sir, I will answer any thing. But, I beseech
    you,
If 't be your pleasure and most wise consent,—   120
As partly, I find, it is,—that your fair daughter,
At this odd-even and dull watch o' the night,
Transported with no worse nor better guard
But with a knave of common hire, a gondolier,

106 **grange**: farmhouse, country house.   107 **In ... soul**:
with sincere intent, i.e. purely for your good.   108–9 i.e. will
not take even good advice from a bad source.   111 **covered**:
copulated with (an animal term).   **Barbary**: Arab; used in
the Saracen countries along the north coast of Africa.   112
nephews: grandsons (Latin *nepos*).   113 **coursers**: stallions,
chargers. **cousins**: (here) direct descendants. **gennets**: (literally)
small Spanish horses.   **germans**: near relatives.   114 **profane**:
foul-mouthed.   116 **making ... backs**: having sexual
intercourse.   118 **answer**: answer for.   122 **odd-even**: time
when night is turning into morning.   **dull watch**: lifeless, dead
time [*N*].   123 **Transported with**: should be carried by.
124 **knave ... hire**: servant for public hire.

To the gross clasps of a lascivious Moor,—   125
If this be known to you, and your allowance,
We then have done you bold and saucy wrongs;
But if you know not this, my manners tell me
We have your wrong rebuke. Do not believe,
That, from the sense of all civility,   130
I thus would play and trifle with your reverence:
Your daughter, if you have not given her leave,
I say again, hath made a gross revolt;
Tying her duty, beauty, wit and fortunes
In an extravagant and wheeling stranger   135
Of here and every where. Straight satisfy yourself:
If she be in her chamber or your house,
Let loose on me the justice of the state
For thus deluding you.
    Brabantio.   Strike on the tinder, ho!
Give me a taper! call up all my people!   140
This accident is not unlike my dream;
Belief of it oppresses me already.
Light, I say! light!   *[Exit, from above.*
    Iago.   Farewell, for I must leave you:
It seems not meet nor wholesome to my place
To be produc'd, as, if I stay, I shall,   145
Against the Moor; for, I do know the state,
However this may gall him with some check,
Cannot with safety cast him; for he's embark'd
With such loud reason to the Cyprus wars,—

---

126 your allowance : has your approval.   **127 saucy :** insolent.
128 manners : sense of polite usage.   **130 from . . . civility :**
contrary to all civilized behaviour.   **134 wit :** intelligence.
135 In : i.e. up in. **extravagant :** wandering, vagrant. **wheeling :**
gadabout.   **141 accident :** occurrence.   **142** i.e. I credit what
you say enough to feel worried already.   **144 meet :** fitting.
wholesome to my place : suitable to my position (i.e. as ensign).
145 produc'd : i.e. as evidence.   **147 gall . . . check :** annoy him
by some reproof. **148 cast :** dismiss. **149 loud :** urgent, obvious.

Which even now stands in act,—that, for their souls,   150
Another of his fathom they have none,
To lead their business; in which regard,
Though I do hate him as I do hell-pains,
Yet, for necessity of present life,
I must show out a flag and sign of love,   155
Which is indeed but sign. That you shall surely find him,
Lead to the Sagittary the raised search;
And there will I be with him. So, farewell.   [*Exit.*

Enter below, BRABANTIO, *and* Servants *with
torches.*

Brabantio. It is too true an evil: gone she is,
And what's to come of my despised time   160
Is nought but bitterness. Now, Roderigo,
Where didst thou see her? O, unhappy girl!
With the Moor, sayst thou? Who would be a father!
How didst thou know 'twas she? O, she deceives me
Past thought. What said she to you? Get more tapers!
Raise all my kindred! Are they married, think you?   166
   Roderigo. Truly, I think they are.
   Brabantio. O heaven! How got she out? O, treason of
      the blood:
Fathers, from hence trust not your daughters' minds
By what you see them act. Are there not charms   170
By which the property of youth and maidhood

---

   150 stands in act: is in progress.   **for their souls:** for all
their need [*N*].   **151 fathom:** ability.   **154 necessity** . . .
life: immediate needs of living.   **155 show out . . . love:**
i.e. pretend to love him ('show out' = display).   **157 raised
search:** the search-party which has been organized [*N*].   **160
despised time:** the little time I have to live [*N*].   **168 treason
of the blood:** rebellion of daughter against father [*N*].   **170 act:**
do.   **charms:** spells, witchery (cf. i. ii. 65).   **171 property:**
quality proper to.

May be abus'd? Have you not read, Roderigo,
Of some such thing?

  Roderigo.   Yes, sir, I have indeed.

  Brabantio. Call up my brother. O! that you had had her.
Some one way, some another! Do you know   175
Where we may apprehend her and the Moor?

  Roderigo. I think I can discover him, if you please
To get good guard and go along with me.

  Brabantio. Pray you, lead on. At every house I'll call;
I may command at most. Get weapons, ho!   180
And raise some special officers of night.
On, good Roderigo; I'll deserve your pains.   [*Exeunt.*

Scene II. ANOTHER STREET

  Enter OTHELLO, IAGO, *and* Attendants, *with torches.*

  Iago. Though in the trade of war I have slain men,
Yet do I hold it very stuff o' the conscience
To do no contriv'd murder: I lack iniquity
Sometimes to do me service. Nine or ten times
I had thought to have yerk'd him here under the ribs.   5

  Othello. 'Tis better as it is.

  Iago.   Nay, but he prated,
And spoke such scurvy and provoking terms
Against your honour
That, with the little godliness I have,
I did full hard forbear him. But, I pray, sir,   10

    172 **abus'd**: deceived.   174 **you**: (emphatic), rather than
he.   180 **I may ... most**: I have authority with most of
them.   181 **officers of night**: officers (constables) operating
at night (to keep the peace).   182 **deserve**: i.e. reward.
2 **very stuff ... conscience**: (the) essential quality of the conscience.   3 **contriv'd**: intended.   4 **do me service**: act
to my own advantage.   5 **yerk'd**: stabbed.   7 **scurvy**:
abusive.   10 **forbear him**: i.e. from striking him.

Are you fast married? Be assur'd of this,
That the magnifico is much belov'd,
And hath in his effect a voice potential
As double as the duke's; he will divorce you,
Or put upon you what restraint and grievance   15
The law—with all his might to enforce it on—
Will give him cable.

   Othello.   Let him do his spite:
My services which I have done the signiory
Shall out-tongue his complaints. 'Tis yet to know,
Which when I know that boasting is an honour   20
I shall promulgate, I fetch my life and being
From men of royal siege, and my demerits
May speak unbonneted to as proud a fortune
As this that I have reach'd; for know, Iago,
But that I love the gentle Desdemona,   25
I would not my unhoused free condition
Put into circumscription and confine
For the sea's worth. But, look! what lights come yond?

   Iago. Those are the raised father and his friends:
You were best go in.

   Othello.   Not I; I must be found: 30
My parts, my title, and my perfect soul
Shall manifest me rightly. Is it they?

   Iago. By Janus, I think no.

11 **fast**: firmly.   12 **magnifico**: one of the chief men of
Venice.   13 **potential**: in its power [*N*].   17 **give him
cable**: allow him (as we use 'rope').   **his spite**: his worst.
18 **signiory**: governing body of Venice.   19 **'Tis yet to
know**: it waits to be known.   21 **promulgate**: make public.
22 **siege**: rank [*N*].   22–4 **my demerits . . . reach'd**: i.e. my
merits are not unworthy of the high position I hold here [*N*].
26 **unhoused**: without home, roving.   **condition**: state of life.
27 i.e. make it circumscribed and confined by the responsibilities of
marriage.   29 **raised**: aroused from sleep.   31 **parts**:
natural gifts.   **title**: legal right.   **perfect soul**: consciousness
of innocence.

Enter CASSIO *and certain* Officers, *with torches.*

Othello. The servants of the duke, and my lieutenant.
The goodness of the night upon you, friends!   35
What is the news?
  Cassio.   The duke does greet you, general,
And he requires your haste-post-haste appearance,
Even on the instant.
  Othello.   What is the matter, think you?
  Cassio. Something from Cyprus, as I may divine.
It is a business of some heat; the galleys   40
Have sent a dozen sequent messengers
This very night at one another's heels,
And many of the consuls, rais'd and met,
Are at the duke's already. You have been hotly call'd for;
When, being not at your lodging to be found,   45
The senate hath sent about three several quests
To search you out.
  Othello.   'Tis well I am found by you.
I will but spend a word here in the house,
And go with you.   [*Exit.*
  Cassio.   Ancient, what makes he here?
  Iago. Faith, he to-night hath boarded a land carrack; 50
If it prove lawful prize, he's made for ever.
  Cassio. I do not understand.
  Iago.   He's married.
  Cassio.   To who?

Re-enter OTHELLO.

  Iago. Marry, to—Come, captain, will you go?

35 (may) **the goodness of the night** (rest) **upon you.**   37
haste-post-haste: immediate [*N*].   40 **heat:** urgency.   41
sequent: successive.   45 **being:** since you were.   46 **quests:**
search parties.   49 **makes:** does.   50 **boarded:** captured.
carrack: merchant ship [*N*].   51 **prize:** capture.   **he's**
made for ever: his future is assured.   53 **Marry:** indeed! (a
mild oath, with pun on 'married').   **will you go:** shall we go?

Othello.   Have with you.
Cassio. Here comes another troop to seek for you.
Iago. It is Brabantio. General, be advis'd;   55
He comes to bad intent.

Enter BRABANTIO, RODERIGO, *and* Officers, *with
torches and weapons.*

Othello.   Holla! stand there!
Roderigo. Signior, it is the Moor.
Brabantio.   Down with him, thief!
                                   [*They draw on both sides.*
Iago. You, Roderigo! come sir, I am for you.
Othello. Keep up your bright swords, for the dew will
   rust them.
Good signior, you shall more command with years   60
Than with your weapons.
   Brabantio. O thou foul thief! where hast thou stow'd my
   daughter?
Damn'd as thou art, thou hast enchanted her;
For I'll refer me to all things of sense,
If she in chains of magic were not bound,   65
Whether a maid so tender, fair, and happy,
So opposite to marriage that she shunn'd
The wealthy curled darlings of our nation,
Would ever have, to incur a general mock,
Run from her guardage to the sooty bosom   70

54 **Have with you:** yes, I'm coming.   55 **advis'd:** warned.
56 **to bad intent:** intending no good to you.   **stand:** stop.
58 **I am for you:** I'll take you on.   59 **Keep up:** sheathe [*N*].
60-1 **you shall . . . weapons:** your age entitles you to a respect
which your weapons cannot enforce.   64 **things of sense:**
matters of common understanding [*N*].   66 **tender:** young.
67 **opposite:** opposed.   68 **curled darlings:** fashionable,
eligible young men.   69 **to incur:** at the risk of incurring
('to' = 'so as to', not 'in order to').   **mock:** mockery.   70 **her
guardage:** the guardianship (of her parent).

Of such a thing as thou; to fear, not to delight.
Judge me the world, if 'tis not gross in sense
That thou hast practis'd on her with foul charms,
Abus'd her delicate youth with drugs or minerals
That weaken motion: I'll have't disputed on;   75
'Tis probable, and palpable to thinking.
I therefore apprehend and do attach thee
For an abuser of the world, a practiser
Of arts inhibited and out of warrant.
Lay hold upon him: if he do resist,   80
Subdue him at his peril.
   Othello.   Hold your hands,
Both you of my inclining, and the rest:
Were it my cue to fight, I should have known it
Without a prompter. Where will you that I go
To answer this your charge?
   Brabantio.   To prison; till fit time   85
Of law and course of direct session
Call thee to answer.
   Othello.   What if I do obey?
How may the duke be therewith satisfied,
Whose messengers are here about my side,
Upon some present business of the state   90
To bring me to him?
   Officer.   'Tis true, most worthy signior;
The duke's in council, and your noble self,
I am sure, is sent for.

72 **Judge me the world**: let the common sense of men decide
(for me) (cf. I. i. 49).   **gross in sense**: obvious.   73 **practis'd
on**: deceived.   74 **minerals**: i.e. mineral (strong) medicines.
75 **motion**: the will [N].   **disputed on**: argued in a law court.
76 **palpable to thinking**: readily perceived.   77 **attach**: arrest.
78 **abuser**: corrupter.   79 **arts inhibited … warrant**: forbidden and unlawful practices (i.e. witchcraft).   82 **inclining**:
following, party.   83 **cue**: part, proper course.   86 **course
of direct session**: due process of law.   90 **present**: urgent.

Brabantio.   How! the duke in council!
In this time of the night! Bring him away.
Mine's not an idle cause: the duke himself,   95
Or any of my brothers of the state,
Cannot but feel this wrong as 'twere their own;
For if such actions may have passage free,
Bond-slaves and pagans shall our statesmen be. [*Exeunt.*

Scene III. A COUNCIL CHAMBER. THE DUKE AND
SENATORS SITTING AT A TABLE. OFFICERS ATTENDING

Duke. There is no composition in these news
That gives them credit.
   First Senator.   Indeed, they are disproportion'd;
My letters say a hundred and seven galleys.
   Duke. And mine, a hundred and forty.
   Second Senator.   And mine, two hundred:
But though they jump not on a just account,—   5
As in these cases, where the aim reports,
'Tis oft with difference,—yet do they all confirm
A Turkish fleet, and bearing up to Cyprus.
   Duke. Nay, it is possible enough to judgment:
I do not so secure me in the error,   10
But the main article I do approve
In fearful sense.

95 **idle cause**: trifling matter.   96 **brothers . . . state**:
fellow-magnificoes.   98 **may . . . free**: be allowed.   99
pagans: heathens, not law-abiding Christians.   1 **composition**:
consistency.   2 **disproportion'd**: inconsistent.   5 **jump**:
agree.   **just**: exact.   6–7 **As . . . difference**: in cases where
the report is founded on a guess, such discrepancies often occur [N].
8 **bearing up to**: making for.   9 **it is . . . judgment**: the report
is reasonable enough to be accepted [N].   10 **I . . . error**:
I do not persuade myself of safety because of the discrepancy.
11 **main article**: substance.   **approve**: accept.   12 **In fearful sense**: as giving cause for great alarm.

Sailor. [*Within.*] What, ho! what, ho! what, ho!
Officer. A messenger from the galleys.

Enter a Sailor.

Duke.   Now, what's the business?
Sailor. The Turkish preparation makes for Rhodes;
So was I bid report here to the state   15
By Signior Angelo.
Duke. How say you by this change?
First Senator.   This cannot be,
By no assay of reason; 'tis a pageant
To keep us in false gaze. When we consider
The importancy of Cyprus to the Turk,   20
And let ourselves again but understand,
That as it more concerns the Turk than Rhodes,
So may he with more facile question bear it,
For that it stands not in such war-like brace,
But altogether lacks the abilities   25
That Rhodes is dress'd in: if we make thought of this,
We must not think the Turk is so unskilful
To leave that latest which concerns him first,
Neglecting an attempt of ease and gain,
To wake and wage a danger profitless.   30
Duke. Nay, in all confidence, he's not for Rhodes.
Officer. Here is more news.

Enter a Messenger.

Messenger. The Ottomites, reverend and gracious,

14 **preparation**: fleet.   17 **How ... by**: what do you
think of?   18 **assay of reason**: reasonable test.   18–19
a pageant ... gaze: a show, or blind, to distract our attention.
20 **importancy**: importance.   23 **more facile question**: lighter
opposition.   **bear it**: take it.   24 **brace**: state of
defence.   25 **abilities**: warlike equipment.   30 **wake**:
start upon.   **wage**: risk.   31 **in all confidence**: we may be
confident.   33 **Ottomites**: Turks.

Steering with due course toward the isle of Rhodes,
Have there injointed them with an after fleet.   35

  First Senator. Ay, so I thought. How many, as you
     guess?

  Messenger. Of thirty sail; and now they do re-stem
Their backward course, bearing with frank appearance
Their purposes toward Cyprus. Signior Montano,
Your trusty and most valiant servitor,   40
With his free duty recommends you thus,
And prays you to believe him.

  Duke. 'Tis certain then, for Cyprus.
Marcus Luccicos, is not he in town?

  First Senator. He's now in Florence.   45

  Duke. Write from us to him; post-post-haste dispatch.

  First Senator. Here comes Brabantio and the valiant
     Moor.

         Enter BRABANTIO, OTHELLO, IAGO, RODERIGO,
                 and Officers.

  Duke. Valiant Othello, we must straight employ you
Against the general enemy Ottoman.
[*To* BRABANTIO.] I did not see you; welcome, gentle
     signior;   50
We lack'd your counsel and your help to-night.

  Brabantio. So did I yours. Good your grace, pardon me;
Neither my place nor aught I heard of business
Hath rais'd me from my bed, nor doth the general care

---

34 **due**: direct.   35 **injointed them**: joined up.   **after
fleet**: fleet coming later.   37–8 **re-stem ... course**: turn
round and go back again.   38–9 **bearing ... purposes**:
carrying out their intention openly.   41 **With ... duty**:
with an assurance of his willing service.   **recommends**: in-
forms.   48 **straight**: immediately.   49 **Ottoman**: Turkish.
53 **place**: position (as senator).   54 **general care**: concern
for the public good.

Take hold of me, for my particular grief   55
Is of so flood-gate and o'erbearing nature
That it engluts and swallows other sorrows
And it is still itself.

 Duke.   Why, what's the matter?

 Brabantio. My daughter! O! my daughter.

 Duke.   Dead?

 Senators.

 Brabantio.   Ay, to me;
She is abus'd, stol'n from me, and corrupted   60
By spells and medicines bought of mountebanks;
For nature so preposterously to err,
Being not deficient, blind, or lame of sense,
Sans witchcraft could not.

 Duke. Whoe'er he be that in this foul proceeding   65
Hath thus beguil'd your daughter of herself
And you of her, the bloody book of law
You shall yourself read in the bitter letter
After your own sense; yea, though our proper son
Stood in your action.

 Brabantio.   Humbly I thank your Grace.   70
Here is the man, this Moor; whom now, it seems,
Your special mandate for the state affairs,
Hath hither brought.

 Duke.   We are very sorry for it.

 Senators.

---

55 Take ... me : fill my thoughts. 56 flood-gate : torrential.
o'erbearing : overwhelming. 57 engluts : ingulfs. 58 i.e. it
is so great that other sorrows are lost in it. 60 abus'd : deceived.
61 mountebanks : quacks. 62 preposterously : unnaturally.
62-4 For ... could not : i.e. Desdemona's nature, not being deficient
etc., could not err so wildly without the use of witchcraft [N].
63 lame : weak. 66 beguil'd : cheated (cf. 156). 67 bloody :
stern [N]. 68-9 read ... sense : interpret in the hardest and most
literal way you can. 69 proper : own. 70 Stood ... action :
were accused by you. 72 mandate : command (to attend).

Duke. [*To* OTHELLO.] What, in your own part, can you
    say to this?

Brabantio. Nothing, but this is so.   75

Othello. Most potent, grave, and reverend signiors,
My very noble and approv'd good masters,
That I have ta'en away this old man's daughter,
It is most true; true, I have married her:
The very head and front of my offending   80
Hath this extent, no more. Rude am I in my speech,
And little bless'd with the soft phrase of peace;
For since these arms of mine had seven years' pith,
Till now some nine moons wasted, they have us'd
Their dearest action in the tented field;   85
And little of this great world can I speak,
More than pertains to feats of broil and battle;
And therefore little shall I grace my cause
In speaking for myself. Yet, by your gracious patience,
I will a round unvarnish'd tale deliver   90
Of my whole course of love; what drugs, what charms,
What conjuration, and what mighty magic,
For such proceeding I am charg'd withal,
I won his daughter.

   Brabantio.   A maiden never bold;
Of spirit so still and quiet, that her motion   95
Blush'd at herself; and she, in spite of nature,

---

74 part: defence.   **76 potent**: powerful [*N*].   **77 approv'd**: proved by experience (to be).   **80 head and
front**: foremost part.   **81 Rude**: plain, unpolished.   **82 soft**:
elegant.   **83 pith**: strength.   **84 Till ... wasted**:
until nine months ago.   **85 dearest**: best, hardest.   **tented
field**: the pitched tents of war.   **90 round**: straightforward.
unvarnish'd: plain.   **91 what drugs**: by what drugs.
92 conjuration: charms.   **93** i.e. For with such conduct
I am charged.   **95–6 her motion ... herself**: she was
even shy of her own natural impulses ('herself' refers to motion).
Cf. I. ii. 75.

Of years, of country, credit, every thing,
To fall in love with what she fear'd to look on!
It is a judgment maim'd and most imperfect
That will confess perfection so could err   100
Against all rules of nature, and must be driven
To find out practices of cunning hell,
Why this should be. I therefore vouch again
That with some mixtures powerful o'er the blood,
Or with some dram conjur'd to this effect,   105
He wrought upon her.

    Duke.   To vouch this, is no proof,
Without more certain and more overt test
Than these thin habits and poor likelihoods
Of modern seeming do prefer against him.

    First Senator. But, Othello, speak: 110
Did you by indirect and forced courses
Subdue and poison this young maid's affections;
Or came it by request and such fair question
As soul to soul affordeth?

    Othello.   I do beseech you,
Send for the lady to the Sagittary,   115

---

97 years: i.e. her youth. **credit**: her reputation. **98 To
fall**: fancy supposing she could fall! **99–100 It is ... confess**:
Only a most infirm and imperfect judgement could agree.
101 and must: and it (i.e. judgement) must. **102 practices**:
plots. **103 vouch**: avouch, assert. **104 powerful ...
blood**: strongly affecting the emotions. **105 dram**: dose.
conjur'd: (accented on second syllable) charmed, bewitched.
107 more overt: i.e. stronger. **test**: proof, testimony. **108
thin habits**: literally, thin garb, hence ill-supported accusations.
poor likelihoods: weak probabilities. **109 modern**:
trashy, untested [*N*]. **seeming**: appearances. **prefer**: bring
forward. **111 indirect and forced courses**: tricky and
forcible means. **113 by request**: unforced. **fair question**:
pleasant conversation. **114 As ... affordeth**: such as
one soul exchanges with another. **115 Sagittary**: see Commentary on I. i. 157.

And let her speak of me before her father:
If you do find me foul in her report,
The trust, the office I do hold of you,
Not only take away, but let your sentence
Even fall upon my life.

    Duke.   Fetch Desdemona hither.   120

    Othello. Ancient, conduct them; you best know the place.

                        [*Exeunt* IAGO *and* Attendants.

And, till she come, as truly as to heaven
I do confess the vices of my blood,
So justly to your grave ears I'll present
How I did thrive in this fair lady's love,   125
And she in mine.

    Duke. Say it, Othello.

    Othello. Her father lov'd me; oft invited me,
Still question'd me the story of my life
From year to year, the battles, sieges, fortunes   130
That I have pass'd.
I ran it through, even from my boyish days
To the very moment that he bade me tell it;
Wherein I spake of most disastrous chances,
Of moving accidents by flood and field,   135
Of hair-breadth 'scapes i' the imminent deadly breach,
Of being taken by the insolent foe
And sold to slavery, of my redemption thence
And portance in my travel's history;
Wherein of antres vast and deserts idle,   140
Rough quarries, rocks and hills whose heads touch heaven,

---

    123 blood: passions (cf. 104).   **124 justly:** exactly.
129 still: constantly.   **134 chances:** events.   **135 moving
accidents:** exciting adventures. **by flood and field:** on sea and
land.   **136 'scapes:** escapes.   **i' the imminent deadly
breach:** at an assault when death threatens every moment.
137 insolent: exulting.   **139 portance:** behaviour.   **140 antres:** caves [*N*].   **idle:** barren *or* solitary.   **141 quarries:**
precipices (natural).

It was my hint to speak, such was the process;
And of the Cannibals that each other eat,
The Anthropophagi, and men whose heads
Do grow beneath their shoulders. This to hear   145
Would Desdemona seriously incline;
But still the house-affairs would draw her thence;
Which ever as she could with haste dispatch,
She'd come again, and with a greedy ear
Devour up my discourse. Which I observing,   150
Took once a pliant hour, and found good means
To draw from her a prayer of earnest heart
That I would all my pilgrimage dilate,
Whereof by parcels she had something heard,
But not intentively: I did consent;   155
And often did beguile her of her tears,
When I did speak of some distressful stroke
That my youth suffer'd. My story being done,
She gave me for my pains a world of sighs;
She swore, in faith, 'twas strange, 'twas passing strange;
'Twas pitiful, 'twas wondrous pitiful: 161
She wish'd she had not heard it, yet she wish'd
That heaven had made her such a man; she thank'd me,
And bade me, if I had a friend that lov'd her,
I should but teach him how to tell my story,   165
And that would woo her. Upon this hint I spake:
She lov'd me for the dangers I had pass'd,

142 **hint**: opportunity.   **such was the process**: this was what
went on.   144 **Anthropophagi**: man-eaters [N].   146 **incline**: bend (her attention).   148 **as** (soon as) **she could.**
151 **pliant hour**: suitable moment.   152 **prayer** ... **heart**:
whole-hearted request.   153 **dilate**: tell at length.   154 **parcels**: small portions.   155 **intentively**: as a whole.
160 **passing**: very.   162–3 **she wish'd ... a man**:
either she wished she had been made a man of this sort, *or*
she wished she could have such a man as husband ('her' = for
her).

And I lov'd her that she did pity them.
This only is the witchcraft I have us'd:
Here comes the lady; let her witness it.   170

Enter DESDEMONA, IAGO, *and* Attendants.

Duke. I think this tale would win my daughter too.
Good Brabantio,
Take up this mangled matter at the best;
Men do their broken weapons rather use
Than their bare hands.
Brabantio.   I pray you, hear her speak: 175
If she confess that she was half the wooer,
Destruction on my head, if my bad blame
Light on the man! Come hither, gentle mistress:
Do you perceive in all this noble company
Where most you owe obedience?
Desdemona.   My noble father,   180
I do perceive here a divided duty:
To you I am bound for life and education;
My life and education both do learn me
How to respect you; you are the lord of duty,
I am hitherto your daughter: but here's my husband; 185
And so much duty as my mother show'd
To you, preferring you before her father,
So much I challenge that I may profess
Due to the Moor my lord.
Brabantio.   God be with you! I have done.
Please it your Grace, on to the state affairs: 190
I had rather to adopt a child than get it.

168 **that**: for that, because.   173 **Take ... best**: make the
best of this unfortunate matter.   174–5 **Men ... hands**: i.e. men
make the best of what is left to them.   182 **education**: up-
bringing.   183 **learn**: teach.   184 **you are the lord of duty**: I
owe obedience to you as my father.   188 **challenge**: claim.
189 **God ... you**: i.e. Very well! [*N*].   190 **on**: let us get on
to.   191 **had rather to**: would prefer to.   **get**: beget.

Come hither, Moor:
I here do give thee that with all my heart
Which, but thou hast already, with all my heart
I would keep from thee. For your sake, jewel,   195
I am glad at soul I have no other child;
For thy escape would teach me tyranny,
To hang clogs on them. I have done, my lord.
    Duke. Let me speak like yourself and lay a sentence,
Which as a grize or step, may help these lovers   200
Into your favour.
When remedies are past, the griefs are ended
By seeing the worst, which late on hopes depended.
To mourn a mischief that is past and gone
Is the next way to draw new mischief on.   205
What cannot be preserv'd when Fortune takes,
Patience her injury a mockery makes.
The robb'd that smiles steals something from the thief;
He robs himself that spends a bootless grief.
    Brabantio. So let the Turk of Cyprus us beguile;   210
We lose it not so long as we can smile.
He bears the sentence well that nothing bears
But the free comfort which from thence he hears;

194 **but thou hast** (it) **already**: if you had not already got it.
195 **For your sake**: because of you [*N*].   197 **escape**:
escapade, elopement.   199 **like yourself**: as if I were in your
position.   **lay a sentence**: offer some maxims (*sentence* = prudential saying, or maxim (Latin *sententia*)).   200 **grize**: (= grece)
stairway.   202–3 **When . . . depended**: What can no longer be
mended ceases to be a source of grief; for the worst has happened, and
we no longer endure the uncertainty of hope [*N*].   205 **next**:
nearest.   206–7 **when . . . makes**: by being resigned, we make
the injury Fortune does us seem a trifle ('takes' = robs; 'her' = Fortune's).   208 **The robb'd**: the man robbed.   209 **spends
. . . grief**: wastes time on unavailing sorrow.   **bootless**: useless.
210 **So**: In that case.   **beguile**: cheat (cf. 156).   212–13 **He
bears . . . hears**: a man who is not personally concerned in the
matter can well draw comfort from such maxims.

But he bears both the sentence and the sorrow
That, to pay grief, must of poor patience borrow.   215
These sentences, to sugar, or to gall,
Being strong on both sides, are equivocal:
But words are words; I never yet did hear
That the bruis'd heart was pierced through the ear.
I humbly beseech you, proceed to the affairs of state.   220
   Duke. The Turk with a most mighty preparation
makes for Cyprus. Othello, the fortitude of the place
is best known to you; and though we have there a
substitute of most allowed sufficiency, yet opinion,
a sovereign mistress of effects, throws a more safer   225
voice on you: you must therefore be content to slub-
ber the gloss of your new fortunes with this more
stubborn and boisterous expedition.
   Othello. The tyrant custom, most grave senators,
Hath made the flinty and steel couch of war   230
My thrice-driven bed of down: I do agnize
A natural and prompt alacrity
I find in hardness, and do undertake
These present wars against the Ottomites.
Most humbly therefore bending to your state,   235

214-15 **But ... borrow:** But the man who can only rely on
patience to console him, has to put up with both the maxim and
the sorrow.   216-17 **These ... equivocal:** These maxims are
ambiguous, because they can either console or annoy strongly.
219 **pierced:** reached (with consolation) [N].   222 **fortitude:**
strength.   224 **allowed:** admitted.   224-5 **opinion
... effects:** public opinion, which is the essential guide to the
measures we must take.   225-6 **throws ... you:** thinks you are
a better man for the work [N].   226-7 **slubber ... fortunes:**
tarnish the first gloss of your marriage.   228 **stubborn:** harsh,
difficult.   **boisterous:** rough, violent.   231 **thrice-
driven:** softest [N].   **agnize:** confess.   232-3 **prompt ...
hardness:** i.e. Othello is disposed with cheerful readiness to endure
hardship.   235 **bending ... state:** obeying your decision
('state' = authority).

I crave fit disposition for my wife,
Due reference of place and exhibition,
With such accommodation and besort
As levels with her breeding.
   Duke.   If you please,
Be't at her father's.
   Brabantio.   I'll not have it so.   240
   Othello. Nor I.
   Desdemona.   Nor I; I would not there reside,
To put my father in impatient thoughts
By being in his eye. Most gracious duke,
To my unfolding lend your gracious ear;
And let me find a charter in your voice   245
To assist my simpleness.
   Duke. What would you, Desdemona?
   Desdemona. That I did love the Moor to live with him,
My downright violence and storm of fortunes
May trumpet to the world; my heart's subdu'd   250
Even to the very quality of my lord;
I saw Othello's visage in his mind,
And to his honours and his valiant parts
Did I my soul and fortunes consecrate.
So that, dear lords, if I be left behind,   255
A moth of peace, and he go to the war,
The rights for which I love him are bereft me,

---

236 **disposition**: arrangements.   237 **Due ... place:**
either proper accommodation, *or* place in rank, precedency.   **exhibition**: allowance for maintenance.   238 **accommodation:**
provision, entertainment.   **besort**: attendance (of ladies).
239 **As levels with**: as is fitting for.   244 **unfolding**: explanation [*N*].   245 **charter ... voice**: 'let your favour
privilege me' (Johnson).   249 **downright violence**: violent
breach of filial obedience.   **storm of fortunes**: taking of the
future into my own hands.   251 **very quality**: true
nature [*N*].   253 **parts**: attributes.   256 **moth**: parasite [*N*].   257 **rights**: way of life [*N*].

And I a heavy interim shall support
By his dear absence. Let me go with him.
   Othello. Let her have your voices.   260
Vouch with me, heaven, I therefore beg it not
To please the palate of my appetite,
Nor to comply with heat the young affects
In my defunct and proper satisfaction,
But to be free and bounteous to her mind;   265
And heaven defend your good souls that you think
I will your serious and great business scant
For she is with me. No, when light-wing'd toys
Of feather'd Cupid seel with wanton dulness
My speculative and offic'd instrument,   270
That my disports corrupt and taint my business,
Let housewives make a skillet of my helm,
And all indign and base adversities
Make head against my estimation!
   Duke. Be it as you shall privately determine,   275
Either for her stay or going. The affair cries haste,
And speed must answer it.
   First Senator. You must away to-night.
   Othello.   With all my heart.
   Duke. At nine i' the morning here we'll meet again.
Othello, leave some officer behind,   280

259 **dear**: grievous.   260 **voices**: approval.   261 **Vouch with me**: bear witness to me.   262 **appetite**: (sexual) desires [*N*].   263 **comply**: carry out. **with heat**: as soon as possible. **young affects**: newly-born desires.   264 **defunct**: performed [*N*]. **proper**: natural, legitimate.   265 **free**: generous.   266 **defend . . . think**: forbid that you should think.   267 **scant**: neglect. 268 **For**: because. **toys**: trifles.   269 **seel**: blind (properly a word from falconry). **wanton dulness**: lethargy resulting from indulgence.   270 **My . . . instrument**: the clear perception which it is my duty to maintain, *or* which belongs to my office. 271 **That**: so that. **disports**: pleasure.   272 **skillet**: saucepan. **helm**: helmet.   273 **indign**: shameful.   274 **Make head against**: attack. **estimation**: reputation.

And he shall our commission bring to you;
With such things else of quality and respect
As doth import you.

  Othello.   So please your Grace, my ancient;
A man he is of honesty and trust:
To his conveyance I assign my wife,   285
With what else needful your good grace shall think
To be sent after me.

  Duke.   Let it be so.
Good night to every one.   [*To* BRABANTIO.]
               And, noble signior,
If virtue no delighted beauty lack,
Your son-in-law is far more fair than black.   290

  First Senator. Adieu, brave Moor! use Desdemona well.

  Brabantio. Look to her, Moor, if thou hast eyes to see:
She has deceiv'd her father, and may thee.

               [*Exeunt* DUKE, Senators, Officers, &c.

  Othello. My life upon her faith! Honest Iago,
My Desdemona must I leave to thee: 295
I prithee, let thy wife attend on her;
And bring them after in the best advantage.
Come, Desdemona; I have but an hour
Of love, of worldly matters and direction,
To spend with thee: we must obey the time.   300

            [*Exeunt* OTHELLO *and* DESDEMONA.

  Roderigo. Iago!

  Iago. What sayst thou, noble heart?

  Roderigo. What will I do, think'st thou?

  282–3 **such . . . you:** i.e. such other things as fit your rank and
position.   289 i.e. If virtue includes all other beauties that
delight.   290 **fair:** attractive (with a play on 'fair' = blond).
297 **in . . . advantage:** as time will best serve.   299 **direction:** i.e. orders to give about my affairs.   300 **obey
the time:** comply with, make the best of, the time available.
303 **will:** must, can.

Iago. Why, go to bed, and sleep.

Roderigo. I will incontinently drown myself.   305

Iago. Well, if thou dost, I shall never love thee
after. Why, thou silly gentleman!

Roderigo. It is silliness to live when to live is torment; and then have we a prescription to die when
death is our physician.   310

Iago. O! villanous; I have looked upon the world
for four times seven years, and since I could distinguish betwixt a benefit and an injury, I never
found man that knew how to love himself. Ere I
would say, I would drown myself for the love of a   315
guinea-hen, I would change my humanity with
a baboon.

Roderigo. What should I do? I confess it is my
shame to be so fond; but it is not in my virtue to
amend it.   320

Iago. Virtue! a fig! 'tis in ourselves that we are
thus, or thus. Our bodies are our gardens, to the
which our wills are gardeners; so that if we will plant
nettles or sow lettuce, set hyssop and weed up thyme,
supply it with one gender of herbs or distract it   325
with many, either to have it sterile with idleness or
manured with industry, why, the power and corrigible authority of this lies in our wills. If the
balance of our lives had not one scale of reason to
poise another of sensuality, the blood and baseness of   330

---

305 incontinently: immediately.   **309-10 then ... physician**:
i.e. when death is the only cure we have a right to commit suicide [*N*].
316 guinea-hen: (loose) woman, a 'skirt'.   **316 change**: exchange.   **319 fond**: infatuated.   **virtue**: power.   **321 a fig**:
Nonsense! [*N*].   **324 set**: plant.   **hyssop**: an aromatic herb [*N*].
325 gender: species.   **distract**: divide up.   **326-7 with**:
through.   **327 manured**: tilled.   **corrigible**: corrective.
328-9 the balance of our lives: our life like a set of scales.
330 poise: counterbalance.   **blood and baseness**: base passions.

our natures would conduct us to most preposterous
conclusions; but we have reason to cool our raging
motions, our carnal stings, our unbitted lusts, where-
of I take this that you call love to be a sect or scion.   335

Roderigo. It cannot be.

Iago. It is merely a lust of the blood and a permission of the will. Come, be a man. Drown thyself!
drown cats and blind puppies. I have professed me
thy friend, and I confess me knit to thy deserving
with cables of perdurable toughness; I could never   340
better stead thee than now. Put money in thy purse;
follow these wars; defeat thy favour with a usurped
beard; I say, put money in thy purse. It cannot be
that Desdemona should long continue her love to the
Moor,—put money in thy purse,—nor he his to her.   345
It was a violent commencement in her, and thou shalt
see an answerable sequestration; put but money in
thy purse. These Moors are changeable in their wills;
—fill thy purse with money:—the food that to him
now is as luscious as locusts, shall be to him shortly   350
as acerbe as coloquintida. She must change for
youth: when she is sated with his body, she will find
the error of her choice. She must have change, she
must: therefore put money in thy purse. If thou
wilt needs damn thyself, do it a more delicate way   355
than drowning. Make all the money thou canst. If

332 **conclusions** : results.   333 **motions** : desires.   **unbitted** : unbridled.   334 **sect** : cutting, part.   **scion** : shoot,
twig.   339 **me** : myself.   340 **perdurable** : everlasting.
341 **stead** : be of use to.   342 **follow these wars** : enlist.
defeat : disguise.   **favour** : appearance.   **usurped** : false.
347 **sequestration** : separation.   350 **locusts** : sweet fruit.
351 **acerbe** : bitter (which F reads) [*N*].   **coloquintida** : bitter
drug [*N*].   351-2 **change for youth** : i.e. change Othello for
a younger man.   355 **delicate** : attractive (as indicated in
ll. 361-3 below).

sanctimony and a frail vow betwixt an erring barbarian and a supersubtle Venetian be not too hard
for my wits and all the tribe of hell, thou shalt
enjoy her; therefore make money. A pox of drowning   360
thyself! it is clean out of the way: seek thou rather
to be hanged in compassing thy joy than to be
drowned and go without her.

Roderigo. Wilt thou be fast to my hopes, if I depend on the issue?   365

Iago. Thou art sure of me: go, make money.
I have told thee often, and I re-tell thee again and
again, I hate the Moor: my cause is hearted: thine
hath no less reason. Let us be conjunctive in our
revenge against him; if thou canst cuckold him, thou   370
dost thyself a pleasure, me a sport. There are many
events in the womb of time which will be delivered.
Traverse; go: provide thy money. We will have
more of this to-morrow. Adieu.

Roderigo. Where shall we meet i' the morning?   375

Iago. At my lodging.

Roderigo. I'll be with thee betimes.

Iago. Go to; farewell. Do you hear, Roderigo?

Roderigo. What say you?

Iago. No more of drowning, do you hear?   380

Roderigo. I am changed. I'll sell all my land.

Iago. Go to; farewell! put money enough in your purse.

[*Exit* RODERIGO.

357 **sanctimony**: holiness [*N*].   **vow**: i.e. marriage-vow.
erring: roving.   358 **supersubtle**: delicate, refined [*N*].
360 **A pox of**: to hell with.   361 **clean . . . way**: quite out of
the question.   362 **compassing**: achieving.   364 **be fast
to**: firmly support.   364–5 **depend . . . issue**: rely upon
the outcome (of your promise).   368 **hearted**: deeply
felt.   369 **conjunctive**: closely united.   373 **Traverse**:
a military command; perhaps 'Dismiss'.   377 **betimes**: early.
378 **Go to**: well then.

Thus do I ever make my fool my purse;
For I mine own gain'd knowledge should profane,
If I would time expend with such a snipe   385
But for my sport and profit. I hate the Moor,
And it is thought abroad that 'twixt my sheets
He has done my office: I know not if't be true,
But I, for mere suspicion in that kind,
Will do as if for surety. He holds me well;   390
The better shall my purpose work on him.
Cassio's a proper man; let me see now:
To get his place; and to plume up my will
In double knavery; how, how? Let's see:
After some time to abuse Othello's ear   395
That he is too familiar with his wife:
He hath a person and a smooth dispose
To be suspected; framed to make women false.
The Moor is of a free and open nature,
That thinks men honest that but seem to be so,   400
And will as tenderly be led by the nose
As asses are.
I have't; it is engender'd: hell and night
Must bring this monstrous birth to the world's light.
                                                    [*Exit.*

383 **make ... purse**: get money out of fools [*N*].   384 **profane**: make poor use of.   385 **snipe**: fool.   387 **abroad**:
commonly.   387–8 **'twixt ... office**: i.e. been to bed with
my wife.   389 **in that kind**: of that sort.   390 **Will do
... surety**: will act as if it were a certainty.   **holds me well**:
thinks well of me.   392 **proper**: fine, handsome.   393–4
plume ... knavery: (perhaps) make the most of my powers for
a double purpose [*N*].   395 **abuse ... ear**: lie to Othello.
397 **person**: figure, appearance.   **smooth dispose**: easy manner
[*N*].   399 **free**: noble, generous.   401 **tenderly**: easily.

ACT II

Scene I. A SEA-PORT TOWN IN CYPRUS. AN OPEN
PLACE NEAR THE QUAY

Enter MONTANO *and two* Gentlemen.

Montano. What from the cape can you discern at sea?
First Gentleman. Nothing at all: it is a high-wrought flood;
I cannot 'twixt the heaven and the main
Descry a sail.
   Montano. Methinks the wind hath spoke aloud at land;   5
A fuller blast ne'er shook our battlements;
If it hath ruffian'd so upon the sea,
What ribs of oak, when mountains melt on them,
Can hold the mortise? what shall we hear of this?
  Second Gentleman. A segregation of the Turkish fleet;   10
For do but stand upon the foaming shore,
The chidden billow seems to pelt the clouds;
The wind-shak'd surge, with high and monstrous mane,
Seems to cast water on the burning Bear
And quench the guards of the ever-fixed pole: 15
I never did like molestation view
On the enchafed flood.
  Montano.   If that the Turkish fleet
Be not enshelter'd and embay'd, they are drown'd;
It is impossible they bear it out.

2 **high-wrought:** highly worked-up, turbulent.   3 **main:**
sea.   5 **at land:** on land.   7 **ruffian'd:** played the ruffian.
9 **hold the mortise:** keep the joints from splitting.   **what:**
what news.   10 **segregation:** dispersal.   12 **chidden:**
buffeted.   13 **mane:** the crest (of the waves).   14 **Bear:**
i.e. the constellation Ursa Major [N].   15 **guards:** two stars
pointing to the Pole Star [N].   16 **molestation:** trouble.
17 **enchafed:** furious.   18 **enshelter'd and embay'd:** safe in
a bay.   19 **bear it out:** should survive.

Enter a third Gentleman.

Third Gentleman. News, lads! our wars are done.   20
The desperate tempest hath so bang'd the Turks
That their designment halts; a noble ship of Venice
Hath seen a grievous wrack and sufferance
On most part of their fleet.
  Montano. How! is this true?
  Third Gentleman.   The ship is here put in, 25
A Veronesa: Michael Cassio,
Lieutenant to the war-like Moor Othello,
Is come on shore: the Moor himself's at sea,
And is in full commission here for Cyprus.
  Montano. I am glad on't; 'tis a worthy governor.   30
  Third Gentleman. But this same Cassio, though he speak
    of comfort
Touching the Turkish loss, yet he looks sadly
And prays the Moor be safe; for they were parted
With foul and violent tempest.
  Montano.   Pray heaven he be;
For I have serv'd him, and the man commands   35
Like a full soldier. Let's to the sea-side, ho!
As well to see the vessel that's come in
As to throw out our eyes for brave Othello,
Even till we make the main and the aerial blue
An indistinct regard.
  Third Gentleman. Come, let's do so;   40
For every minute is expectancy
Of more arrivance.

22 **designment**: intention.   23 **wrack**: (= wreck) destruction.   **sufferance**: damage.   26 **Veronesa**: ship of Verona
[*N*].   29 **is** . . . **Cyprus**: is entrusted with full powers as
governor of Cyprus.   32 **Touching**: as regards.   36 **full**: able.
38 **throw** . . . **eyes**: look out for.   39–40 **Even** . . . **regard**:
i.e. until we cannot distinguish sea from sky.   39 **the aerial**:
scan as 'th' erial'.   42 **arrivance**: ships or people arriving.

Enter CASSIO.

Cassio. Thanks, you the valiant of this war-like isle,
That so approve the Moor. O! let the heavens
Give him defence against the elements,   45
For I have lost him on a dangerous sea.
    Montano. Is he well shipp'd?
    Cassio. His bark is stoutly timber'd, and his pilot
Of very expert and approv'd allowance;
Therefore my hopes, not surfeited to death,   50
Stand in bold cure.

                [*Within*, 'A sail!—a sail!—a sail!'

Enter a Messenger.

    Cassio. What noise?
    Messenger. The town is empty; on the brow o' the sea
Stand ranks of people, and they cry, 'A sail!'
    Cassio. My hopes do shape him for the governor.   55
                      [*Guns heard.*
    Second Gentleman. They do discharge their shot of
      courtesy;
Our friends at least.
    Cassio.   I pray you, sir, go forth,
And give us truth who 'tis that is arriv'd.
    Second Gentleman. I shall.   [*Exit.*
    Montano. But, good lieutenant, is your general wiv'd?
    Cassio. Most fortunately: he hath achiev'd a maid   61

---

    44 approve: esteem.   **49 Of very ... allowance**: acknow-
ledged to be experienced and skilful.   **50–1 Therefore ... cure**:
i.e. I haven't been hoping for so long that I despair of his safety [*N*].
53 brow o': cliff above.   **55 hopes ... governor**: i.e. I hope
this will prove to be the governor ('him' = the occupant of the ship).
56 shot of courtesy: ceremonial salute of guns.   **57** i.e.
therefore they are at least friends.   **60 wiv'd**: married.

That paragons description and wild fame;
One that excels the quirks of blazoning pens,
And in th' essential vesture of creation
Does tire the ingener.

Re-enter second Gentleman.

　　　　　　　　　　　How now! who has put in ?   65
Second Gentleman. 'Tis one Iago, ancient to the general.
　Cassio. He has had most favourable and happy speed:
Tempests themselves, high seas, and howling winds,
The gutter'd rocks, and congregated sands,
Traitors ensteep'd to clog the guiltless keel,   70
As having sense of beauty, do omit
Their mortal natures, letting go safely by
The divine Desdemona.
　Montano.　　　　　　　What is she ?
　Cassio. She that I spake of, our great captain's captain,
Left in the conduct of the bold Iago,   75
Whose footing here anticipates our thoughts
A se'nnight's speed. Great Jove, Othello guard,
And swell his sail with thine own powerful breath,
That he may bless this bay with his tall ship,
Make love's quick pants in Desdemona's arms,   80
Give renew'd fire to our extincted spirits,
And bring all Cyprus comfort!

62 **paragons** : excels. [*N*].　　　**description** : all that description could say of her.　　**wild fame** : the most exaggerated accounts. 63 **quirks** : subtleties, flourishes.　　**blazoning** : eulogizing [*N*]. 64–5 **And in ... ingener**: and her quality, as nature made her, excels all that art could invent ('ingener' = inventer) [*N*].　　65 **put in :** i.e. into harbour.　　67 **speed** : fortune.　　69 **gutter'd** : jagged. **congregated sands** : sand-banks.　　70 **ensteep'd** : lying under the water.　　71 **sense of** : a feeling for.　　71–2 **omit ...** **natures** : forbear to exercise their deadly natures.　　75 **conduct :** escort.　　76 **footing** : landing.　　77 **a se'nnight's speed** : by a week.　　79 **bless** : make happy.　　**tall** : splendid.　　81 **extincted** : extinguished, depressed.

Enter DESDEMONA, EMILIA, IAGO, RODERIGO,
                and Attendants.

                                    O! behold,
The riches of the ship is come on shore.
Ye men of Cyprus, let her have your knees.
Hail to thee, lady! and the grace of heaven,   85
Before, behind thee, and on every hand,
Enwheel thee round!
    Desdemona.   I thank you, valiant Cassio.
What tidings can you tell me of my lord?
    Cassio. He is not yet arriv'd; nor know I aught
But that he's well, and will be shortly here.   90
    Desdemona. O! but I fear—How lost you company?
    Cassio. The great contention of the sea and skies
Parted our fellowship. But hark! a sail.
                    [*Cry within,* 'A sail!—a sail!' *Guns heard.*
    Second Gentleman. They give their greeting to the citadel:
This likewise is a friend.
    Cassio.   See for the news!   95
                                          [*Exit* Gentleman.
Good ancient, you are welcome:—[*To* EMILIA.] welcome,
        mistress.
Let it not gall your patience, good Iago,
That I extend my manners; 'tis my breeding
That gives me this bold show of courtesy.   [*Kissing her.*
    Iago. Sir, would she give you so much of her lips   100
As of her tongue she oft bestows on me,
You'd have enough.
    Desdemona.   Alas! she has no speech.

---

84 **let . . . knees**: i.e. kneel to her.   87 **Enwheel**: encircle.
95 **likewise**: see l. 56.   **See for**: go and ask for.   97 **gall**
your patience: annoy you.   98 **extend my manners**: i.e.
take the liberty of politeness so far as to (kiss your wife) [*N*].

Iago. In faith, too much;
I find it still when I have list to sleep:
Marry, before your ladyship, I grant,   105
She puts her tongue a little in her heart,
And chides with thinking.

Emilia. You have little cause to say so.

Iago. Come on, come on; you are pictures out of doors,
Bells in your parlours, wild cats in your kitchens,   110
Saints in your injuries, devils being offended,
Players in your housewifery, and housewives in your beds.

Desdemona. O! fie upon thee, slanderer.

Iago. Nay, it is true, or else I am a Turk:
You rise to play and go to bed to work.   115

Emilia. You shall not write my praise.

Iago.   No, let me not.

Desdemona. What wouldst thou write of me, if thou
    shouldst praise me?

Iago. O gentle lady, do not put me to't,
For I am nothing if not critical.

Desdemona. Come on; assay. There's one gone to the
    harbour?   120

Iago. Ay, madam.

Desdemona. I am not merry, but I do beguile
The thing I am by seeming otherwise. [*Aside.*]
Come, how wouldst thou praise me?

---

104 **still**: always.   **list**: desire.   106–7 **She . . . thinking :**
i.e. she keeps her tongue somewhat to herself, and only scolds in
her thoughts.   109 **Come on**: now, now!   **pictures :**
pleasant to look at, demure [*N*].   110 **Bells**: noisy as bells,
talkers.   **wild cats**: tyrants to your domestics.   111 **Saints**
. . . injuries : 'when you have a mind to do injuries you put on an
air of sanctity' (Johnson).   112 **Players . . . housewifery :**
lazy in domestic affairs.   **housewives . . . beds :** (forward) hussies
in bed [*N*].   116 **my praise**: a character or eulogy of me.
119 **critical**: censorious.   120 **assay**: try [*N*].   122–3
I do . . . am : i.e. disguise my sorrow.

Iago. I am about it; but indeed my invention   125
Comes from my pate as birdlime does from frieze;
It plucks out brains and all: but my muse labours,
And thus she is deliver'd.
If she be fair and wise, fairness and wit,
The one's for use, the other useth it.   130

   Desdemona. Well prais'd! How if she be black and
      witty?

Iago. If she be black, and thereto have a wit,
She'll find a white that shall her blackness fit.

   Desdemona. Worse and worse.

   Emilia. How if fair and foolish?   135

Iago. She never yet was foolish that was fair,
For even her folly help'd her to an heir.

   Desdemona. These are old fond paradoxes to make fools
laugh i' the alehouse. What miserable praise hast thou for
her that's foul and foolish?   140

Iago. There's none so foul and foolish thereunto
But does foul pranks which fair and wise ones do.

   Desdemona. O heavy ignorance! thou praisest the worst
best. But what praise couldst thou bestow on a deserving
woman indeed, one that in the authority of her merit, did
justly put on the vouch of very malice itself?   146

   Iago. She that was ever fair and never proud,

125: **about it**: thinking what to say.   125–6 **invention . . .
frieze**: my thoughts come out of my head with as much difficulty as
bird-lime does from coarse material.   127 **plucks . . . all**: i.e. the
effort of thinking paralyses expression.   **labours**: is in travail,
labour.   129–30 i.e. if she is beautiful and intelligent, she will
use her intelligence to exploit her beauty. ('The one' = wit, 'the
other' = fairness.)   132–3 i.e. if she is dark and intelligent she
will find a man to suit her. ('white' may suggest 'wight' = person,
as in 157.)   137 **folly**: (1) foolishness, (2) sexual looseness.
138 **fond**: silly.   **paradoxes**: puns, verbal tricks.   140 **foul**:
ugly.   141 **thereunto**: in addition.   142 **foul pranks**:
sexual misdemeanours.   146 **put on . . . itself**: force the
acknowledgement of merit even from malice itself.

Had tongue at will and yet was never loud,
Never lack'd gold and yet went never gay,
Fled from her wish and yet said 'Now I may,'   150
She that being anger'd, her revenge being nigh,
Bade her wrong stay and her displeasure fly,
She that in wisdom never was so frail
To change the cod's head for the salmon's tail,
She that could think and ne'er disclose her mind,   155
See suitors following and not look behind,
She was a wight, if ever such wight were,—
    Desdemona. To do what?
    Iago. To suckle fools and chronicle small beer.   159
    Desdemona. O most lame and impotent conclusion! Do not
learn of him, Emilia, though he be thy husband. How say
you, Cassio? is he not a most profane and liberal counsellor?
    Cassio. He speaks home, madam; you may relish him
more in the soldier than in the scholar.
    Iago. [*Aside.*] He takes her by the palm; ay, well   165
said, whisper; with as little a web as this will I en-
snare as great a fly as Cassio. Ay, smile upon her, do;
I will gyve thee in thine own courtship. You say
true, 'tis so, indeed. If such tricks as these strip you
out of your lieutenantry, it had been better you had   170
not kissed your three fingers so oft, which now again
you are most apt to play the sir in. Very good; well

---

148 **Had ... will**: was eloquent.   149 **went never gay**:
was never flamboyantly dresssed.   150 i.e. did not allow herself
to follow her inclination till it was permissible.   152 **her
wrong**: her sense of the wrong done to her.   **stay**: be restrained.
154 **To change ... tail**: as to exchange something solid for a
dubious delicacy [*N*].   159 **chronicle small beer**: talk about
petty matters [*N*].   160 **impotent**: weak.   162 **profane**:
coarse.   **liberal**: gross.   163 **home**: bluntly.   164 **in**
(the shape of) **the soldier**: as a soldier.   165-6 **well said**:
well done.   168 **gyve**: fetter.   **courtship**: good manners
[*N*].   172 **play ... in**: act the gentleman in doing.

kissed! an excellent courtesy! 'tis so, indeed. Yet
again your fingers to your lips? would they were
clyster-pipes for your sake! [*A trumpet heard.*]   175
The Moor! I know his trumpet,

  Cassio. 'Tis truly so.

  Desdemona. Let's meet him and receive him.

  Cassio. Lo! where he comes.

      Enter OTHELLO *and* Attendants.

  Othello. O my fair warrior!

  Desdemona.   My dear Othello!   180

  Othello. It gives me wonder great as my content
To see you here before me. O my soul's joy!
If after every tempest come such calms,
May the winds blow till they have waken'd death!
And let the labouring bark climb hills of seas   185
Olympus-high, and duck again as low
As hell's from heaven! If it were now to die,
'Twere now to be most happy, for I fear
My soul hath her content so absolute
That not another comfort like to this   190
Succeeds in unknown fate.

  Desdemona.   The heavens forbid
But that our loves and comforts should increase
Even as our days do grow!

  Othello.   Amen to that, sweet powers!
I cannot speak enough of this content;
It stops me here; it is too much of joy: 195
And this, and this, the greatest discords be,

                      [*Kissing her.*

That e'er our hearts shall make!

---

   175 **clyster-pipes** : tubes for administering enemas.   191 **Succeeds** : follows.   193 **sweet** : favourable.   196 **this
... be** : let these kisses be our greatest discord, i.e. no discord can
arise between us [*N*].

Iago.   [*Aside.*] O! you are well tun'd now,
But I'll set down the pegs that make this music,
As honest as I am.

Othello.   Come, let us to the castle.   199
News, friends; our wars are done, the Turks are drown'd.
How does my old acquaintance of this isle?
Honey, you shall be well desir'd in Cyprus;
I have found great love amongst them. O my sweet,
I prattle out of fashion, and I dote
In mine own comforts. I prithee, good Iago,   205
Go to the bay and disembark my coffers.
Bring thou the master to the citadel;
He is a good one, and his worthiness
Does challenge much respect. Come, Desdemona,
Once more well met at Cyprus.   210

                    [*Exeunt all except* IAGO *and* RODERIGO.

Iago. Do thou meet me presently at the harbour.
Come hither. If thou be'st valiant, as they say base
men being in love have then a nobility in their
natures more than is native to them, list me. The
lieutenant to-night watches on the court of guard: 215
first, I must tell thee this, Desdemona is directly in
love with him.

Roderigo. With him! why, 'tis not possible.

Iago. Lay thy finger thus, and let thy soul be
instructed. Mark me with what violence she first   220

197-9 **O!...am**: i.e. you are well-attuned to one another
now, but I will alter all this—honest man as I am! (ironical) [*N*].
201 **acquaintance**: friends.   202 **desir'd**: welcome.   204 **out
of fashion**: *either* unbecomingly, *or* incoherently [*N*].   204-5
dote in: talk foolishly because of.   206 **coffers**: chests.
207 **master**: the captain of the ship.   209 **challenge**:
claim.   214 **native**: natural.   **list me**: heed what I say.
215 **watches ... guard**: is on duty in the guardroom [*N*].
216 **directly**: certainly [*N*].   219 **thus**: across the lips, i.e.
keep it secret.   220 **Mark me**: notice (cf. I. i. 49).

loved the Moor but for bragging and telling her
fantastical lies; and will she love him still for
prating? let not thy discreet heart think it. Her
eyes must be fed; and what delight shall she
have to look on the devil? When the blood is made   225
dull with the act of sport, there should be, again
to inflame it, and to give satiety a fresh appetite,
loveliness in favour, sympathy in years, manners,
and beauties; all which the Moor is defective in.
Now, for want of these required conveniences, her   230
delicate tenderness will find itself abused, begin to
heave the gorge, disrelish and abhor the Moor;
very nature will instruct her in it, and compel
her to some second choice. Now, sir, this granted,
as it is a most pregnant and unforced position, who   235
stands so eminently in the degree of this fortune
as Cassio does? a knave very voluble, no further
conscionable than in putting on the mere form of
civil and humane seeming, for the better compassing
of his salt and most hidden loose affection? why,   240
none; why, none: a slipper and subtle knave, a
finder-out of occasions, that has an eye can stamp

221 **but for**: only because of (his).   222 **still**: always.
223 **discreet**: wise.   225 **the blood**: desire [N].   226 **dull**: sati-
ated.   **the act of sport**: copulation.   228 **favour**: face, appearance.   230 **conveniences**: compatibilities.   231 **abused**:
cheated.   232 **heave the gorge**: reject (literally 'sick up').
233 **very nature**: nature herself.   235 **pregnant**: full of probabi-
lity.   **unforced**: obvious.   **position**: proposition.   236 **in the**
.↑. . **fortune**: on the ladder leading to this position.   237 **voluble**:
glib [N].   237–8 **no further . . . on**: no more scrupulous than is
involved in putting on.   239 **civil**: well-mannered.   **humane**:
courteous.   **seeming**: appearance.   **compassing**: achievement.
240 **salt**: lecherous.   **loose**: unrestrained.   **affection**: desire.
241 **slipper**: slippery.   **subtle**: crafty.   242 **finder-out of**
occasions: maker of opportunities (for gratifying his desires).
an eye can: an eye which can.   **stamp**: coin, (here) invent.

and counterfeit advantages, though true advantage
never present itself; a devilish knave! Besides, the
knave is handsome, young, and hath all those   245
requisites in him that folly and green minds look
after; a pestilent complete knave! and the woman
hath found him already.

Roderigo. I cannot believe that in her; she is full
of most blessed condition.   250

Iago. Blessed fig's end! the wine she drinks is made of
grapes; if she had been blessed she would never have
loved the Moor; blessed pudding! Didst thou not see her
paddle with the palm of his hand? didst not mark that?

Roderigo. Yes, that I did; but that was but courtesy.

Iago. Lechery, by this hand! an index and obscure   256
prologue to the history of lust and foul thoughts.
They met so near with their lips, that their breaths
embraced together. Villanous thoughts, Roderigo!
when these mutualities so marshal the way, hard at   260
hand comes the master and main exercise, the incorporate conclusion. Pish! But, sir, be you ruled
by me: I have brought you from Venice. Watch
you to-night; for the command, I'll lay't upon you:
Cassio knows you not. I'll not be far from you: do   265
you find some occasion to anger Cassio, either by
speaking too loud, or tainting his discipline; or from

243-4 **counterfeit ... itself**: create for himself favourable opportunities even when such opportunities do not offer themselves.
246 **folly**: wantonness.   **green**: raw, inexperienced.   247
complete: absolute.   248 **found him**: seen through him [*N*].
250 **blessed condition**: noble disposition.   251 **fig's end**:
nonsense.   254 **paddle**: stroke, play fondly with.   256 **index**:
table of contents at the *beginning* of a book, a prelude.   **obscure**: dark [*N*].   260 **mutualities**: intimacies.   **marshal**:
lead.   260-1 **hard at hand**: close by.   261-2 **incorporate
conclusion**: the final union in one body.   264 **for. . . you**:
I'll give you your orders [*N*].   267 **tainting**: disparaging.
discipline: the way he carries out his duties.

what other course you please, which the time shall
more favourably minister.

Roderigo. Well.   270

Iago. Sir, he is rash and very sudden in choler,
and haply may strike at you: provoke him, that
he may; for even out of that will I cause these of
Cyprus to mutiny, whose qualification shall come
into no true taste again but by the displanting of   275
Cassio. So shall you have a shorter journey to your
desires by the means I shall then have to prefer them;
and the impediment most profitably removed,
without the which there were no expectation of our
prosperity.   280

Roderigo. I will do this, if you can bring it to any
opportunity.

Iago. I warrant thee. Meet me by and by at the citadel:
I must fetch his necessaries ashore. Farewell.

Roderigo. Adieu.   [*Exit.*

Iago. That Cassio loves her, I do well believe it;   285
That she loves him, 'tis apt, and of great credit:
The Moor, howbeit that I endure him not,
Is of a constant, loving, noble nature;
And I dare think he'll prove to Desdemona
A most dear husband. Now, I do love her too;
Not out of absolute lust,—though peradventure
I stand accountant for as great a sin,—   290
But partly led to diet my revenge,

268–9 **which . . . minister**: according as the occasion may rise.
271 **choler**: anger.   272 **haply**: perhaps.   274 **qualification**: disloyalty [*N*].   274–5 **come . . . again**: shall not be put
right.   277 **prefer**: promote.   280 **prosperity**: success.
281–2 **bring . . . opportunity**: arrange things.   283 **warrant**:
guarantee.   287 **apt**: likely.   **of great credit**: very credible.
288 **endure him not**: can't stand him.   292 **absolute**: mere.
293 **accountant for**: accountable for, guilty of.   294 **led**:
because I am led.   **diet**: feed.

For that I do suspect the lusty Moor   295
Hath leap'd into my seat; the thought whereof
Doth like a poisonous mineral gnaw my inwards;
And nothing can or shall content my soul
Till I am even'd with him, wife for wife;
Or failing so, yet that I put the Moor   300
At least into a jealousy so strong
That judgment cannot cure. Which thing to do,
If this poor trash of Venice, whom I trash
For his quick hunting, stand the putting-on,
I'll have our Michael Cassio on the hip;   305
Abuse him to the Moor in the rank garb,
For I fear Cassio with my night-cap too,
Make the Moor thank me, love me, and reward me
For making him egregiously an ass
And practising upon his peace and quiet   310
Even to madness. 'Tis here, but yet confus'd:
Knavery's plain face is never seen till us'd.   [*Exit.*

Scene II. A STREET

Enter a Herald *with a proclamation;* People *following.*

Herald. It is Othello's pleasure, our noble and
valiant general, that, upon certain tidings now

297 **mineral** : cf. I. ii. 74.   **inwards** : inward parts [N].   300
failing so : i.e. if I cannot seduce Desdemona.   302 **judgment** :
reason.   303–4 **whom ... hunting** : whom I hold back from his
over-hasty pursuit of Desdemona ('for' = because of) [N].   304
stand the putting-on : is up to the incitement.   305 **on the hip** :
where I want him [N].   306 **Abuse** : slander.   **rank garb** :
grossest manner [N].   307 **with my night-cap** : i.e. that he has
cuckolded me.   309 **egregiously** : conspicuously.   310
practising upon : plotting against, injuring.   311 **to madness** :
to maddening him.   **'Tis here** : this is my plan.   **confus'd** : not
worked out in detail.   312 i.e. villainy is never seen clearly
until it is put into practice.   2 **upon** : in consequence of.

arrived, importing the mere perdition of the Turkish
fleet, every man put himself into triumph; some to
dance, some to make bonfires, each man to what   5
sport and revels his mind leads him; for, besides
these beneficial news, it is the celebration of his
nuptial. So much was his pleasure should be proclaimed. All offices are open, and there is full
liberty of feasting from this present hour of five till   10
the bell have told eleven. Heaven bless the isle of
Cyprus and our noble general Othello!   [*Exeunt.*

Scene III. A HALL IN THE CASTLE

Enter OTHELLO, DESDEMONA, CASSIO, *and*
Attendants.

Othello. Good Michael, look you to the guard to-night:
Let's teach ourselves that honourable stop,
Not to outsport discretion.
    Cassio. Iago hath direction what to do;
But, notwithstanding, with my personal eye   5
Will I look to't.
    Othello.   Iago is most honest.
Michael, good night; to-morrow with your earliest
Let me have speech with you. [*To* DESDEMONA.]Come, my
        dear love,
The purchase made, the fruits are to ensue;
That profit's yet to come 'twixt me and you.   10
Good night.
          [*Exeunt* OTHELLO, DESDEMONA, *and* Attendants.

3 **mere perdition**: total loss.   **put ... triumph**: take part
in public rejoicings.   9 **offices**: kitchens, butteries.   11
have: shall have.   2–3 i.e. let us learn when to stop, an excellent
lesson, so that we do not revel beyond proper bounds.   7 **with
your earliest**: as early as possible.   9 **purchase made**: prize
obtained.   10 i.e. we have not yet enjoyed our wedding-night.

Enter IAGO.

Cassio. Welcome, Iago; we must to the watch.

Iago. Not this hour, lieutenant; 'tis not yet ten o' the clock. Our general cast us thus early for the love of his Desdemona, who let us not therefore blame; he hath not yet made wanton the night with her, and she is sport for Jove.

Cassio. She's a most exquisite lady.   17

Iago. And, I'll warrant her, full of game.

Cassio. Indeed, she is a most fresh and delicate creature.

Iago. What an eye she has! methinks it sounds a parley of provocation.   21

Cassio. An inviting eye; and yet methinks right modest.

Iago. And when she speaks, is it not an alarum to love?

Cassio. She is indeed perfection.   24

Iago. Well, happiness to their sheets! Come, lieutenant, I have a stoup of wine, and here without are a brace of Cyprus gallants that would fain have a measure to the health of black Othello.

Cassio. Not to-night, good Iago: I have very poor and unhappy brains for drinking: I could well wish courtesy would invent some other custom of entertainment.   31

Iago. O! they are our friends; but one cup: I'll drink for you.

Cassio. I have drunk but one cup to-night, and that was craftily qualified too, and, behold, what innovation it makes here: I am unfortunate in the infirmity, and dare not task my weakness with any more.   37

---

13 **Not this hour** : not for an hour.   14 **cast** : dismissed (as in I. i. 148).   18 **game** : amorous sport.   20-1 **sounds ... provocation** : speaks provocative language, invites to love.   23 **alarum to love** : rousing call to love.   26 **stoup** : tankard (of two quarts). 27 **gallants** : (young) gentlemen.   **have a measure** : drink a toast.   30 **unhappy brains** : a poor head.   **courtesy** : polite custom.   35 **craftily qualified** : carefully diluted.   **innovation** : disorder.   36 **here** : (he points to his head).   37 **task** : put a strain on.

Iago. What, man! 'tis a night of revels; the gallants
desire it.

Cassio. Where are they?   40

Iago. Here at the door; I pray you, call them in.

Cassio. I'll do't; but it dislikes me.   [*Exit.*

Iago. If I can fasten but one cup upon him,
With that which he hath drunk to-night already,
He'll be as full of quarrel and offence   45
As my young mistress' dog. Now, my sick fool Roderigo,
Whom love has turn'd almost the wrong side out,
To Desdemona hath to-night carous'd
Potations pottle deep; and he's to watch.
Three lads of Cyprus, noble swelling spirits,   50
That hold their honours in a wary distance,
The very elements of this war-like isle,
Have I to-night fluster'd with flowing cups.
And they watch too. Now, 'mongst this flock of drunkards,
Am I to put our Cassio in some action   55
That may offend the isle. But here they come.
If consequence do but approve my dream,
My boat sails freely, both with wind and stream.

Re-enter CASSIO, *with him* MONTANO, *and* Gentlemen.
Servant *following with wine.*

Cassio. 'Fore God, they have given me a rouse already.

42 **it dislikes me:** I dislike it.   43 **fasten... upon him:** persuade
him to accept.   45 **offence:** readiness to take offence, and/or to give it.
46 **my young mistress' dog:** any young lady's (spoilt) dog (cf. 71).
47 **the ... out:** upside down.   48 **carous'd:** swilled.   49 **pottle
deep:** to the bottom of a two-quart pot.   **watch:** see II. i. 263.
50 **lads:** bright boys [*N*].   **noble ... spirits:** fine high-spirited
fellows.   51 **hold...distance:** are not too easy-going (i.e. are
very touchy) about their honour [*N*].   52 **elements ... isle:**
typical Cypriot hot-heads [*N*].   53 **flowing:** abundant.   55 **Am
I:** I propose.   56 **offend:** disturb (the peace of).   57 **consequence:** what follows.   **approve my dream:** confirm my hopes.
58 **stream:** current.   59 **rouse:** full draught.

Montano. Good faith, a little one; not past a pint, as
I am a soldier.   61
  Iago. Some wine, ho!

> And let me the canakin clink, clink;
> And let me the canakin clink:
>> A soldier's a man;   65
>> A life's but a span;
> Why then let a soldier drink.

Some wine, boys!
  Cassio. 'Fore God, an excellent song.   69
  Iago. I learned it in England, where indeed they are
most potent in potting; your Dane, your German, and
your swag-bellied Hollander,—drink, ho!—are nothing to
your English.   73
  Cassio. Is your Englishman so exquisite in his drinking?
  Iago. Why, he drinks you with facility your Dane dead
drunk; he sweats not to overthrow your Almain; he
gives your Hollander a vomit ere the next pottle can be
filled.
  Cassio. To the health of our general!   79
  Montano. I am for it, lieutenant; and I'll do you justice.
  Iago. O sweet England!

> King Stephen was a worthy peer,
>> His breeches cost him but a crown;
> He held them sixpence all too dear,
>> With that he call'd the tailor lown.   85

---

63 let me :]et's have.   **canakin :** small tankard.   **66 span :**
short time [*N*].   **71 potent in potting :** mighty tipplers.
your Dane : i.e. a Dane, any Dane [*N*].   **72 swag-bellied :**
pot-bellied.   **74 exquisite :** first-class [*N*].   **76 sweats
not to :** i.e. finds it easy to.   **Almain :** German.   **77 gives
. . . vomit :** i.e. lets the Dutchman have as handicap a vomit [*N*].
80 do you justice : equal you in drinking.   **82 peer :** lord
[*N*].   **84 held :** thought.   **85 lown :** fool.

> He was a wight of high renown,
>> And thou art but of low degree:
> 'Tis pride that pulls the country down,
>> Then take thine auld cloak about thee.

Some wine, ho!   90

Cassio. Why, this is a more exquisite song than the other.

Iago. Will you hear't again?

Cassio. No; for I hold him to be unworthy of his place that does those things. Well, God's above all; and there be souls must be saved, and there be souls must not be saved.   96

Iago. It's true, good lieutenant.

Cassio. For mine own part,—no offence to the general, nor any man of quality,—I hope to be saved.

Iago. And so do I too, lieutenant.   100

Cassius. Ay; but, by your leave, not before me; the lieutenant is to be saved before the ancient. Let's have no more of this; let's to our affairs. God forgive us our sins! Gentlemen, let's look to our business. Do not think, gentlemen, I am drunk: this is my   105 ancient; this is my right hand, and this is my left hand. I am not drunk now; I can stand well enough, and speak well enough.

All. Excellent well.   109

Cassio. Why, very well, then; you must not think then that I am drunk.   [*Exit.*

Montano. To the platform, masters; come, let's set the watch.

Iago. You see this fellow that is gone before;
He is a soldier fit to stand by Caesar

---

86 **wight**: man.   89 **auld**: Scottish form of 'old'.   91 **exquisite**: witty.   95 **souls must**: i.e. which must. 99 **quality**: rank.   112 **platform**: the gun-platform, used as station for sentries (*Hamlet* I. ii. 251).   **set the watch**: relieve and mount guard.

And give direction; and do but see his vice;   115
'Tis to his virtue a just equinox,
The one as long as the other; 'tis pity of him.
I fear the trust Othello puts him in,
On some odd time of his infirmity,
Will shake this island.
   Montano.   But is he often thus?   120
   Iago. 'Tis evermore the prologue to his sleep:
He'll watch the horologe a double set,
If drink rock not his cradle.
   Montano.   It were well
The general were put in mind of it.
Perhaps he sees it not; or his good nature   125
Prizes the virtue that appears in Cassio,
And looks not on his evils. Is not this true?

Enter RODERIGO.

   Iago. [*Aside to him.*] How now, Roderigo!
I pray you, after the lieutenant; go.   [*Exit* RODERIGO.
   Montano. And 'tis great pity that the noble Moor   130
Should hazard such a place as his own second
With one of an ingraft infirmity;
It were an honest action to say
So to the Moor.
   Iago.   Not I, for this fair island: 135
I do love Cassio well, and would do much
To cure him of this evil. But hark! what noise?
[*Cry within,* 'Help! Help!'

---

115 **direction**: orders in battle.   116 **equinox**: exactly
equal [*N*].   117 **of him**: about him, in his case.   118
trust: position of responsibility.   119 **some odd time**: some
time or other.   122 **watch . . . set**: be awake for two rounds
of the clock.   131 i.e. risk having as his second in command.
132 **ingraft**: ingrafted, firmly implanted.   133 **honest**:
honourable.

Re-enter CASSIO, *driving in* RODERIGO.

Cassio. You rogue! you rascal!

Montano.   What's the matter, lieutenant?

Cassio. A knave teach me my duty!

I'll beat the knave into a twiggen bottle.   139

Roderigo. Beat me!

Cassio.   Dost thou prate, rogue?

                     [*Striking* RODERIGO.

Montano.   [*Staying him.*] Nay, good lieutenant;

I pray you, sir, hold your hand.

Cassio.   Let me go, sir,

Or I'll knock you o'er the mazzard.

Montano.   Come, come; you're drunk.

Cassio. Drunk!   [*They fight.*

Iago. [*Aside to* RODERIGO.] Away, I say! go out, and

     cry a mutiny.   [*Exit* RODERIGO.

Nay, good lieutenant! God's will, gentlemen!   145

Help, ho! Lieutenant! sir! Montano! sir!

Help, masters! Here's a goodly watch indeed!

                       [*Bell rings.*

Who's that that rings the bell? *Diablo*, ho!

The town will rise: God's will! lieutenant, hold!

You will be sham'd for ever.

Re-enter OTHELLO *and* Attendants.

Othello.   What is the matter here? 150

Montano. 'Zounds! I bleed still; I am hurt to the death.

---

139 **beat . . . twiggen bottle**: i.e. chase him into the smallest
hole ('twiggen' = made of twigs) [*N*].   140 **prate**: (here)
answer back.   142 **mazzard**: head (slang).   144 **cry a
mutiny**: call out that a riot is taking place.   145 **God's will**:
let God's will be done, i.e. Peace! (a mild protest).   147
goodly: fine (ironical).   148 **Diablo**: what the devil! (Spanish).
149 **rise**: i.e. in riot.   **hold**: stop!   151 **'Zounds**: God's
wounds! (an oath).

Othello. Hold, for your lives!

Iago. Hold, ho, lieutenant! Sir! Montano! gentlemen!
Have you forgot all sense of place and duty?
Hold! the general speaks to you; hold for shame!   155
    Othello. Why, how now, ho! from whence ariseth this?
Are we turn'd Turks, and to ourselves do that
Which heaven hath forbid the Ottomites?
For Christian shame put by this barbarous brawl;
He that stirs next to carve for his own rage   160
Holds his soul light; he dies upon his motion.
Silence that dreadful bell! it frights the isle
From her propriety. What is the matter, masters?
Honest Iago, that look'st dead with grieving,
Speak, who began this? on thy love, I charge thee.   165
    Iago. I do not know; friends all but now, even now,
In quarter and in terms like bride and groom
Devesting them for bed; and then, but now,—
As if some planet had unwitted men,—
Swords out, and tilting one at other's breast,   170
In opposition bloody. I cannot speak
Any beginning to this peevish odds,
And would in action glorious I had lost
Those legs that brought me to a part of it!
    Othello. How comes it, Michael, you are thus forgot? 175
    Cassio. I pray you, pardon me; I cannot speak.

154 **sense of place**: feeling for where you are.   158 i.e.
by destroying their fleet [*N*].   160 **carve . . . rage**: satisfy
his anger [*N*].   161 **soul**: life.   **upon his motion**: as soon
as he moves.   162 **dreadful**: causing fear.   163 **propriety**: natural state (of quiet).   164 **dead**: i.e. deadly pale
[*N*].   166 **friends . . . now**: they were friends only a moment
ago.   167 **In quarter**: (probably) on good terms.   **in terms
like**: on such a footing as.   **groom**: bridegroom.   168 **devesting them**(selves): undressing.   169 **unwitted**: deprived of
wits [*N*].   171 **speak**: tell of.   172 **peevish odds**:
stupid quarrel [*N*].   175 **you . . . forgot**: you forgot yourself
thus.

Othello. Worthy Montano, you were wont be civil;
The gravity and stillness of your youth
The world hath noted, and your name is great
In mouths of wisest censure: what's the matter,   180
That you unlace your reputation thus
And spend your rich opinion for the name
Of a night-brawler? give me answer to it.
   Montano. Worthy Othello, I am hurt to danger;
Your officer, Iago, can inform you,   185
While I spare speech, which something now offends me,
Of all that I do know; nor know I aught
By me that's said or done amiss this night,
Unless self-charity be sometimes a vice,
And to defend ourselves it be a sin   190
When violence assails us.
   Othello.   Now, by heaven,
My blood begins my safer guides to rule,
And passion, having my best judgment collied,
Assays to lead the way. If I once stir,
Or do but lift this arm, the best of you   195
Shall sink in my rebuke. Give me to know
How this foul rout began, who set it on;
And he that is approv'd in this offence,
Though he had twinn'd with me—both at a birth—
Shall lose me. What! in a town of war,   200

177 **wont be civil**: accustomed to be well behaved.   178
stillness: sobriety.   180 **mouths of wisest censure**: people
whose opinion is worth having.   181 **unlace**: ruin [*N*].
182 **spend**: throw away.   **your rich opinion**: the excellent
opinion people have of you.   186 **spare**: am sparing of.   **something**: to some extent.   **offends**: hurts.   189 **self-charity**:
looking after oneself.   192 **blood**: anger.   **safer guides**: i.e.
reason, judgement.   193 **collied**: darkened [*N*].   194 **Assays**:
attempts.   196 **sink ... rebuke**: feel the weight of my punishment.
197 **rout**: uproar.   **set it on**: started it.   198 **approv'd**:
shown to be guilty.   199 **twinn'd**: been born as a twin.   200 **lose
me**: lose my confidence.   **of war**: under military law.

Yet wild, the people's hearts brimful of fear,
To manage private and domestic quarrel,
In night, and on the court and guard of safety!
'Tis monstrous. Iago, who began't?

   Montano. If partially affin'd, or leagu'd in office,   205
Thou dost deliver more or less than truth,
Thou art no soldier.

   Iago.   Touch me not so near;
I had rather have this tongue cut from my mouth
Than it should do offence to Michael Cassio;
Yet, I persuade myself, to speak the truth   210
Shall nothing wrong him. Thus it is, general.
Montano and myself being in speech,
There comes a fellow crying out for help,
And Cassio following with determin'd sword
To execute upon him. Sir, this gentleman   215
Steps in to Cassio, and entreats his pause;
Myself the crying fellow did pursue,
Lest by his clamour, as it so fell out,
The town might fall in fright; he, swift of foot,
Outran my purpose, and I return'd the rather   220
For that I heard the clink and fall of swords,
And Cassio high in oath, which till 'to-night
I ne'er might say before. When I came back,—
For this was brief,—I found them close together,

201 **Yet wild:** still disturbed.   202 **manage:** conduct.
domestic: personal.   203 **on the court . . . safety:** (probably) on duty in the guard-room and responsible for safety [*N*].
205 **partially affin'd:** bound by ties of friendship.   **leagu'd in
office:** i.e. because you have a bond as brother-officers.   206
deliver: report.   207 **Touch . . . near:** i.e. do not remind
me so sharply (of my feeling for Cassio).   214–15 **determin'd . . .
execute:** sword determined to wreak his anger.   215 **this gentleman:** i.e. Montano.   216 **entreats his pause:** asks him to stop.
217 **crying:** shouting.   219 **in:** into.   220 **Outran my
purpose:** was too fast for me.   **the rather:** the more quickly.
221 **fall:** clash.   222 **high:** loud.

At blow and thrust, even as again they were   225
When you yourself did part them.
More of this matter can I not report:
But men are men; the best sometimes forget:
Though Cassio did some little wrong to him,
As men in rage strike those that wish them best,   230
Yet, surely Cassio, I believe, receiv'd
From him that fled some strange indignity,
Which patience could not pass.
    Othello.   I know, Iago,
Thy honesty and love doth mince this matter,
Making it light to Cassio. Cassio, I love thee;   235
But never more be officer of mine.

Enter DESDEMONA, *attended.*

Look! if my gentle love be not rais'd up;
[*To* CASSIO.] I'll make thee an example.
    Desdemona.   What's the matter?
    Othello. All's well now, sweeting; come away to bed.
Sir, for your hurts, myself will be your surgeon.   240
Lead him off.   [MONTANO *is led off.*
Iago, look with care about the town,
And silence those whom this vile brawl distracted.
Come, Desdemona; 'tis the soldiers' life,
To have their balmy slumbers wak'd with strife.   245
                    [*Exeunt all but* IAGO *and* CASSIO.
    Iago. What! are you hurt, lieutenant?
    Cassio. Ay; past all surgery.
    Iago. Marry, heaven forbid!
    Cassio. Reputation, reputation, reputation! O! I
have lost my reputation. I have lost the immortal part 250

---

  232 **strange**: unusual.   **indignity**: insult.   233 **pass**:
endure.   234 **mince**: minimize.   237 **rais'd**: roused.
240 **myself ... surgeon**: I will look after you.

of myself, and what remains is bestial. My reputation,
Iago my reputation!

Iago. As I am an honest man, I thought you had
received some bodily wound; there is more offence in
that than in reputation. Reputation is an idle and   255
most false imposition; oft got without merit, and lost
without deserving: you have lost no reputation at
all, unless you repute yourself such a loser. What!
man; there are ways to recover the general again;
you are but now cast in his mood, a punishment more   260
in policy than in malice; even so as one would beat
his offenceless dog to affright an imperious lion.
Sue to him again, and he is yours.

Cassio. I will rather sue to be despised than to
deceive so good a commander with so slight, so   265
drunken, and so indiscreet an officer. Drunk! and
speak parrot! and squabble, swagger, swear, and
discourse fustian with one's own shadow! O thou
invisible spirit of wine! if thou hast no name to be
known by, let us call thee devil!   270

Iago. What was he that you followed with your
sword? What had he done to you?

Cassio. I know not.

Iago. Is't possible?

Cassio. I remember a mass of things, but nothing   275
distinctly; a quarrel, but nothing wherefore. O

---

254 **offence** : damage.   255 **idle** : empty.   256 **imposition** :
attribution (by the public).   259 **recover** : reconcile yourself
with.   260 **cast** : dismissed.   **mood** : anger.   260–1 **punishment . . . malice** : i.e. a punishment dictated more by policy than
by real disgust with you.   262 **imperious** : majestic [*N*].
264–5 **than to deceive** : slightly ungrammatical for 'than deceive' or
'than be given the opportunity again to deceive'.   265 **slight** :
worthless.   267 **speak parrot** : talk nonsense.   268 **fustian** :
rubbish (literally a cheap cloth).   **with one's own shadow** : some
unreal opponent, *or* one's self.   276 **wherefore** : as to its cause.

God! that men should put an enemy in their mouths
to steal away their brains; that we should, with joy,
pleasance, revel, and applause, transform ourselves
into beasts.   280

Iago. Why, but you are now well enough; how came
you thus recovered?

Cassio. It hath pleased the devil drunkenness to give
place to the devil wrath; one unperfectness shows me
another, to make me frankly despise myself.   285

Iago. Come, you are too severe a moraler. As the time
the place, and the condition of this country stands,
I could heartily wish this had not befallen, but since
it is as it is, mend it for your own good.

Cassio. I will ask him for my place again; he shall   290
tell me I am a drunkard! Had I as many mouths as
Hydra, such an answer would stop them all. To be
now a sensible man, by and by a fool, and presently
a beast! O strange! Every inordinate cup is un-
blessed and the ingredient is a devil.   295

Iago. Come, come; good wine is a good familiar
creature if it be well used; exclaim no more against it.
And, good lieutenant, I think you think I love you.

Cassio. I have well approved it, sir. I drunk!

Iago. You or any man living may be drunk at   300
some time, man. I'll tell you what you shall do. Our
general's wife is now the general: I may say so in this
respect, for that he hath devoted and given up himself
to the contemplation, mark, and denotement of her
parts and graces: confess yourself freely to her; impor- 305

---

279 **pleasance**: pleasure.   **applause**: approval.   286
moraler: moralizer.   292 **Hydra**: a many-headed monster [N].
293 **presently**: immediately after.   294 **inordinate**: excessive.
295 **ingredient**: chief component.   296 **familiar**: friendly [N].
299 **approved**: proved.   304 **mark**: observation.   **denotement**: noting, study [N].   305 **parts**: virtues, merits.

tune her; she'll help to put you in your place again.
She is of so free, so kind, so apt, so blessed a disposition, that she holds it a vice in her goodness not to do
more than she is requested. This broken joint between
you and her husband entreat her to splinter; and my   310
fortunes against any lay worth naming, this crack of
your love shall grow stronger than it was before.

   Cassio. You advise me well.

   Iago. I protest, in the sincerity of love and honest
kindness.   315

   Cassio. I think it freely; and betimes in the morning
I will beseech the virtuous Desdemona to undertake for
me. I am desperate of my fortunes if they check me here.

   Iago. You are in the right. Good night, lieutenant;
I must to the watch.   320

   Cassio. Good night, honest Iago!   [*Exit.*

   Iago. And what's he then that says I play the villain?
When this advice is free I give and honest,
Probal to thinking and indeed the course
To win the Moor again? For 'tis most easy   325
The inclining Desdemona to subdue
In any honest suit; she's fram'd as fruitful
As the free elements. And then for her
To win the Moor, were't to renounce his baptism,
All seals and symbols of redeemed sin,   330

   307 free: generous.   **apt**: willing.   **310 splinter**: make a
splint for, i.e. mend [*N*].   **311 lay**: bet.   **314 protest**: assure you
(that it is).   **316 freely**: willingly.   **betimes**: early.   **317
undertake**: plead.   **318 I am . . . here**: i.e. I despair
of retrieving my position if I fail to get Desdemona on my side.
322 what's he: who is he.   **323 free**: frank.   **324 Probal**:
probable (here only).   **326 inclining**: gracious.   **subdue**:
win over.   **327 suit**: plea, cause.   **fram'd**: is by nature.   **fruitful**: benevolent.   **328 free**: bountiful.   **329 were't to
renounce**: even if it meant renouncing.   **330 All ... sin**: (and)
all the outward signs and symbols which show he is redeemed from
sin (i.e. a baptized Christian).

His soul is so enfetter'd to her love,
That she may make, unmake, do what she list,
Even as her appetite shall play the god
With his weak function. How am I then a villain
To counsel Cassio to this parallel course,   335
Directly to his good? Divinity of hell!
When devils will the blackest sins put on,
They do suggest at first with heavenly shows,
As I do now; for while this honest fool
Plies Desdemona to repair his fortunes,   340
And she for him pleads strongly to the Moor,
I'll pour this pestilence into his ear
That she repeals him for her body's lust;
And, by how much she strives to do him good,
She shall undo her credit with the Moor.   345
So will I turn her virtue into pitch,
And out of her own goodness make the net
That shall enmesh them all.

Re-enter RODERIGO.

How now, Roderigo!
Roderigo. I do follow here in the chase, not like
a hound that hunts, but one that fills up the cry.   350
My money is almost spent; I have been to-night
exceedingly well cudgelled; and I think the issue
will be, I shall have so much experience for my

332 **list**: like.   333–4 **Even . . . function**: just as his passion
for her governs (like a god) his mind, which is thus weakened [*N*].
335–6 **parallel . . . good**: course of action which is in line with his
welfare [*N*].   336 **Divinity of hell**: hellish theology [*N*].
337 **put on**: instigate.   338 **suggest**: tempt.   **shows**:
appearances.   342 **pestilence**: poison.   343 **repeals**:
calls back into favour.   344 **by how much**: in proportion as.
345 **undo**: ruin.   **credit**: reputation.   349–50 i.e. I am
merely a subordinate in this, a mere voice ('cry' = a pack of
hounds).

pains; and so, with no money at all and a little more
wit, return again to Venice.   355

Iago. How poor are they that have not patience!
What wound did ever heal but by degrees?
Thou know'st we work by wit and not by witchcraft,
And wit depends on dilatory time.
Does't not go well? Cassio hath beaten thee,   360
And thou by that small hurt hast cashiered Cassio.
Though other things grow fair against the sun,
Yet fruits that blossom first will first be ripe:
Content thyself awhile. By the mass, 'tis morning;
Pleasure and action make the hours seem short.   365
Retire thee; go where thou art billeted:
Away, I say; thou shalt know more hereafter:
Nay, get thee gone. [*Exit* RODERIGO.] Two things are to
     be done,
My wife must move for Cassio to her mistress;
I'll set her on;   370
Myself the while to draw the Moor apart,
And bring him jump when he may Cassio find
Soliciting his wife: ay, that's the way:
Dull not device by coldness and delay.   [*Exit.*

355 **wit**: sense.   358 **wit**: brains, intelligence.   359 **dilatory**: which moves slowly.   362–3 **Though ... ripe**: i.e. (probably) other things (the plot against Othello and Desdemona) are
doing well enough; but the fruits coming from the first blossoms
(the plot against Cassio) will mature first [*N*].   364 **Content
... awhile**: be patient.   369 **move for**: appeal on behalf of.
372 **jump when**: exactly at the time when.   373 **soliciting**:
pleading to.   374 i.e. strike while the iron is hot. ('device' = plan).

ACT III

Scene I. CYPRUS. BEFORE THE CASTLE

Enter CASSIO, *and some* Musicians.

Cassio. Masters, play here, I will content your pains;
Something that's brief; and bid 'Good morrow, general.'

Enter Clown.   [*Music.*

Clown. Why, masters, have your instruments been in
Naples, that they speak i' the nose thus?

First Musician. How, sir, how?   5

Clown. Are these, I pray you, wind-instruments?

First Musician. Ay, marry, are they, sir.

Clown. O! thereby hangs a tail.

First Musician. Whereby hangs a tale, sir?   9

Clown. Marry, sir, by many a wind-instrument that
I know. But, masters, here's money for you; and the
general so likes your music, that he desires you, for love's
sake, to make no more noise with it.

First Musician. Well, sir, we will not.   14

Clown. If you have any music that may not be heard,
to't again; but, as they say, to hear music the general does
not greatly care.

First Musician. We have none such, sir.   18

Clown. Then put up your pipes in your bag, for I'll
away. Go; vanish into air; away!   [*Exeunt* Musicians.

---

1 Masters: gentlemen.   **content your pains**: pay you for your
trouble.   **4 speak i' the nose**: have a nasal quality [*N*].
7 marry: oath by the Virgin Mary.   **8 hangs a tail**: there is
more to say about that.   **10 wind-instrument**: the Clown
refers to the *anus*.   **16 to't**: to it, i.e. start up.   **general**:
both (i) the general, Othello, and (ii) people in general, the public.
19 put . . . bag: i.e. stop playing (a pun on bagpipes).

Cassio. Dost thou hear, mine honest friend?

Clown. No, I hear not your honest friend; I hear you.

Cassio. Prithee, keep up thy quillets. There's a poor piece of gold for thee. If the gentlewoman that attends the general's wife be stirring, tell her there's one Cassio entreats her a little favour of speech: wilt thou do this?

Clown. She is stirring, sir: if she will stir hither, I shall seem to notify unto her.

Cassio. Do, good my friend.   [*Exit* Clown.

Enter IAGO.

In happy time, Iago.

Iago. You have not been a-bed, then?   30

Cassio. Why, no; the day had broke
Before we parted. I have made bold, Iago,
To send in to your wife; my suit to her
Is, that she will to virtuous Desdemona
Procure me some access.

Iago.   I'll send her to you presently; 35
And I'll devise a mean to draw the Moor
Out of the way, that your converse and business
May be more free.

Cassio. I humbly thank you for't. [*Exit* IAGO.] I never
        knew
A Florentine more kind and honest.   40

Enter EMILIA.

Emilia. Good morrow, good lieutenant: I am sorry
For your displeasure; but all will sure be well.
The general and his wife are talking of it,

23 **keep up** : put away. **quillets** : quibbles.   23–4 **poor piece** : Cassio excuses the tip.   26 **entreats** : begs.   28 **seem to** : make it my business to [*N*].   29 **In happy time** : you have come just at the right time.   35 **presently** : at once.   36 **mean** : means.   42 **For your displeasure** : for your being out of favour. **sure** : surely.

And she speaks for you stoutly: the Moor replies
That he you hurt is of great fame in Cyprus   45
And great affinity, and that in wholesome wisdom
He might not but refuse you; but he protests he loves
    you,
And needs no other suitor but his likings
To take the saf'st occasion by the front
To bring you in again.

Cassio.   Yet, I beseech you,   50
If you think fit, or that it may be done,
Give me advantage of some brief discourse
With Desdemona alone.

Emilia.   Pray you, come in:
I will bestow you where you shall have time
To speak your bosom freely.

Cassio.   I am much bound to you. 55
                                     [*Exeunt.*

Scene II. A ROOM IN THE CASTLE

Enter OTHELLO, IAGO, *and* Gentlemen.

Othello. These letters give, Iago, to the pilot,
And by him do my duties to the senate;
That done, I will be walking on the works;
Repair there to me.

Iago.   Well, my good lord, I'll do't.

Othello. This fortification, gentlemen, shall we see't?   5

Gentlemen. We'll wait upon your lordship.   [*Exeunt.*

46 (of) **great affinity**: highly connected. **in wholesome wisdom**:
as a matter of wise policy.   47 **might . . . you**: could not but cashier
you.   49 **take . . . front**: take the first safe opportunity ('front' =
forelock) [*N*].   50 **bring . . . again**: restore you.   53 **Desdemona** [Q. Desdemon]: The final -a is elided before the following
vowel for metrical purposes.   54 **bestow**: place.   55 **speak
your bosom**: unburden yourself. **bound**: obliged.   2 **do my
duties**: pay my respects.   3 **works**: fortifications.   4 **repair**:
come back. **Well**: very good.

Scene III. BEFORE THE CASTLE

Enter DESDEMONA, CASSIO, *and* EMILIA.

Desdemona. Be assur'd, good Cassio, I will do
All my abilities in thy behalf.
   Emilia. Good madam, do: I warrant it grieves my
      husband,
As if the cause were his.
   Desdemona. O! that's an honest fellow. Do not doubt,
      Cassio,   5
But I will have my lord and you again
As friendly as you were.
   Cassio.   Bounteous madam,
Whatever shall become of Michael Cassio,
He's never anything but your true servant.
   Desdemona. I know't; I thank you. You do love my
      lord;   10
You have known him long; and be you well assur'd
He shall in strangeness stand no further off
Than in a politic distance.
   Cassio.   Ay, but, lady,
That policy may either last so long,
Or feed upon such nice and waterish diet,   15
Or breed itself so out of circumstance,
That, I being absent and my place supplied,
My general will forget my love and service.
   Desdemona. Do not doubt that; before Emilia here
I give thee warrant of thy place. Assure thee,   20
If I do vow a friendship, I'll perform it

2 **All my abilities**: the best I can.   4 **cause**: affair, matter.
12–13 **He ... distance**: he shall be no colder towards you than
policy demands.   15 **feed ... diet**: be maintained for such
trivial and weak reasons.   16 **breed ... circumstance**: be
kept up by mere accidents to such an extent [*N*].   17 **supplied**:
filled.   19 **doubt**: fear.   20 **warrant**: assurance.

To the last article; my lord shall never rest;
I'll watch him tame, and talk him out of patience;
His bed shall seem a school, his board a shrift;
I'll intermingle every thing he does   25
With Cassio's suit. Therefore be merry, Cassio;
For thy solicitor shall rather die
Than give thy cause away.

Enter OTHELLO, *and* IAGO *at a distance.*

Emilia. Madam, here comes my lord.
Cassio. Madam, I'll take my leave.   30
Desdemona. Why, stay, and hear me speak.
Cassio. Madam, not now; I am very ill at ease,
Unfit for mine own purposes.
Desdemona. Well, do your discretion.   [*Exit* CASSIO.
Iago. Ha! I like not that.
Othello.   What dost thou say?   35
Iago. Nothing, my lord: or if—I know not what.
Othello. Was not that Cassio parted from my wife?
Iago. Cassio, my lord? No, sure, I cannot think it
That he would steal away so guilty-like,
Seeing you coming.
Othello.   I do believe 'twas he.   40
Desdemona. How now, my lord!
I have been talking with a suitor here,
A man that languishes in your displeasure.
Othello. Who is't you mean?
Desdemona. Why, your lieutenant, Cassio. Good my
lord,   45

22 **article**: detail.   23 **watch him tame**: keep him awake
until he agrees [*N*].   24 **board**: table, i.e. meals.   **shrift**:
confessional[*N*].   27 **solicitor**: advocate.   28 **give . . .
away**: abandon.   33 **for . . . purposes**: i.e. to plead my case.
34 **do your discretion**: do as you think fit.   42 **suitor**: peti-
tioner.   43 **languishes in**: suffers under.

If I have any grace or power to move you,
His present reconciliation take;
For if he be not one that truly loves you,
That errs in ignorance and not in cunning,
I have no judgment in an honest face.   50
I prithee call him back.

   Othello.   Went he hence now?

   Desdemona. Ay, sooth; so humbled,
That he hath left part of his grief with me,
To suffer with him. Good love, call him back.   54

   Othello. Not now, sweet Desdemona; some other time.

   Desdemona. But shall't be shortly?

   Othello.   The sooner, sweet, for you.

   Desdemona. Shall't be to-night at supper?

   Othello.   No, not to-night.

   Desdemona. To-morrow dinner then?

   Othello.   I shall not dine at home;
I meet the captains at the citadel.

   Desdemona. Why then, to-morrow night; or Tuesday
     morn;   60
On Tuesday noon, or night; on Wednesday morn:
I prithee name the time, but let it not
Exceed three days: in faith, he's penitent;
And yet his trespass, in our common reason,—
Save that they say, the wars must make examples   65
Out of their best,—is not almost a fault
To incur a private check. When shall he come?
Tell me, Othello; I wonder in my soul,
What you could ask me that I should deny,

<hr>

47 **His . . . take:** accept his immediate repentance.   **49 in
cunning:** knowingly.   50 **in:** as to.   51 **prithee:** pray
you.   52 **sooth:** indeed.   56 **for:** because of.   58 **dinner:**
i.e. at midday.   64 **trespass:** offence.   **in . . . reason:** judging
by normal standards.   65–6 **the wars . . . best:** i.e. examples must
be made of the best soldiers to preserve discipline.   66–7 i.e.
hardly deserves a private (let alone a public) rebuke.

Or stand so mammering on. What! Michael Cassio,   70
That came a wooing with you, and so many a time,
When I have spoke of you dispraisingly,
Hath ta'en your part; to have so much to do
To bring him in! Trust me, I could do much.—
  Othello. Prithee, no more; let him come when he will; 75
I will deny thee nothing.
  Desdemona.   Why, this is not a boon;
'Tis as I should entreat you wear your gloves,
Or feed on nourishing dishes, or keep you warm,
Or sue to you to do peculiar profit
To your own person; nay, when I have a suit   80
Wherein I mean to touch your love indeed,
It shall be full of poise and difficult weight,
And fearful to be granted.
  Othello.   I will deny thee nothing:
Whereon, I do beseech thee, grant me this,
To leave me but a little to myself.   85
  Desdemona. Shall I deny you? no: farewell, my lord.
  Othello. Farewell, my Desdemona: I'll come to thee
    straight.
  Desdemona. Emilia, come. Be as your fancies teach you;
Whate'er you be, I am obedient.   [*Exit, with* EMILIA.
  Othello. Excellent wretch! Perdition catch my soul   90
But I do love thee! and when I love thee not,
Chaos is come again.

---

70 **mammering** : hesitating, dithering.   73 **so much to do** :
so much difficulty.   74 **bring him in** : restore him.   76 **boon** :
favour.   77 **as** : as if.   78 **you** : yourself.   79 **peculiar** :
personal (Latin *peculiaris* = one's own).   81 **touch** : test.   82
poise : weight, importance.   **difficult weight** : so weighty that it will
be difficult to decide upon.   83 **fearful ... granted** : occasioning
doubt as to whether it can be granted.   84 **Whereon** : in return
for which.   87 **straight** : immediately.   88 **Be ... you** : do as
you think best.   90 **Perdition** : i.e. hell [*N*].   91 **when
... not** : if I should not.   92 **is come** : would be come [*N*].

Iago. My noble lord,—
Othello. What dost thou say, Iago?
Iago. Did Michael Cassio, when you woo'd my lady,
Know of your love? 95
Othello. He did, from first to last: why dost thou ask?
Iago. But for a satisfaction of my thought;
No further harm.
Othello. Why of thy thought, Iago?
Iago. I did not think he had been acquainted with her.
Othello. O! yes; and went between us very oft. 100
Iago. Indeed!
Othello. Indeed! ay, indeed; discern'st thou aught in that?
Is he not honest?
Iago. Honest, my lord?
Othello. Honest! ay, honest.
Iago. My lord, for aught I know. 104
Othello. What dost thou think?
Iago. Think, my lord!
Othello. Think, my lord!
By heaven, he echoes me,
As if there were some monster in his thought
Too hideous to be shown. Thou dost mean something:
I heard thee say but now, thou lik'dst not that,
When Cassio left my wife; what didst not like? 110
And when I told thee he was of my counsel
In my whole course of wooing, thou criedst 'Indeed!'
And didst contract and purse thy brow together,
As if thou then hadst shut up in thy brain
Some horrible conceit. If thou dost love me, 115
Show me thy thought.
Iago. My lord, you know I love you.
Othello. I think thou dost;

---

100 **went between us:** i.e. with letters, messages, etc.
103 **honest:** honourable. 109 **but now:** just now (l. 35) [*N*].
111 **of my counsel:** in my confidence. 115 **conceit:** idea.

And, for I know thou art full of love and honesty,
And weigh'st thy words before thou giv'st them breath,
Therefore these stops of thine fright me the more; 120
For such things in a false disloyal knave
Are tricks of custom, but in a man that's just
They are close dilations, working from the heart
That passion cannot rule.

Iago.   For Michael Cassio,
I dare be sworn I think that he is honest. 125
　Othello. I think so too.
　Iago.   Men should be what they seem;
Or those that be not, would they might seem none!
　Othello. Certain, men should be what they seem.
　Iago. Why then, I think Cassio's an honest man.
　Othello. Nay, yet there's more in this. 130
I pray thee, speak to me as to thy thinkings,
As thou dost ruminate, and give thy worst of thoughts
The worst of words.

Iago.   Good my lord, pardon me;
Though I am bound to every act of duty,
I am not bound to that all slaves are free to. 135
Utter my thoughts? Why, say they are vile and false;
As where's that palace whereinto foul things
Sometimes intrude not? who has a breast so pure
But some uncleanly apprehensions
Keep leets and law days, and in session sit 140
With meditations lawful?

120 **stops**: pauses, hesitations.　　**122 tricks of custom**:
common tricks.　　123 **close**: secret.　　**dilations**: movements
of the heart [*N*].　　124 **passion** ... **rule**: that cannot
govern its feelings [*N*].　　127 **seem none**: (probably) not
look like men.　　131-2 **speak** ... **ruminate**: tell me about
your thoughts just as they are.　　135 **I am** ... **free to**: I
am not bound in that in respect of which even slaves are free.
139 **apprehensions**: thoughts.　　140 **Keep leets and law days**:
hold court [*N*].　　**in session**: on the bench.

Othello. Thou dost conspire against thy friend, Iago,
If thou but think'st him wrong'd, and mak'st his
    ear
A stranger to thy thoughts.
  Iago. I do beseech you,
Though I perchance am vicious in my guess,—   145
As, I confess, it is my nature's plague
To spy into abuses, and oft my jealousy
Shapes faults that are not,—that your wisdom yet,
From one that so imperfectly conceits,
Would take no notice, nor build yourself a trouble   150
Out of his scattering and unsure observance.
It were not for your quiet nor your good,
Nor for my manhood, honesty, or wisdom,
To let you know my thoughts.
  Othello. What dost thou mean?
  Iago. Good name in man and woman, dear my lord, 155
Is the immediate jewel of their souls:
Who steals my purse steals trash; 'tis something,
    nothing;
'Twas mine, 'tis his, and has been slave to thousands;
But he that filches from me my good name
Robs me of that which not enriches him,   160
And makes me poor indeed.
  Othello. By heaven, I'll know thy thoughts.
  Iago. You cannot, if my heart were in your hand;
Nor shall not, whilst 'tis in my custody.
  Othello. Ha!
  Iago. O! beware, my lord, of jealousy;   165

145 i.e. even if I have put the worst construction on what I
saw [*N*].   146 **plague**: weakness, curse.   147 **jealousy**:
suspiciousness.   149 **conceits**: forms ideas.   151
scattering: random. **observance**: observation.   152 **were
not**: would not be.   155 **Good name**: reputation, honour.
156 **immediate**: most prized.   158 **has been slave to**: i.e.
money (the contents of the purse) has been owned by.

It is the green-ey'd monster which doth mock
The meat it feeds on; that cuckold lives in bliss
Who, certain of his fate, loves not his wronger;
But, O! what damned minutes tells he o'er
Who dotes, yet doubts; suspects, yet soundly loves!   170
   Othello. O misery!

   Iago. Poor and content is rich, and rich enough,
But riches fineless is as poor as winter
To him that ever fears he shall be poor.
Good heaven, the souls of all my tribe defend   175
From jealousy!
   Othello.   Why, why is this?
Think'st thou I'd make a life of jealousy,
To follow still the changes of the moon
With fresh suspicions? No; to be once in doubt
Is once to be resolved. Exchange me for a goat   180
When I shall turn the business of my soul
To such exsufflicate and blown surmises,
Matching thy inference. 'Tis not to make me jealous
To say my wife is fair, feeds well, loves company,
Is free of speech, sings, plays, and dances well;   185
Where virtue is, these are more virtuous:

166-7 which ... feeds on: i.e. which plays with (and so torments) the man who entertains it [*N*].   **167 cuckold:** husband of an unfaithful wife.   **168 his wronger:** i.e. his wife.   **169 what ... o'er:** what moments of agony he passes through ('tells o'er' = counts over).   **172 Poor:** to be poor.   **173 fineless:** infinite.   **175 all my tribe:** me and my family.   **177 make ... jealousy:** live in a state of jealousy.   **178-9 To follow ... suspicions:** and be a prey to fresh suspicions every time the moon changes.   **180 to be resolved:** to settle the matter once and for all [*N*].   **Exchange ... goat:** i.e. I should be no better than a goat (= lustful animal).   **181 the business ... soul:** my serious preoccupation.   **182 exsufflicate:** exaggerated.   **blown:** inflated [*N*].   **183 Matching thy inference:** as your allegations.   **'Tis not to:** it does not.   **185 free:** open, frank.   **186 these ... virtuous:** these things add to virtue.

Nor from mine own weak merits will I draw
The smallest fear, or doubt of her revolt;
For she had eyes, and chose me. No, Iago;
I'll see before I doubt; when I doubt, prove; 190
And, on the proof, there is no more but this,
Away at once with love or jealousy!

Iago. I am glad of it; for now I shall have reason
To show the love and duty that I bear you
With franker spirit; therefore, as I am bound, 195
Receive it from me; I speak not yet of proof.
Look to your wife; observe her well with Cassio;
Wear your eyes thus, not jealous nor secure:
I would not have your free and noble nature
Out of self-bounty be abus'd; look to't: 200
I know our country disposition well;
In Venice they do let heaven see the pranks
They dare not show their husbands; their best conscience
Is not to leave't undone, but keep't unknown.

Othello. Dost thou say so? 205

Iago. She did deceive her father, marrying you;
And when she seem'd to shake and fear your looks,
She lov'd them most.

Othello. And so she did.

Iago. Why, go to, then;
She that so young could give out such a seeming,
To seel her father's eyes up close as oak, 210

187 from ... merits : because my merits are few.   188 doubt : suspicion.   revolt : unfaithfulness.   195 bound : i.e. in duty. 198 Wear ... thus : i.e. behave as if you were.   secure : careless, over-confident.   199 free : frank.   200 self-bounty : innate generosity.   abus'd : tricked.   look to't : watch it. 201 our ... disposition : the nature of (the women of) our country. 202 pranks : behaviour, games ('sexual' implied) [N].   203 their best conscience : the highest that conscience dictates to them. 208 Why ... then : well, then.   209 give ... seeming : assume such a false appearance.   210 seel ... up : blind [N].

He thought 'twas witchcraft; but I am much to blame;
I humbly do beseech you of your pardon
For too much loving you.

Othello.   I am bound to thee for ever.

Iago. I see, this hath a little dash'd your spirits.

Othello. Not a jot, not a jot.

Iago.   I' faith, I fear it has.   215
I hope you will consider what is spoke
Comes from my love. But, I do see you're mov'd;
I am to pray you not to strain my speech
To grosser issues nor to larger reach
Than to suspicion.   220

Othello. I will not.

Iago.   Should you do so, my lord,
My speech should fall into such vile success
As my thoughts aim not at. Cassio's my worthy friend—
My lord, I see you're mov'd.

Othello.   No, not much mov'd:
I do not think but Desdemona's honest.   225

Iago. Long live she so! and long live you to think so!

Othello. And, yet, how nature erring from itself,—

Iago. Ay, there's the point: as, to be bold with you,
Not to affect many proposed matches
Of her own clime, complexion, and degree,   230
Whereto, we see, in all things nature tends;
Foh! one may smell in such, a will most rank,

---

213 **bound** : obliged.   218 **I ... pray** : I must ask.   **strain** :
exaggerate.   219 **To grosser issues** : stronger conclusions.
larger reach : greater meaning.   222 **My speech ... success** :
my words would have such dreadful consequences [*N*].   225 **but** :
but that, otherwise than that.   227 **nature** : i.e. human
nature (so in 231).   **erring** : wandering away from [*N*].   228 **as** :
so as (goes with 'nature erring').   **to ... you** : to speak plainly to
you.   229 **affect** : incline to.   230 **clime** : country.   **complexion** : (here) colour (of skin).   **degree** : rank.   232 **such** :
such people.   **will** : appetite.   **rank** : wanton (cf. II. i. 306).

Foul disproportion, thoughts unnatural.
But pardon me; I do not in position
Distinctly speak of her, though I may fear   235
Her will, recoiling to her better judgment,
May fall to match you with her country forms
And happily repent.

   Othello.   Farewell, farewell:
If more thou dost perceive, let me know more;
Set on thy wife to observe. Leave me, Iago.   240

   Iago. My lord, I take my leave.   *[Going.*

   Othello. Why did I marry? This honest creature,
    doubtless,
Sees and knows more, much more, than he unfolds.

   Iago. [*Returning.*] My lord, I would I might entreat
    your honour
To scan this thing no further; leave it to time.   245
Although 'tis fit that Cassio have his place,
For, sure he fills it up with great ability,
Yet, if you please to hold him off awhile,
You shall by that perceive him and his means:
Note if your lady strain his entertainment   250
With any strong or vehement importunity;
Much will be seen in that. In the mean time,
Let me be thought too busy in my fears,
As worthy cause I have to fear I am,
And hold her free, I do beseech your honour.   255

   Othello. Fear not my government.

   Iago. I once more take my leave.   *[Exit.*

   233 disproportion: unsuitability.   **234 position:** my affir-
mation (cf. II. i. 235).   **235 Distinctly:** individually.   **236
recoiling:** reverting.   **237 fall to:** begin to.   **match:** compare.   **her country forms:** the appearance of her countrymen [*N*].
238 happily: haply, perhaps.   **245 scan:** consider.   **249
means:** methods.   **250 strain his entertainment:** presses you to
take him back [*N*].   **253 busy:** officious, anxious.   **254 worthy:**
good.   **255 free:** guiltless.   **256 government:** discretion.

Othello. This fellow's of exceeding honesty,
And knows all qualities, with a learned spirit,
Of human dealings; if I do prove her haggard,   260
Though that her jesses were my dear heart-strings,
I'd whistle her off and let her down the wind,
To prey at fortune. Haply, for I am black,
And have not those soft parts of conversation
That chamberers have, or, for I am declin'd   265
Into the vale of years—yet that's not much—
She's gone, I am abus'd; and my relief
Must be to loathe her. O curse of marriage!
That we can call these delicate creatures ours,
And not their appetites. I had rather be a toad,   270
And live upon the vapour of a dungeon,
· Than keep a corner in the thing I love
For others' uses. Yet, 'tis the plague of great ones;
Prerogativ'd are they less than the base;
'Tis destiny unshunnable, like death: 275
Even this forked plague is fated to us
When we do quicken.

                Look! where she comes.

259–60 **knows all ... dealings**: is deeply skilled in matters of human behaviour.   260 **haggard**: untamed (of a hawk).   261 **jesses**: short straps attached to the hawk's legs and the wrist of the trainer or hunter [*N*].   **heart-strings**: 'in old notions of anatomy, the tendons or nerves supposed to brace and sustain the heart' (*O.E.D.*).   262 **whistle her off**: send her off.   **let ... wind**: with the wind behind her, i.e. dismiss her [*N*].   263 **prey at fortune**: take her chance ('at fortune' = where she likes).   **Haply**: perhaps. **for**: because [*N*].   264 **soft ... conversation**: drawing-room accomplishments, including speech.   265 **chamberers**: gallants [*N*].   267 **gone**: i.e. unfaithful.   **abus'd**: cuckolded. **relief**: my only outlet [*N*].   270 **appetites**: (sexual) desires. 271 **vapour**: foul air.   274 i.e. they are even worse off in this respect than the humble ('Prerogativ'd' = privileged) [*N*].   276–7 i.e. even at the very moment that we are conceived (*or* born), we are destined to be cuckolded ('forked plague' = cuckold's horns) [*N*].

If she be false, O! then heaven mocks itself.
I'll not believe it.

Re-enter DESDEMONA *and* EMILIA.

Desdemona.   How now, my dear Othello!
Your dinner and the generous islanders   280
By you invited, do attend your presence.
    Othello. I am to blame.
    Desdemona.   Why do you speak so faintly?
Are you not well?
    Othello. I have a pain upon my forehead here.
    Desdemona. Faith, that's with watching;' twill away
        again: 285
Let me but bind it hard, within this hour
It will be well.
    Othello.   Your napkin is too little:
                        [*She drops her handkerchief.*
Let it alone. Come, I'll go in with you.
    Desdemona. I am very sorry that you are not well.
                        [*Exeunt* OTHELLO *and* DESDEMONA.
    Emilia. I am glad I have found this napkin;   290
This was her first remembrance from the Moor;
My wayward husband hath a hundred times
Woo'd me to steal it, but she so loves the token,
For he conjur'd her she should ever keep it,
That she reserves it evermore about her   295
To kiss and talk to. I'll have the work ta'en out,
And give't Iago:

278 **mocks**: i.e. in making her [*N*].   280 **generous**: noble.
281 **attend**: wait for.   282 **faintly**: indistinctly.   285
watching: sleeplessness [*N*].   287 **napkin**: handkerchief.
291 **remembrance**: keepsake.   292 **wayward**: unpredict-
able [*N*].   293 **Woo'd**: cajoled.   294 **conjúr'd**: solemnly made
her swear.   295 **reserves**: keeps.   296 **work**: embroidery.
ta'en out: copied [*N*].

What he will do with it heaven knows, not I;
I nothing but to please his fantasy.

Enter IAGO.

Iago. How now! what do you here alone?   300
Emilia. Do not you chide; I have a thing for you.
Iago. A thing for me? It is a common thing—
Emilia. Ha!
Iago. To have a foolish wife.
Emilia. O! is that all? What will you give me now 305
For that same handkerchief?
Iago.   What handkerchief?
Emilia. What handkerchief!
Why, that the Moor first gave to Desdemona:
That which so often you did bid me steal.
Iago. Hast stol'n it from her?   310
Emilia. No, faith; she let it drop by negligence,
And, to the advantage, I, being there, took't up.
Look, here it is.
Iago.   A good wench; give it me.
Emilia. What will you do with't, that you have been so
    earnest
To have me filch it?   315
Iago. Why, what's that to you?   [*Snatches it.*
Emilia. If it be not for some purpose of import
Give't me again; poor lady! she'll run mad
When she shall lack it.
Iago. Be not acknown on't; I have use for it.   320
Go, leave me.   [*Exit* EMILIA.
I will in Cassio's lodging lose this napkin,

---

299 **I ... fantasy**: I only do it for his whim [*N*].   302 **common thing**: (i) ordinary, and (ii) shared by everybody [*N*].
312 **to the advantage**: luckily.   313 **A good wench**: that's a
good girl.   317 **import**: importance.   319 **lack**: miss.
320 **Be ... on't**: admit no knowledge of it [*N*].   322 **lose**: drop.

And let him find it; trifles light as air
Are to the jealous confirmations strong
As proofs of holy writ; this may do something.   325
The Moor already changes with my poison:
Dangerous conceits are in their natures poisons,
Which at the first are scarce found to distaste,
But with a little act upon the blood,
Burn like the mines of sulphur. I did say so: 330
Look! where he comes!

Enter OTHELLO.

                            Not poppy, nor mandragora,
Nor all the drowsy syrups of the world,
Shall ever medicine thee to that sweet sleep
Which thou ow'dst yesterday.
    Othello.   Ha! ha! false to me?
    Iago. Why how now, general! no more of that.   335
    Othello. Avaunt! be gone! thou hast set me on the rack;
I swear 'tis better to be much abus'd
Than but to know't a little.
    Iago.   How now, my lord!
    Othello. What sense had I of her stol'n hours of lust?
I saw't not, thought it not, it harm'd not me;   340
I slept the next night well, was free and merry;
I found not Cassio's kisses on her lips;

325 **proofs of holy writ**: things vouched for by the Bible.
326 **with**: under the influence of.   327 **conceits**: thoughts,
imaginings.   328 **distaste**: offend the taste.   329 **act**:
action.   331 **poppy**: i.e. opium.   **mandragora**: the mandrake
(a plant having narcotic properties) [*N*].   332 **drowsy
syrups**: drugs causing sleep.   333 **medicine**: drug (verb).
334 **ow'dst**: possessed, enjoyed (owe = own).   336 **Avaunt**:
away! (a word usually addressed to a devil or a witch).   **rack**: i.e.
of torture.   338 **know't**: know of it.   339 **sense**: knowledge.   **stol'n**: secret.   341 **free**: untroubled.

He that is robb'd, not wanting what is stol'n,
Let him not know't and he's not robb'd at all.

Iago. I am sorry to hear this.   345

Othello. I had been happy, if the general camp,
Pioners and all, had tasted her sweet body,
So I had nothing known. O! now, for ever
Farewell the tranquil mind; farewell content!
Farewell the plumed troop and the big wars   350
That make ambition virtue! O, farewell!
Farewell the neighing steed, and the shrill trump,
The spirit-stirring drum, the ear-piercing fife,
The royal banner, and all quality,
Pride, pomp, and circumstance of glorious war!   355
And, O you mortal engines, whose rude throats
The immortal Jove's dread clamours counterfeit,
Farewell! Othello's occupation's gone!

Iago. Is it possible, my lord?

Othello. Villain, be sure thou prove my love a whore, 360
Be sure of it; give me the ocular proof;
Or, by the worth of mine eternal soul,
Thou hadst been better have been born a dog
Than answer my wak'd wrath.

Iago.   Is't come to this?

Othello. Make me to see't; or, at the least, so prove it, 365
That the probation bear no hinge nor loop
To hang a doubt on; or woe upon thy life!

Iago. My noble lord,—

343 **wanting**: missing.   346 **general**: whole.   347 **Pionérs**:
labourers [*N*].   350 **plumed troop**: troops fine with plumes
in their helmets.   **big**: stirring.   351 **make ... virtue**:
turn ambition into a virtue.   352 **trump**: trumpet.   354
quality: attributes.   355 **Pride**: magnificence.   **circumstance**: pageantry, ceremony.   356 **mortal**: deadly.   **engines**:
machines, i.e. cannon.   **rude**: loud-mouthed.   357 **counterfeit**: imitate [*N*].   361 **ocular proof**: proof to the eyes.
362 **eternal**: immortal.   366 **probation**: proof [*N*].

Othello. If thou dost slander her and torture me,
Never pray more; abandon all remorse;   370
On horror's head horrors accumulate;
Do deeds to make heaven weep, all earth amaz'd;
For nothing canst thou to damnation add
Greater than that.

Iago.   O grace! O heaven forgive me!
Are you a man! have you a soul or sense?   375
God be wi' you; take mine office. O wretched fool!
That liv'st to make thine honesty a vice.
O monstrous world! Take note, take note, O world!
To be direct and honest is not safe.
I thank you for this profit, and, from hence   380
I'll love no friend, sith love breeds such offence.

Othello. Nay, stay; thou shouldst be honest.

Iago. I should be wise; for honesty's a fool,
And loses that it works for.

Othello.   By the world,
I think my wife be honest and think she is not;   385
I think that thou art just and think thou art not.
I'll have some proof. Her name, that was as fresh
As Dian's visage, is now begrim'd and black
As mine own face. If there be cords or knives,
Poison or fire or suffocating streams,   390
I'll not endure it. Would I were satisfied!

Iago. I see, sir, you are eaten up with passion.

---

370 **remorse:** pity [*N*].   373 **damnation:** i.e. your own
damnation.   374 **grace:** i.e. God's grace.   376 **God . . .
you:** goodbye! (as it scans).   **office:** i.e. post as ensign.
377 **That . . . vice:** i.e. who has lived long enough to find out that
being honest is a handicap.   380 **profit:** gain, i.e. lesson.
381 **sith:** since.   382 **shouldst:** i.e. by all appearances.
384 **loses . . . works for:** i.e. honesty gets a man nowhere
('that' = that which).   388 **Dian's:** Diana's (goddess of the
moon and of chastity).   390 **suffocating:** that kill by drowning.
391 **satisfied:** i.e. of her guilt.

I do repent me that I put it to you.
You would be satisfied?

  Othello.   Would! nay, I will.

  Iago. And may; but how? how satisfied, my lord?   395
Would you, the supervisor, grossly gape on;
Behold her topp'd?

  Othello.   Death and damnation! O!

  Iago. It were a tedious difficulty, I think,
To bring them to that prospect; damn them then,
If ever mortal eyes do see them bolster   400
More than their own! What then? how then?
What shall I say? Where's satisfaction?
It is impossible you should see this,
Were they as prime as goats, as hot as monkeys,
As salt as wolves in pride, and fools as gross   405
As ignorance made drunk; but yet, I say,
If imputation, and strong circumstances,
Which lead directly to the door of truth,
Will give you satisfaction, you may have it.

  Othello. Give me a living reason she's disloyal.   410

  Iago. I do not like the office;
But, sith I am enter'd in this cause so far,
Prick'd to't by foolish honesty and love,
I will go on. I lay with Cassio lately;
And, being troubled with a raging tooth,   415

393 **put it to you**: (presumably) brought the matter to your attention.   396 **supervisor**: onlooker.   **grossly**: (i) coarsely, and (ii) stupidly (cf. 405).   397 **topp'd**: 'covered', as one animal by another [*N*].   399 **To ... prospect**: to contrive that you should see them thus ('prospect' = thing seen).   **damn them then**: i.e. they would be poor fools if.   400 **bolster**: lie in bed. 404 **prime**: lecherous.   405 **salt**: hot.   **in pride**: on heat. 406 **ignorance ... drunk**: people in drunken indifference.   407 i.e. imputation of guilt based on strong circumstantial evidence. 410 **living**: vital, real.   411 **office**: job.   412 **cause**: matter.   413 **Prick'd to't**: urged on to it.   414 **lay with**: slept in the same bed with [*N*].

I could not sleep.
There are a kind of men so loose of soul
That in their sleeps will mutter their affairs;
One of this kind is Cassio.
In sleep I heard him say, 'Sweet Desdemona,   420
Let us be wary, let us hide our loves!'
And then, sir, would he gripe and wring my hand,
Cry, 'O, sweet creature!' and then kiss me hard,
As if he pluck'd up kisses by the roots,
That grew upon my lips; then laid his leg   425
Over my thigh, and sigh'd, and kiss'd; and then
Cried, 'Cursed fate, that gave thee to the Moor!'

   Othello. O monstrous! monstrous!

   Iago.   Nay, this was but his dream.

   Othello. But this denoted a foregone conclusion:
'Tis a shrewd doubt, though it be but a dream.   430

   Iago. And this may help to thicken other proofs
That do demonstrate thinly.

   Othello.   I'll tear her all to pieces.

   Iago. Nay, but be wise; yet we see nothing done;
She may be honest yet. Tell me but this:
Have you not sometimes seen a handkerchief   435
Spotted with strawberries in your wife's hand?

   Othello. I gave her such a one; 'twas my first gift.

   Iago. I know not that; but such a handkerchief—
I am sure it was your wife's—did I to-day
See Cassio wipe his beard with.

   Othello.   If it be that,—   440

---

417 loose of soul: i.e. incapable of keeping their thoughts to
themselves [*N*].   **422 gripe:** grip hard.   **429 denoted ...
conclusion:** indicated what had gone before (not quite the modern
sense of the phrase).   **430 shrewd doubt:** strong (reason for)
suspicion.   **431 thicken:** strengthen.   **432: demónstrate
thinly:** are weak as proofs.   **433 yet:** as yet.   **see:** i.e. have
seen.   **434 yet:** still.   **but:** only.   **436 spotted with strawberries:** i.e. worked with a pattern of strawberries.

Iago. If it be that, or any that was hers,
It speaks against her with the other proofs.

Othello. O! that the slave had forty thousand lives;
One is too poor, too weak for my revenge.
Now do I see 'tis true. Look here, Iago;   445
All my fond love thus do I blow to heaven:
'Tis gone.
Arise, black vengeance, from thy hollow cell!
Yield up, O love! thy crown and hearted throne
To tyrannous hate. Swell, bosom, with thy fraught,   450
For 'tis of aspics' tongues!

Iago.   Yet be content.

Othello. O! blood, blood, blood!

Iago. Patience, I say; your mind, perhaps, may change.

Othello. Never, Iago. Like to the Pontick sea,
Whose icy current and compulsive course   455
Ne'er feels retiring ebb, but keeps due on
To the Propontic and the Hellespont,
Even so my bloody thoughts, with violent pace,
Shall ne'er look back, ne'er ebb to humble love,
Till that a capable and wide revenge   460
Swallow them up.   [*Kneels.*
            Now, by yond marble heaven,
In the due reverence of a sacred vow
I here engage my words.

Iago.   Do not rise yet.   [*Kneels.*
Witness, you ever-burning lights above!
You elements that clip us round about!   465

443 **the slave**: i.e. Cassio.   446 **fond**: foolish [*N*].   449
hearted throne: throne seated in the heart [*N*].   450 **tyrannous**: pitiless.   **Swell**: i.e. as with poison.   **fraught**: burden.
451 **aspics'**: asps' (poisonous snakes) [*N*].   **content**: calm.
455 **compulsive**: onward pressing [*N*].   460 **capable**: compre-
hensive.   461 **marble**: shining [*N*].   462 **In the due reverence**: with all the solemnity.   463 **engage**: pledge.   464
lights: i.e. stars and planets.   465 **clip**: surround, embrace [*N*].

Witness, that here Iago doth give up
The execution of his wit, hands, heart,
To wrong'd Othello's service! Let him command,
And to obey shall be in me remorse,
What bloody business ever.

Othello.   I greet thy love,   470
Not with vain thanks, but with acceptance bounteous,
And will upon the instant put thee to't:
Within these three days let me hear thee say
That Cassio's not alive.

Iago. My friend is dead; 'tis done at your request: 475
But let her live.

Othello.   Damn her, lewd minx! O, damn her!
Come, go with me apart; I will withdraw
To furnish me with some swift means of death
For the fair devil. Now art thou my lieutenant.

Iago. I am your own for ever.   [*Exeunt.*

Scene IV. BEFORE THE CASTLE

Enter DESDEMONA, EMILIA, *and* Clown.

Desdemona. Do you know, sirrah, where Lieutenant
Cassio lies?

Clown. I dare not say he lies any where.

Desdemona. Why, man?   4

Clown. He is a soldier; and for one to say a soldier lies,
is stabbing.

Desdemona. Go to; where lodges he?

---

466 **give up**: dedicate.   467 **execution**: operation, exercise.
469 **remorse**: a matter of conscience [*N*].   470 **What . . .
ever**: whatever it may be.   471 **vain**: empty.   **bounteous**:
whole-hearted.   472 **upon the instant**: at once.   **put . . . to't**:
i.e. to the test.   475 **is**: is as good as.   1 **sirrah**: my
good man.   2 **lies**: lodges.   3 **lies**: a pun on telling lies.
6 **is stabbing**: would get me stabbed.   7 **Go to**: come, come.

Clown. To tell you where he lodges is to tell you where
I lie.

Desdemona. Can anything be made of this? 　　　　　10

Clown. I know not where he lodges, and for me to devise
a lodging, and say he lies here or he lies there, were to lie
in mine own throat.

Desdemona. Can you inquire him out, and be edified by
report? 　　　　　15

Clown. I will catechize the world for him; that is, make
questions, and by them answer.

Desdemona. Seek him, bid him come hither; tell him
I have moved my lord in his behalf, and hope all will
be well. 　　　　　20

Clown. To do this is within the compass of man's wit,
and therefore I will attempt the doing it. 　　　　　[*Exit.*

Desdemona. Where should I lose that handkerchief,
　　Emilia?

Emilia. I know not, madam.

Desdemona. Believe me, I had rather have lost my
　　purse 　　　　　25
Full of cruzadoes; and, but my noble Moor
Is true of mind, and made of no such baseness
As jealous creatures are, it were enough
To put him to ill thinking.

Emilia. 　　　　　Is he not jealous? 　　　　　29

Desdemona. Who! he? I think the sun where he was born
Drew all such humours from him.

Emilia. 　　　　　Look! where he comes.

8–9 **where I lie**: i.e. what I don't know. 　　11 **devise**: imagine.
13 **in . . . throat**: wilfully, deeply [*N*]. 　　14 **inquire him out**:
find out where he is. 　　14–15 **edified by report**: instructed by
what you hear [*N*]. 　　16–17 **catechize . . . for him**: ask everywhere for him [*N*]. 　　19 **moved**: pleaded with. 　　21 **compass**: range. 　　23 **where . . . lose**: where could I have lost. 　　26
cruzadoes: Portuguese coin, then current in England [*N*]. **but**: but
for the fact that. 　　31 **humours**: (i) disposition, (ii) moisture [*N*].

Desdemona. I will not leave him now till Cassio
Be call'd to him.

Enter OTHELLO.

How is't with you, my lord?

Othello. Well, my good lady. [*Aside.*] O! hardness to
   dissemble.
How do you, Desdemona?

   Desdemona.   Well, my good lord.   **35**
   Othello. Give me your hand. This hand is moist, my lady.
   Desdemona. It yet has felt no age nor known no sorrow.
   Othello. This argues fruitfulness and liberal heart;
Hot, hot, and moist; this hand of yours requires
A sequester from liberty, fasting and prayer,   **40**
Much castigation, exercise devout;
For here's a young and sweating devil here,
That commonly rebels. 'Tis a good hand,
A frank one.

   Desdemona.   You may, indeed, say so;
For 'twas that hand that gave away my heart.   **45**
   Othello. A liberal hand; the hearts of old gave hands,
But our new heraldry is hands not hearts.

   Desdemona. I cannot speak of this. Come now, your
   promise.
   Othello. What promise, chuck?
   Desdemona. I have sent to bid Cassio come speak with you.

34 dissemble: pretend (not to know) [N].   **38 argues:** indicates [N].   **fruitfulness:** here in sexual sense.   **liberal:** (i) generous,
(ii) licentious.   **40 sequester:** seclusion.   **41 exercise devout:** acts of devotion and abstinence.   **42–3 For ... rebels:**
i.e. This hot hand indicates a passionate nature which is likely to
give unrestrained liberty to its (sexual) desires [N].   **44 frank:**
free and open.   **46–7 the hearts ... not hearts:** in olden days,
when the hand was given, the heart was behind it; but it is now
fashionable to give the hand without the heart [N].   **48 I cannot ... this:** I can't follow you [N].   **49 chuck:** term of
endearment.

Othello. I have a salt and sorry rheum offends me.   51
Lend me thy handkerchief.

Desdemona.   Here, my lord.

Othello. That which I gave you.

Desdemona.   I have it not about me.

Othello. Not?

Desdemona.   No, indeed, my lord.

Othello.   That is a fault.
That handkerchief   55
Did an Egyptian to my mother give;
She was a charmer, and could almost read
The thoughts of people; she told her, while she kept it,
'Twould make her amiable and subdue my father
Entirely to her love, but if she lost it   60
Or made a gift of it, my father's eye
Should hold her loathed, and his spirits should hunt
After new fancies. She dying gave it me;
And bid me, when my fate would have me wive,
To give it her. I did so; and take heed on't;   65
Make it a darling like your precious eye;
To lose't or give't away, were such perdition
As nothing else could match.

Desdemona.   Is't possible?

Othello. 'Tis true; there's magic in the web of it;
A sibyl, that had number'd in the world   70
The sun to course two hundred compasses,
In her prophetic fury sew'd the work;

51 **salt and sorry rheum :** a miserable running cold.   **offends :**
which troubles.   57 **charmer :** sorceress.   58 **while :**
as long as.   59 **amiable :** lovable.   62 **hold her :** regard
her as.   **spirits :** desires.   63 **fancies :** loves.   65 **her :**
my wife.   66 **Make it a darling :** cherish it.   67 **were :**
would be.   **perdition :** dreadful loss.   69 **web :** texture.
70 **sibyl :** prophetess [N].   70-1 **number'd ... compasses :**
lived so long as to count two hundred revolutions of the sun [N].
72 **fury :** inspiration.

The worms were hallow'd that did breed the silk,
And it was dy'd in mummy which the skilful
Conserv'd of maidens' hearts.

    Desdemona.   Indeed! is't true?   75

    Othello. Most veritable; therefore look to't well.

    Desdemona. Then would to heaven that I had never
        seen it!

    Othello. Ha! wherefore?

    Desdemona. Why do you speak so startingly and rash?

    Othello. Is't lost? is't gone? speak, is it out o' the way?

    Desdemona. Heaven bless us!

    Othello.   Say you?   81

    Desdemona. It is not lost: but what an if it were?

    Othello. How!

    Desdemona. I say, it is not lost.

    Othello.   Fetch't, let me see't.

    Desdemona. Why, so I can, sir, but I will not now.   85
This is a trick to put me from my suit:
Pray you let Cassio be receiv'd again.

    Othello. Fetch me the handkerchief; my mind misgives.

    Desdemona. Come, come;
You'll never meet a more sufficient man.   90

    Othello. The handkerchief!

    Desdemona.   I pray, talk me of Cassio.

    Othello. The handkerchief!

    Desdemona.   A man that all his time
Hath founded his good fortunes on your love,
Shar'd dangers with you —

---

    73 worms : silkworms.   **hallow'd :** sacred.   **74 mummy :**
medicinal preparation made out of dead bodies.   **75 Conserv'd
. . . hearts :** made into a conserve out of the hearts of virgins [*N*].
76 look to't : look after it.   **79 startingly :** abruptly.   **rash :**
excitedly (adj. for adv. ; the 'ly' of 'startlingly' carries on).   80
out o' the way : mislaid.   **82 an :** if (tautology).   **83 How :**
What!   **88 misgives :** (me), is disturbed.   **90 sufficient :**
capable.   **91 talk me :** talk, I beg you.

Othello. The handkerchief!

Desdemona.   In sooth you are to blame. 95

Othello. Away!   [*Exit.*

Emilia. Is not this man jealous?

Desdemona. I ne'er saw this before.

Sure, there's some wonder in this handkerchief;

I am most unhappy in the loss of it.   100

Emilia. 'Tis not a year or two shows us a man;

They are all but stomachs, and we all but food;

They eat us hungerly, and when they are full

They belch us. Look you! Cassio and my husband.

Enter IAGO *and* CASSIO.

Iago. There is no other way; 'tis she must do't: 105

And, lo! the happiness: go and importune her.

Desdemona. How now, good Cassio! what's the news

    with you?

Cassio. Madam, my former suit: I do beseech you

That by your virtuous means I may again

Exist, and be a member of his love   110

Whom I with all the office of my heart

Entirely honour; I would not be delay'd.

If my offence be of such mortal kind

That nor my service past, nor present sorrows,

Nor purpos'd merit in futurity,   115

---

95 **In sooth**: truly [*N*].   96 **Away!** Out of my sight!
101 i.e. we don't find out what men are like at once.   102 **They
are**: (read as one syllable). **but**: merely [*N*].   103 **hungerly**:
hungrily.   104 **belch us**: reject us.   106 **lo! the happiness**:
what good luck (to find her). **importune**: plead your case with.
109 **virtuous means**: powerful aid [*N*].   110 **be a member
of**: share in [*N*].   111 **office**: service, duty [*N*].   112
delay'd: kept in suspense.   113 **mortal**: fatal, i.e. not to be
atoned for.   114 **nor ... nor**: neither ... nor.   115 i.e.
nor the services I intend to do in the future.

Can ransom me into his love again,
But to know so must be my benefit;
So shall I clothe me in a forc'd content,
And shut myself up in some other course
To fortune's alms.
   Desdemona.   Alas! thrice-gentle Cassio!   120
My advocation is not now in tune;
My lord is not my lord; nor should I know him,
Were he in favour as in humour alter'd.
So help me every spirit sanctified,
As I have spoken for you all my best   125
And stood within the blank of his displeasure
For my free speech. You must awhile be patient;
What I can do I will, and more I will
Than for myself I dare; let that suffice you.
   Iago. Is my lord angry?
   Emilia.   He went hence but now,   130
And, certainly in strange unquietness.
   Iago. Can he be angry? I have seen the cannon,
When it hath blown his ranks into the air,
And, like the devil, from his very arm
Puff'd his own brother; and can he be angry?   135
Something of moment then; I will go meet him;
There's matter in't indeed, if he be angry.

---

116 **ransom me:** bring me back.   117 **But ... benefit:** only to know this would be a relief.   118 **clothe ... content:** accept the inevitable.   119 **shut ... course:** content myself with some other occupation [N].   120 **To fortune's alms:** whatever fortune may offer me.   **thrice-gentle:** dear.   121 **advocation:** advocacy, plea.   **in tune:** timely.   123 **favour:** face, appearance.   **humour:** mood.   124-5 **So ... As:** May all the saints help me as surely as.   126 **stood ... blank:** made myself the target [N].   127 **free speech:** freedom of speech, i.e. (here) importunity.   131 **unquietness:** perturbation.   134 **from ... arm:** from immediately beside him [N]. 135 **puff'd:** blown.   **brother:** i.e. brother-in-arms [N].   136 **of moment:** important.

Desdemona. I prithee, do so. [*Exit* IAGO.] Something, sure, of state,
Either from Venice, or some unhatch'd practice
Made demonstrable here in Cyprus to him,   140
Hath puddled his clear spirit; and, in such cases
Men's natures wrangle with inferior things,
Though great ones are their object. 'Tis even so;
For let our finger ache, and it indues
Our other healthful members ev'n to that sense   145
Of pain. Nay, we must think men are not gods,
Nor of them look for such observancy
As fits the bridal. Beshrew me much, Emilia,
I was—unhandsome warrior as I am—
Arraigning his unkindness with my soul;   150
But now I find I had suborn'd the witness,
And he's indicted falsely.

Emilia. Pray heaven it be state-matters, as you think,
And no conception, nor no jealous toy
Concerning you.   155

Desdemona. Alas the day! I never gave him cause.

Emilia. But jealous souls will not be answer'd so;

138 **Something ... state**: State business.   139 **unhatch'd practice**: plot not yet ripe.   140 **Made demonstrable**: uncovered.   141 **puddled**: made muddy, disturbed.   **clear**: serene.   142 **wrangle with inferior things**: are irritable about trifles.   143 **their object**: the real cause of their trouble.   **'Tis even so**: Yes, of course, that's it.   144 **let ... and**: suppose ... then.   144-6 **indues ... pain**: gives even the healthy parts of our bodies a feeling of pain ('indue' = lead on).   146 **think**: bear in mind that.   147 **observancy**: eager attentions.   148 **the bridal**: the wedding-day [N].   **Beshrew me much**: How silly I am!   149 **unhandsome**: unfair and inexpert [N].   150-1 **Arraigning ... witness**: accusing him in my mind of unkindness; but now I find I have induced my thoughts to give false witness.   152 **indicted**: charged [N].   154 **conception**: fancy.   **toy**: whim, freak.

They are not ever jealous for the cause,
But jealous for they are jealous; 'tis a monster
Begot upon itself, born on itself.   160
  Desdemona. Heaven keep that monster from Othello's
    mind!
  Emilia. Lady, amen.
  Desdemona. I will go seek him. Cassio, walk here-
    about;
If I do find him fit, I'll move your suit
And seek to effect it to my uttermost.   165
  Cassio. I humbly thank your ladyship.
             [*Exeunt* DESDEMONA *and* EMILIA.

Enter BIANCA.

  Bianca. Save you, friend Cassio!
  Cassio.   What make you from home?
How is it with you, my most fair Bianca?
I' faith, sweet love, I was coming to your house.
  Bianca. And I was going to your lodging, Cassio.   170
What! keep a week away? seven days and nights?
Eight score eight hours? and lovers' absent hours,
More tedious than the dial eight score times?
O weary reckoning!
  Cassio.   Pardon me, Bianca,
I have this while with leaden thoughts been press'd,   175
But I shall, in a more continuate time,

158-9 **They ... are jealous**: they are never jealous with
reason, but jealous because it is their nature to be jealous.
160 **Begot ... on itself**: self-generated and produced.   164 **fit**:
in a favourable mood.   **move your suit**: put your case to him
[*N*].   167 **Save you**: i.e. God save you.   **make you**: are
you doing.   172-3 **lovers' ... times**: the separation of lovers
seems much longer than the hours told by the clock (dial) [*N*].
175 **press'd**: weighed down.   176 **continuate**: uninter-
rupted.

Strike off this score of absence. Sweet Bianca.

[*Giving her* DESDEMONA's *handkerchief*.

Take me this work out.

Bianca.   O Cassio! whence came this?
This is some token from a newer friend;
To the felt absence now I feel a cause;   180
Is't come to this? Well, well.

Cassio.   Go to, woman!
Throw your vile guesses in the devil's teeth,
From whence you have them. You are jealous now,
That this is from some mistress, some remembrance:
No, in good troth, Bianca.

Bianca.   Why, whose is it?   185

Cassio. I know not, sweet; I found it in my chamber.
I like the work well; ere it be demanded,—
As like enough it will,—I'd have it copied;
Take it and do't; and leave me for this time.

Bianca. Leave you! wherefore?   190

Cassio. I do attend here on the general,
And think it no addition nor my wish
To have him see me woman'd.

Bianca.   Why, I pray you?

Cassio. Not that I love you not.

Bianca.   But that you do not love me.
I pray you, bring me on the way a little   195
And say if I shall see you soon at night.

Cassio. 'Tis but a little way that I can bring you,
For I attend here; but I'll see you soon.

Bianca. 'Tis very good; I must be circumstanc'd. [*Exeunt*.

177 **Strike off this score**: make up for this record against me.
178 **Take me ... out**: copy this embroidery for me.   180 **To the
felt absence**: for the failure to visit me that I noticed.   184 **remembrance**: token of love.   185 **in good troth**: honestly.
191 **attend on**: wait for.   192 **addition**: credit to me.   193
woman'd: in the company of a woman.   195 **bring ... little**: come
part of the way with me.   199 **be circumstanc'd**: put up with things.

ACT IV

Scene I. CYPRUS. BEFORE THE CASTLE

Enter OTHELLO *and* IAGO.

Iago. Will you think so?
Othello.   Think so, Iago!
Iago.   What!
To kiss in private?
Othello.   An unauthoriz'd kiss.
Iago. Or to be naked with her friend a-bed
An hour or more, not meaning any harm?
  Othello. Naked a-bed, Iago, and not mean harm?   5
It is hypocrisy against the devil:
They that mean virtuously, and yet do so,
The devil their virtue tempts, and they tempt heaven.
  Iago. If they do nothing, 'tis a venial slip;
But if I give my wife a handkerchief,—   10
  Othello. What then?
  Iago. Why, then, 'tis hers, my lord; and, being hers,
She may, I think, bestow't on any man.
  Othello. She is protectress of her honour too;
May she give that?   15
  Iago. Her honour is an essence that's not seen;
They have it very oft that have it not:
But for the handkerchief,—
  Othello. By heaven, I would most gladly have forgot it:—
Thou said'st,—O! it comes o'er my memory,   20

1 **Will you:** are you determined to [*N*].   6 **hypocrisy ...
devil:** a sham intended to cheat the devil [*N*].   8 **they ...
heaven:** i.e. they put themselves into such a situation that even
Heaven can scarcely save them.   14 **honour:** chastity.   17
They ... not: i.e. they appear to have it when they have not.
18 **But for:** but as to.

As doth the raven o'er the infectious house,
Boding to all,—he had my handkerchief.

   Iago. Ay, what of that?

   Othello.   That's not so good now.

   Iago.   What,
If I had said I had seen him do you wrong?
Or heard him say, as knaves be such abroad,   25
Who having, by their own importunate suit,
Or voluntary dotage of some mistress,
Convinced or supplied them, cannot choose
But they must blab.

   Othello.   Hath he said any thing?

   Iago. He hath, my lord; but be you well assur'd,   30
No more than he'll unswear.

   Othello.   What hath he said?

   Iago. Faith, that he did—I know not what he did.

   Othello. What? what?

   Iago. Lie—

   Othello.   With her?

   Iago.   With her, on her; what you will.

   Othello. Lie with her! lie on her! We say, lie on   35
her, when they belie her. Lie with her! that's fulsome. Handkerchief,—confessions,—handkerchief!
To confess, and be hanged for his labour. First, to
be hanged, and then to confess: I tremble at it.

---

21 **infectious**: infected (with disease) [*N*].   22 **Boding:**
ominous (the raven was a bird of ill omen).   25 **as ... abroad:**
as indeed there are such rascals about.   **say:** speak of it.
27 **voluntary dotage:** the willing infatuation.   28 **Convinced or supplied:** overcome their hesitancy or satisfied their
desires.   31 **unswear:** swear he never said.   36 **belie:**
slander [*N*].   **fulsome:** foul, obscene.   38 **confess and be
hanged:** i.e. Cassio's confession of his guilt would naturally result
in his being hanged [*N*].   **for his labour:** i.e. in confessing
(ironical).   38–9 **First ... confess:** i.e. to be hanged without
benefit of confession [*N*].

Nature would not invest herself in such shadowing   40
passion without some instruction. It is not words
that shake me thus. Pish! Noses, ears, and lips. Is it
possible?—Confess!—Handkerchief!—O devil!

[Falls in a trance.

Iago. Work on,
My medicine, work! Thus credulous fools are caught; 45
And many worthy and chaste dames even thus,
All guiltless, meet reproach. What, ho! my lord!
My lord, I say! Othello!

Enter CASSIO.

How now, Cassio!

Cassio. What's the matter?

Iago. My lord is fallen into an epilepsy;   50
This is his second fit; he had one yesterday.

Cassio. Rub him about the temples.

Iago.   No, forbear;
The lethargy must have his quiet course,
If not he foams at mouth, and by and by
Breaks out to savage madness. Look! he stirs;   55
Do you withdraw yourself a little while,
He will recover straight; when he is gone,
I would on great occasion speak with you. *[Exit* CASSIO.
How is it, general? Have you not hurt your head?

Othello. Dost thou mock me?

Iago.   I mock you! no, by heaven. 60
Would you would bear your fortune like a man!

40–1 **Nature ... some instruction :** i.e. my feelings would not
be clothed in such a foreboding (gloomy) frenzy, unless there were
solid reason for it [*N*].   41 **not words :** i.e. but the things
they suggest.   42–3 **Noses ... possible :** i.e. (probably) Can
such physical intimacy have taken place between them ?   43
s.d. trance: swoon.   47 **All :** completely.   **meet reproach :**
incur shame.   53 **lethargy :** coma, fit.   **have ... course :**
run its course without interference.   58 **great occasion : a**
matter of great importance.

Othello. A horned man's a monster and a beast.

Iago. There's many a beast then, in a populous city,
And many a civil monster.

Othello. Did he confess it?

Iago.   Good sir, be a man;   65
Think every bearded fellow that's but yok'd
May draw with you; there's millions now alive
That nightly lie in those unproper beds
Which they dare swear peculiar; your case is better.
O! 'tis the spite of hell, the fiend's arch-mock,   70
To lip a wanton in a secure couch,
And to suppose her chaste. No, let me know;
And knowing what I am I know what she shall be.

Othello. O! thou art wise; 'tis certain.

Iago.   Stand you awhile apart;
Confine yourself but in a patient list.   75
Whilst you were here o'erwhelmed with your grief,—
A passion most unsuiting such a man,—
Cassio came hither; I shifted him away,
And laid good 'scuse upon your ecstasy;
Bade him anon return and here speak with me;   80
The which he promis'd. Do but encave yourself,
And mark the fleers, the gibes, and notable scorns,

64 **civil**: (i) living in a city, citizen, and (ii) well-mannered, orderly [*N*].   66-7 **Think ... with you**: remember every married man may be in your situation (pull the same cart).   68 **unproper**: not theirs only but shared by others [*N*].   69 **Which ... peculiar**: which they confidently believe to be exclusively their own.   71 **lip**: kiss.   **wanton**: unchaste woman.   **secure**: seeming safe, free from suspicion (accented 'sécure').   73 **I am**: viz. a cuckold.   **I know ... be**: i.e. I know what revenge I should take [*N*].   75 i.e. only keep yourself within the bounds of patience ('list' = limit).   78 **shifted him away**: got rid of him.   79 **laid ... ecstasy**: put it down plausibly to your swoon [*N*].   80 **anon**: soon.   81 **encave**: hide [*N*].   82 **fleers**: sneers.   **notable**: open.   **scorns**: contemptuous words or gestures.

That dwell in every region of his face;
For I will make him tell the tale anew,
Where, how, how oft, how long ago, and when   85
He hath, and is again to cope your wife:
I say, but mark his gesture. Marry, patience;
Or I shall say you are all in all in spleen,
And nothing of a man.
  Othello.   Dost thou hear, Iago?
I will be found most cunning in my patience;   90
But—dost thou hear?—most bloody.
  Iago.   That's not amiss;
But yet keep time in all. Will you withdraw?
                       [OTHELLO *goes apart.*

Now will I question Cassio of Bianca,
A housewife that by selling her desires
Buys herself bread and clothes; it is a creature   95
That dotes on Cassio; as 'tis the strumpet's plague
To beguile many and be beguil'd by one.
He, when he hears of her, cannot refrain
From the excess of laughter. Here he comes:

        Re-enter CASSIO.

As he shall smile, Othello shall go mad;   100
And his unbookish jealousy must conster
Poor Cassio's smiles, gestures, and light behaviour
Quite in the wrong. How do you now, lieutenant?

---

86 **cope**: lie with.   87 **gesture**: demeanour, behaviour.
Marry: by the Virgin Mary (a common oath).   88 **all in
spleen**: made up of nothing but anger [N].   92 **keep time**:
don't go too fast.   93 **of**: about.   94 **housewife**: hussy
(cf. II. i. 112).   **her desires**: her (sexual) appetite (and perhaps
also what is desired of her).   95 **it**: contemptuous for 'she'.
96 **as 'tis**: for it is.   100 **As**: in proportion as.   101 **unbookish**: unskilled, inexperienced [N].   **conster**: construe, interpret.   103 **in the wrong**: wrongly.

Cassio. The worse that you give me the addition
Whose want even kills me.   105

Iago. Ply Desdemona well, and you are sure on't.
[*Speaking lower.*] Now, if this suit lay in Bianca's power,
How quickly should you speed!

Cassio.   Alas! poor caitiff!

Othello. [*Aside.*] Look! how he laughs already!

Iago. I never knew woman love man so.   110

Cassio. Alas! poor rogue, I think, i' faith, she loves me.

Othello. [*Aside.*] Now he denies it faintly, and laughs
it out.

Iago. Do you hear, Cassio?

Othello. [*Aside.*]   Now he importunes him.
To tell it o'er: go to; well said, well said.

Iago. She gives it out that you shall marry her;   115
Do you intend it?

Cassio. Ha, ha, ha!

Othello. [*Aside.*] Do you triumph, Roman? do you
triumph?

Cassio. I marry her! what? a customer? I prithee, bear
some charity to my wit; do not think it so unwholesome.
Ha, ha, ha!   121

Othello. [*Aside.*] So, so, so, so. They laugh that win.

Iago. Faith, the cry goes that you shall marry her.

Cassio. Prithee, say true.

104 **addition**: title (i.e. of lieutenant).   105 **Whose want**:
the lack of which.   **even**: is precisely what.   **kills me**: colloquial for 'makes me feel worthless'.   106 **Ply**: keep at her.
107 **power**: i.e. to grant [*N*].   108 **speed**: succeed.   **caitiff**:
wretch (affectionately contemptuous; cf. 111).   112 **faintly**: not
really meaning it.   **laughs it out**: makes a joke of it.   113 **Do
you hear**: (goes on to 115).   114 **go to ... well said**: (derisive
and ironical) that's right! well done!   119 **customer**: prostitute [*N*].   119–20 **bear ... wit**: give me credit for some sense.
120 **unwholesome**: unsound.   122 i.e. 'he laughs best who
laughs last'.   123 **cry**: rumour.   124 **say true**: don't
talk nonsense.

Iago. I am a very villain else.   125

Othello. [*Aside.*] Have you scored me? Well.

Cassio. This is the monkey's own giving out: she is persuaded I will marry her, out of her own love and flattery, not out of my promise.   129

Othello. [*Aside.*] Iago beckons me; now he begins the story.

Cassio. She was here even now; she haunts me in every place. I was the other day talking on the sea bank with certain Venetians, and thither come this bauble, and, by this hand, she falls me thus about my neck;—   135

Othello. [*Aside.*] Crying, 'O dear Cassio!' as it were; his gesture imports it.

Cassio. So hangs and lolls and weeps upon me; so hales and pulls me; ha, ha, ha!   139

Othello. [*Aside.*] Now he tells how she plucked him to my chamber. O! I see that nose of yours, but not the dog I shall throw it to.

Cassio. Well, I must leave her company.

Iago. Before me! look, where she comes.   144

Cassio. 'Tis such another fitchew! marry, a perfumed one.

Enter BIANCA.

What do you mean by this haunting of me?

Bianca. Let the devil and his dam haunt you! What did you mean by that same handkerchief you

125 **very**: complete.   126 **scored**: injured [*N*].   127
monkey's: cf. 108.   **giving out**: report, version.   128–9 **own**
...**flattery**: self-love and good opinion of herself.   130 **beckons**
me: makes a sign to me (to watch).   133 **sea bank**: sea-shore.
134 **bauble**: trifle, light creature.   **by this hand**: as sure as I'm
here.   135 **me**: believe me!   137 **imports**: implies.
140 **plucked**: pulled eagerly.   143 **leave her company**: give
her up.   144 **Before me**: upon my soul [*N*].   145 **'Tis**
...**fitchew**: she's a regular pole-cat [*N*].   **marry**: (here) Phew!
147 **dam**: mother (of animals and devils).

gave me even now? I was a fine fool to take it.
I must take out the work! A likely piece of work,   150
that you should find it in your chamber, and not
know who left it there! This is some minx's token,
and I must take out the work! There, give it your
hobby-horse; wheresoever you had it I'll take out
no work on't.   155

  Cassio. How now, my sweet Bianca! how now, how now!
  Othello. [*Aside.*] By heaven, that should be my hand-
kerchief!
  Bianca. An you'll come to supper to-night, you may;
an you will not, come when you are next prepared for. [*Exit.*
  Iago. After her, after her.   161
  Cassio. Faith, I must; she'll rail in the street else.
  Iago. Will you sup there?
  Cassio. Faith, I intend so.
  Iago. Well, I may chance to see you, for I would very
fain speak with you.   166
  Cassio. Prithee, come; will you?
  Iago. Go to; say no more.   [*Exit* CASSIO.
  Othello. [*Advancing.*] How shall I murder him, Iago?
  Iago. Did you perceive how he laughed at his vice? 170
  Othello. O! Iago!
  Iago. And did you see the handkerchief?
  Othello. Was that mine?
  Iago. Yours, by this hand; and to see how he prizes the
foolish woman your wife! she gave it him, and he hath
given it his whore.   176

---

  150 **the work**: see III. iii. 296; but here Bianca is contemptuous.
A likely ... work: a pretty story!   152 **minx's**: loose
woman's.   154 **hobby-horse**: your (new) mistress [*N*].
156 **How now**: now, now (placatory).   157 **should be**: must
be.   159 **An**: if.   160 **next ... for**: next expected (ironical,
i.e. 'never').   162 **rail**: make a row.   165–6 **would very fain**:
am anxious to [*N*].

Othello. I would have him nine years a-killing. A fine woman! a fair woman! a sweet woman!

Iago. Nay, you must forget that.

Othello. Ay, let her rot, and perish, and be damned   180
to-night; for she shall not live. No, my heart is turned to stone; I strike it, and it hurts my hand. O! the world hath not a sweeter creature; she might lie by an emperor's side and command him tasks.

Iago. Nay, that's not your way.   185

Othello. Hang her! I do but say what she is. So delicate with her needle! An admirable musician! O, she will sing the savageness out of a bear. Of so high and plentous wit and invention!

Iago. She's the worse for all this.   190

Othello. O! a thousand, a thousand times. And then, of so gentle a condition!

Iago. Ay, too gentle.

Othello. Nay, that's certain;—but yet the pity of it, Iago! O! Iago, the pity of it, Iago!   195

Iago. If you are so fond over her iniquity, give her patent to offend; for, if it touch not you, it comes near nobody.

Othello. I will chop her into messes. Cuckold me!

Iago. O! 'tis foul in her.   200

Othello. With mine officer!

Iago. That's fouler.

Othello. Get me some poison, Iago; this night: I'll not

177 **I . . . a-killing**: i.e. kill him slowly to prolong the agony (**a-killing** = in the killing, being killed).   184 **command him tasks**: i.e. he would do anything for her.   185 **that's . . . way**: i.e. you must not think about her charms [*N*].   187 **delicate**: expert.   189 **wit**: sense, wisdom.   **invention**: liveliness of mind.   192 **condition**: nature [*N*].   193 **too gentle**: i.e. too generous in her favours.   196 **fond**: foolish.   **over**: about. 197 **patent**: permission.   197–8 **it comes. . . nobody**: it doesn't matter to anybody else.   199 **messes**: small pieces, gobbets.

expostulate with her, lest her body and beauty unprovide
my mind again. This night, Iago.   205

Iago. Do it not with poison, strangle her in her bed,
even the bed she hath contaminated.

Othello. Good, good; the justice of it pleases; very good.

Iago. And for Cassio, let me be his undertaker; you shall
hear more by midnight.   210

Othello. Excellent good. [*A trumpet within.*] What
trumpet is that same?

Iago. Something from Venice, sure. 'Tis Lodovico,
Come from the duke; and see, your wife is with him.

Enter LODOVICO, DESDEMONA, *and* Attendants.

Lodovico. God save you, worthy general!
Othello.   With all my heart, sir.
Lodovico. The duke and senators of Venice greet you.
                              [*Gives him a packet.*
Othello. I kiss the instrument of their pleasures.   216
                              [*Opens the packet, and reads.*
Desdemona. And what's the news, good cousin Lodovico?
Iago. I am very glad to see you, signior;
Welcome to Cyprus.
Lodovico. I thank you. How does Lieutenant Cassio?
Iago. Lives, sir.   221
Desdemona. Cousin, there's fall'n between him and
my lord
An unkind breach; but you shall make all well.
Othello. Are you sure of that?
Desdemona. My lord?   225
Othello. *This fail you not to do, as you will—*

204 **unprovide**: make unready.   209 **let ... undertaker**:
let me settle with him (the modern sense appears to be later).
214 **With ... heart**: (probably) the same to you.   216 **instrument**: means (i.e. either the packet, or the messenger).   221 **Lives**:
i.e. is here (non-committal).   223 **unkind**: unnatural.

Lodovico. He did not call; he's busy in the paper.
Is there division 'twixt my lord and Cassio?

Desdemona. A most unhappy one; I would do much
To atone them, for the love I bear to Cassio.   230

Othello. Fire and brimstone!

Desdemona.   My lord?

Othello.   Are you wise?

Desdemona. What! is he angry?

Lodovico.   May be the letter mov'd him;
For, as I think, they do command him home,
Deputing Cassio in his government.   234

Desdemona. Trust me, I am glad on't.

Othello.   Indeed!

Desdemona.   My lord?

Othello. I am glad to see you mad.

Desdemona.   Why, sweet Othello?

Othello. Devil!   [*Strikes her.*

Desdemona.   I have not deserved this.

Lodovico. My lord, this would not be believ'd in Venice,
Though I should swear I saw't: 'tis very much;
Make her amends, she weeps.

Othello.   O devil, devil!   240
If that the earth could teem with woman's tears,
Each drop she falls would prove a crocodile.
Out of my sight!

Desdemona.   I will not stay to offend you.   [*Going.*

Lodovico. Truly, an obedient lady;
I do beseech your lordship, call her back.   245

Othello. Mistress!

Desdemona.   My lord?

Othello.   What would you with her, sir?

---

227 **He . . . call**: i.e. he wasn't talking to you.   230 **atone
them**: bring them together.   231 **wise**: i.e. discreet, tactful [*N*].
234 **in his government**: to succeed him [*N*].   239 **very much**:
shocking, monstrous.   241 **teem with**: become pregnant by [*N*].

Lodovico. Who, I, my lord?

Othello. Ay, you did wish that I would make her turn:
Sir, she can turn and turn, and yet go on,
And turn again; and she can weep, sir, weep;   250
And she's obedient, as you say, obedient,
Very obedient. Proceed you in your tears.
Concerning this, sir—O well-painted passion!—
I am commanded home. Get you away;
I'll send for you anon. Sir, I obey the mandate,   255
And will return to Venice. Hence! avaunt!

                                        [*Exit* DESDEMONA.
Cassio shall have my place. And, sir, to-night,
I do entreat that we may sup together;
You are welcome, sir, to Cyprus. Goats and monkeys!

                                                [*Exit.*
Lodovico. Is this the noble Moor whom our full senate
Call all-in-all sufficient? is this the noble nature   261
Whom passion could not shake? whose solid virtue
The shot of accident nor dart of chance
Could neither graze nor pierce?

Iago.   He is much chang'd.

Lodovico. Are his wits safe? is he not light of brain? 265

Iago. He's that he is; I may not breathe my censure
What he might be, if, what he might, he is not,
I would to heaven he were!

Lodovico.   What! strike his wife!

249 **turn and turn**: (i) return, (ii) play false [*N*].   **yet go on**:
follow her own path.   252 **Proceed you**: (to Desdemona).
253 **this**: i.e. the letter of recall (O. speaks alternately to Lodovico
and his wife).   **well-painted passion**: well-assumed grief.
255 **anon**: soon.   256 **avaunt**: be off.   261 **all-in-all**:
in every way.   **sufficient**: fit for an office.   265 **safe**: sound.
light of brain: out of his mind, light-headed [*N*].   266 **that**: that
which.   **breathe**: whisper.   **censure**: opinion.   267–8 **What
... were**: I wish to heaven he were what he well might be (i.e. mad),
if he is not so indeed (i.e. madness would excuse his action) [*N*].

Iago. Faith, that was not so well; yet would I knew
That stroke would prove the worst!

Lodovico.   Is it his use?   270
Or did the letters work upon his blood,
And new-create this fault?

Iago.   Alas, alas!
It is not honesty in me to speak
What I have seen and known. You shall observe him,
And his own courses will denote him so   275
That I may save my speech. Do but go after
And mark how he continues.

Lodovico. I am sorry that I am deceiv'd in him.

[*Exeunt.*

Scene II. A ROOM IN THE CASTLE

Enter OTHELLO *and* EMILIA.

Othello. You have seen nothing, then?

Emilia. Nor ever heard, nor ever did suspect.

Othello. Yes, you have seen Cassio and she together.

Emilia. But then I saw no harm, and then I heard
Each syllable that breath made up between them.   5

Othello. What! did they never whisper?

Emilia.   Never, my lord.

Othello. Nor send you out o' the way?

Emilia.   Never.

Othello. To fetch her fan, her gloves, her mask, nor
  nothing?

Emilia. Never, my lord.

Othello. That's strange.   10

270 **use**: usual behaviour.   271 **blood**: feelings.   273
It ... honesty: it would not be honourable [*N*].   275 **courses**:
actions.   **denote**: reveal.   3 **Yes**: but.   **she**: her [*N*].
5 **breath**: speech.

Emilia. I durst, my lord, to wager she is honest,
Lay down my soul at stake: if you think other,
Remove your thought; it doth abuse your bosom.
If any wretch have put this in your head,
Let heaven requite it with the serpent's curse!   15
For, if she be not honest, chaste, and true,
There's no man happy; the purest of their wives
Is foul as slander.
    Othello.   Bid her come hither; go. [*Exit* EMILIA.
She says enough; yet she's a simple bawd
That cannot say as much. This is a subtle whore,   20
A closet lock and key of villanous secrets;
And yet she'll kneel and pray; I have seen her do't.

           Re-enter EMILIA *with* DESDEMONA.

Desdemona. My lord, what is your will?
Othello.   Pray, chuck, come hither.
Desdemona. What is your pleasure?
Othello.   Let me see your eyes;
Look in my face.
Desdemona.   What horrible fancy's this?   25
Othello. [*To* EMILIA.] Some of your function, mistress,
Leave procreants alone and shut the door;
Cough or cry 'hem' if any body come;
Your mystery, your mystery; nay, dispatch.
                                        [*Exit* EMILIA.

11 **durst:** would dare.   **honest:** chaste (as often hereafter).
12 **Lay...at stake:** would stake my soul upon it.   **other:** otherwise.   13 **abuse your bosom:** deceive you.   18 **foul as
slander:** as foul as slander could make them out to be.   19
enough: i.e. enough to acquit D.   **she's...cannot:** a bawd who
could not...would be a fool.   **bawd:** attendant of a brothel [N].
20 **This:** i.e. Desdemona.   21 i.e. one who keeps closely locked
up all her disreputable secrets ('closet' = cabinet for private papers).
26 **of your function:** i.e. bawds [N].   **mistress:** madam (contemptuous).   27 **procreants:** begetters (of young).   29 **mystery:**
trade (here, of keeping the door).   **dispatch:** get on with it.

Desdemona. Upon my knees, what doth your speech
     import ?   30
I understand a fury in your words,
But not the words.
  Othello. Why, what art thou ?
  Desdemona.   Your wife, my lord ; your true
And loyal wife.
  Othello.   Come, swear it, damn thyself ;
Lest, being like one of heaven, the devils themselves   35
Should fear to seize thee ; therefore be double-damn'd ;
Swear thou art honest.
  Desdemona.   Heaven doth truly know it.
  Othello. Heaven truly knows that thou art false as hell.
  Desdemona. To whom, my lord ? with whom ? how am
     I false ?
  Othello. Ah ! Desdemona ; away, away, away !   40
  Desdemona. Alas, the heavy day !—Why do you weep ?
Am I the motive of these tears, my lord ?
If haply you my father do suspect
An instrument of this your calling back,
Lay not your blame on me ; if you have lost him,   45
Why, I have lost him too.
  Othello.   Had it pleas'd heaven
To try me with affliction, had they rain'd
All kinds of sores, and shames, on my bare head,
Steep'd me in poverty to the very lips,
Given to captivity me and my utmost hopes,   50

30 **import** : mean.   35 **being like . . . heaven** : since you
look like a heavenly being (grammatically with **thee**).   36
double-damn'd : i.e. both for adultery and for swearing falsely.
41 **heavy** : grievous.   42 **motive** : cause.   43 **If haply** : i.e. if
perhaps it is because.   44 **An instrument** : of having had a hand
in.   45 **lost him** : lost his friendship (see I. iii. 128).   47 **they :**
the heavens.   48 **sores** : afflictions [N].   **bare** : defenceless.
49 **to . . . lips** : (as we say 'up to the eyes' in debt etc.).   50
i.e. deprived me of the very least I might have hoped for.

I should have found in some part of my soul
A drop of patience; but, alas! to make me
The fixed figure for the time of scorn
To point his slow unmoving finger at;
Yet could I bear that too; well, very well.   55
But there, where I have garner'd up my heart,
Where either I must live or bear no life,
The fountain from the which my current runs
Or else dries up; to be discarded thence!
Or keep it as a cistern for foul toads   60
To knot and gender in! Turn thy complexion there,
Patience, thou young and rose-lipp'd cherubin;
Ay, here, look grim as hell!

Desdemona. I hope my noble lord esteems me honest.

Othello. O! ay; as summer flies are in the shambles,   65
That quicken even with blowing. O thou weed!
Who art so lovely fair and smell'st so sweet
That the sense aches at thee, would thou hadst ne'er
   been born.

Desdemona. Alas! what ignorant sin have I committed?

Othello. Was this fair paper, this most goodly book,   70
Made to write 'whore' upon? What committed!
Committed! O thou public commoner!
I should make very forges of my cheeks.

53–4 i.e. an object for the scornful world to point at while time
moves on so slowly as to seem motionless [*N*].   56 **garner'd**
... **heart**: treasured up all that I love.   58 **fountain**: spring.
61 **knot**: cluster. **gender**: engender [*N*].   61–3 **Turn ... hell**:
'At such an object do thou, Patience, thyself change colour: at this
do thou, even thou, rosy cherub as thou art, look grim as hell' (Johnson) [*N*].   65 **shambles**: slaughter-house *or* butcher's shop.
66 **quicken ... blowing**: become pregnant again immediately they
have laid their eggs ('blowing': used of flies, depositing their eggs;
cf. fly-blown).   68 **sense**: senses [*N*].   69 **ignorant**:
unknown to me.   70–1 **Was ... upon**: i.e. how can so fair a
woman be a whore?   72 **commoner**: one common to all, whore.
73 **very forges**: regular fires [*N*].

That would to cinders burn up modesty,
Did I but speak thy deeds. What committed!   75
Heaven stops the nose at it and the moon winks,
The bawdy wind that kisses all it meets
Is hush'd within the hollow mine of earth,
And will not hear it. What committed!
Impudent strumpet!
  Desdemona.   By heaven, you do me wrong.   80
  Othello. Are not you a strumpet?
  Desdemona.   No, as I am a Christian.
If to preserve this vessel for my lord
From any other foul unlawful touch
Be not to be a strumpet, I am none.
  Othello. What! not a whore?
  Desdemona.   No, as I shall be sav'd.   85
  Othello. Is it possible?
  Desdemona. O! heaven forgive us.
  Othello.   I cry you mercy, then;
I took you for that cunning whore of Venice
That married with Othello. You, mistress,
That have the office opposite to Saint Peter,   90
And keep the gate of hell!

Re-enter EMILIA.

                    You, you, ay, you!
We have done our course; there's money for your pains.
I pray you, turn the key and keep our counsel. [*Exit.*
  Emilia. Alas! what does this gentleman conceive?
How do you, madam? how do you, my good lady?   95

---

76 winks: closes her eyes (*not* modern sense).   **78 hollow
mine**: the cavern of the winds (a classical conception).   **82
vessel**: i.e. her body [*N*].   **87 forgive us**: (polite for) forgive
you for your imputation.   **I ... mercy**: ask your pardon (ironical).
90 office: duty, post [*N*].   **92 done our course**: finished our
business [*N*].   **93 turn the key**: i.e. let us out (cf. 27).   **keep
our counsel**: keep quiet about us.   **94 conceive**: imagine, think.

Desdemona. Faith, half asleep.

Emilia. Good madam, what's the matter with my lord?

Desdemona. With who?

Emilia. Why, with my lord, madam.

Desdemona. Who is thy lord?

Emilia.   He that is yours, sweet lady.   100

Desdemona. I have none; do not talk to me, Emilia;
I cannot weep, nor answer have I none,
But what should go by water. Prithee, to-night
Lay on my bed my wedding sheets: remember:
·And call thy husband hither.

Emilia.   Here is a change indeed!   105
                                             [*Exit.*

Desdemona. 'Tis meet I should be us'd so, very meet.
How have I been behav'd, that he might stick
The small'st opinion on my greatest abuse?

Re-enter EMILIA, *with* IAGO.

Iago. What is your pleasure, madam? How is it with
you?   110

Desdemona. I cannot tell. Those that do teach young
  babes
Do it with gentle means and easy tasks;
He might have chid me so; for, in good faith,
I am a child to chiding.

Iago.   What's the matter, lady?

Emilia. Alas! Iago, my lord hath so bewhor'd her,   115
Thrown such despite and heavy terms upon her,
As true hearts cannot bear.

103 **go by water**: be expressed in tears.   106 **meet**: just
(ironical).   107 **been behav'd**: behaved myself.   107-8
stick . . . abuse: attach the smallest importance to the worst
things I have done.   114 **a child to chiding**: as sensitive
as a child to scolding.   115 **bewhor'd**: treated as a whore [*N*].
116 **despite**: scorn.   **heavy terms**: insulting language.

Desdemona. Am I that name, Iago?

Iago.   What name, fair lady?

Desdemona. Such as she says my lord did say I was.

Emilia. He call'd her whore; a beggar in his drink   120
Could not have laid such terms upon his callat.

Iago. Why did he so?

Desdemona. I do not know; I am sure I am none such.

Iago. Do not weep, do not weep. Alas the day!

Emilia. Has she forsook so many noble matches,   125
Her father and her country and her friends,
To be call'd whore? would it not make one weep?

Desdemona. It is my wretched fortune.

Iago.   Beshrew him for it!
How comes this trick upon him?

Desdemona.   Nay, heaven doth know.

Emilia. I will be hang'd, if some eternal villain,   130
Some busy and insinuating rogue,
Some cogging cozening slave, to get some office,
Have not devis'd this slander; I'll be hang'd else.

Iago. Fie! there is no such man; it is impossible.   134

Desdemona. If any such there be, heaven pardon him!

Emilia. A halter pardon him, and hell gnaw his bones!
Why should he call her whore? who keeps her company?
What place? what time? what form? what likelihood?
The Moor's abus'd by some most villanous knave,
Some base notorious knave, some scurvy fellow.   140

---

121 **callat**: whore, trull.   125 **forsook ... matches**: given up the chance of so many excellent marriages.   128 **Beshrew**: confound.   129 **trick**: whim.   130 **eternal**: unmitigated (an intensifying adjective, as we use 'everlasting').   131 **busy**: busy-bodying, officious.   **insinuating**: scheming [*N*].   132 **cogging**: cheating.   **cozening**: cheating, wheedling.   **slave**: scoundrel.   136 **A halter ... him**: i.e. the only mercy I'd give him is the rope.   137 **keeps her company**: i.e. is her lover.   138 **what form**: how could it have been contrived [*N*].   140 **notorious**: conspicuous.

O heaven! that such companions thou'dst unfold,
And put in every honest hand a whip
To lash the rascals naked through the world,
Even from the east to the west!

Iago.   Speak within door.

Emilia. O! fie upon them. Some such squire he was   145
That turn'd your wit the seamy side without,
And made you to suspect me with the Moor.

Iago. You are a fool; go to.

Desdemona.   O good Iago,
What shall I do to win my lord again?
Good friend, go to him; for, by this light of heaven,   150
I know not how I lost him. Here I kneel:
If e'er my will did trespass 'gainst his love,
Either in discourse of thought or actual deed,
Or that mine eyes, mine ears, or any sense,
Delighted them in any other form;   155
Or that I do not yet, and ever did,
And ever will, though he do shake me off
To beggarly divorcement, love him dearly,
Comfort forswear me! Unkindness may do much;
And his unkindness may defeat my life,   160
But never taint my love. I cannot say 'whore:'
It does abhor me now I speak the word;
To do the act that might the addition earn

---

141 **that**: would that.   **companions**: rascals.   **unfold**:
expose.   144 **Speak . . . door**: lower your voice.   145
Some such squire: a fine young fool.   146 **seamy side**
without: worst side outwards (i.e. addled your wits).   148 **go**
to: shut up.   152 **trespass**: offend.   153 **discourse of**
thought: process of thinking, thought (cf. *Hamlet* I. ii. 150).
155 **Delighted them**: pleased themselves (reflexive).   **form**:
shape, person (than his).   156 **yet**: still.   158 **divorce-**
ment: separation.   159 **Comfort . . . me**: may I never be
happy again.   160 **defeat**: destroy.   162 **abhor me**: fill
me with disgust [*N*].   163 **addition**: title.

Not the world's mass of vanity could make me.

  Iago. I pray you be content, 'tis but his humour;   165
The business of the state does him offence,
And he does chide with you.

  Desdemona.   If 'twere no other,—

  Iago. 'Tis but so, I warrant.   [*Trumpets.*
Hark! how these instruments summon to supper;
The messengers of Venice stay the meat: 170
Go in, and weep not; all things shall be well.

             [*Exeunt* DESDEMONA *and* EMILIA.

Enter RODERIGO.

How now, Roderigo!

  Roderigo. I do not find that thou dealest justly with me.

  Iago. What in the contrary?

  Roderigo. Every day thou daff'st me with some de-   175
vice, Iago; and rather, as it seems to me now, keepest
from me all conveniency, than suppliest me with the
least advantage of hope. I will indeed no longer endure it, nor am I yet persuaded to put up in peace
what already I have foolishly suffered.   180

  Iago. Will you hear me, Roderigo?

  Roderigo. Faith, I have heard too much, and your
words and performances are no kin together.

  Iago. You charge me most unjustly.

  Roderigo. With nought but truth. I have wasted   185
myself out of my means. The jewels you have had

   164 **mass of vanity**: store of (empty) splendours.   165 **content**: calm.   **humour**: mood.   166 **does him offence**: troubles
him.   167 **does chide**: is angry.   **other**: business (than state
affairs).   170 **stay the meat**: await the meal.   174 **What
in the contrary**: what can you allege to the contrary?   175
daff'st: put me off [*N*].   **device**: pretext.   177 **conveniency**: opportunity (of seeing Desdemona).   178 **advantage
of hope**: likely chance.   179 **put up**: put up with.
185–6 **wasted . . . means**: squandered all my money.

from me to deliver to Desdemona would half have
corrupted a votarist; you have told me she has received them, and returned me expectations and comforts of sudden respect and acquaintance, but   190
I find none.

Iago. Well; go to; very well.

Roderigo. Very well! go to! I cannot go to, man; nor
'tis not very well: by this hand, I say, it is very scurvy,
and begin to find myself fopped in it.   195

Iago. Very well.

Roderigo. I tell you 'tis not very well. I will make myself known to Desdemona; if she will return me my jewels,
I will give over my suit and repent my unlawful solicita-
tion; if not, assure yourself I will seek satisfaction of you.

Iago. You have said now.   201

Roderigo. Ay, and said nothing, but what I protest
intendment of doing.

Iago. Why, now I see there's mettle in thee, and
even from this instant do build on thee a better   205
opinion than ever before. Give me thy hand,
Roderigo; thou hast taken against me a most just
exception; but yet, I protest, I have dealt most
directly in thy affair.

Roderigo. It hath not appeared.   210

Iago. I grant indeed it hath not appeared, and
your suspicion is not without wit and judgment.
But, Roderigo, if thou hast that in thee indeed,

188 **votarist**: nun.   189 **expectations**: promises.   190
sudden: immediate.   **respect**: consideration [N].   **acquaintance**: meeting [N].   193 **I cannot go to**: I am not to be put off
by phrases such as 'go to' (or, perhaps, go to = get at Desdemona).
194 **scurvy**: lousy.   195 **fopped**: fooled [N].   199 **soli-
citation**: suit.   201 **You ... now**: 'Now you're talking'
(Ridley).   202 **protest**: assert.   203 **intendment**: intention.
207–8 **taken ... exception**: found fault with me most justly.
209 **directly**: straightforwardly.   212 **wit**: sense.

which I have greater reason to believe now than
ever, I mean purpose, courage, and valour, this   215
night show it: if thou the next night following enjoy
not Desdemona, take me from this world with
treachery and devise engines for my life.

Roderigo. Well, what is it? is it within reason
and compass?   220

Iago. Sir, there is especial commission come from
Venice to depute Cassio in Othello's place.

Roderigo. Is that true? why, then Othello and
Desdemona return again to Venice.   224

Iago. O, no! he goes into Mauritania, and takes
away with him the fair Desdemona, unless his abode
be lingered here by some accident; wherein none
can be so determinate as the removing of Cassio.

Roderigo. How do you mean, removing of him?

Iago. Why, by making him uncapable of Othello's 230
place; knocking out his brains.

Roderigo. And that you would have me do?

Iago. Ay; if you dare do yourself a profit and
a right. He sups to-night with a harlotry, and
thither will I go to him; he knows not yet of his   235
honourable fortune. If you will watch his going
thence,—which I will fashion to fall out between
twelve and one,—you may take him at your pleasure;
I will be near to second your attempt, and he shall
fall between us. Come, stand not amazed at it, but 240
go along with me; I will show you such a necessity
in his death that you shall think yourself bound
to put it on him. It is now high supper-time, and

---

216 **enjoy**: i.e. sleep with.   218 **devise engines for**: contrive plots against.   220 **compass**: possibility.   226 **lingered**: prolonged.   227 **determinate**: effective.   234
harlotry: harlot.   240 **amazed**: taken aback.   243 **high
supper-time**: high time for supper.

the night grows to waste; about it.

Roderigo. I will hear further reason for this.   245
Iago. And you shall be satisfied.   [*Exeunt.*

Scene III. Another Room in the Castle

Enter OTHELLO, LODOVICO, DESDEMONA,
EMILIA, *and* Attendants.

Lodovico. I do beseech you, sir, trouble yourself no
   further.
Othello. O! pardon me; 'twill do me good to walk.
Lodovico. Madam, good night; I humbly thank your
   ladyship.
Desdemona. Your honour is most welcome.
Othello.   Will you walk, sir?
O! Desdemona,—   5
Desdemona. My lord?
Othello. Get you to bed on the instant; I will be returned
forthwith; dismiss your attendant there; look it be done.
Desdemona. I will, my lord.   9
         [*Exeunt* OTHELLO, LODOVICO, *and* Attendants.
Emilia. How goes it now? he looks gentler than he did.
Desdemona. He says he will return incontinent;
He hath commanded me to go to bed,
And bade me to dismiss you.
Emilia.   Dismiss me!
Desdemona. It was his bidding; therefore, good Emilia,
Give me my nightly wearing, and adieu: 15
We must not now displease him.
Emilia. I would you had never seen him.

---

244 **the night . . . waste**: we are wasting time [*N*].   4 **Will
you walk**: shall we go?   11 **incontinent**: at once.   15
wearing: wear, nightdress.

Desdemona. So would not I; my love doth so approve him,
That even his stubbornness, his checks and frowns,—
Prithee, unpin me,—have grace and favour in them.   20

Emilia. I have laid those sheets you bade me on the bed.

Desdemona. All's one. Good faith! how foolish are our
    minds!
If I do die before thee, prithee, shroud me
In one of those same sheets.

Emilia.   Come, come, you talk.

Desdemona. My mother had a maid call'd Barbara;   25
She was in love, and he she lov'd prov'd mad
And did forsake her; she had a song of 'willow;'
An old thing 'twas, but it express'd her fortune,
And she died singing it; that song to-night
Will not go from my mind; I have much to do   30
But to go hang my head all at one side,
And sing it like poor Barbara. Prithee, dispatch.

Emilia. Shall I go fetch your night-gown?

Desdemona.   No, unpin me here.
This Lodovico is a proper man.

Emilia. A very handsome man.   35

Desdemona. He speaks well.

Emilia. I know a lady in Venice would have walked
barefoot to Palestine for a touch of his nether lip.

Desdemona.
       The poor soul sat sighing by a sycamore tree,
         Sing all a green willow;   40
       Her hand on her bosom, her head on her knee,

---

18 **approve**: approve of, admire.   19 **stubbornness**: harsh-
ness. **checks**: rebukes.   20 **grace and favour**: charm and
attraction.   22 **All's one**: it doesn't matter [N].   24 **Come
... talk**: how foolishly you talk!   26 **mad**: (probably here)
wild, i.e. inconstant.   28 **her fortune**: what happened to her.
30–1 **I ... But**: it is all I can do not to.   32 **dispatch**: hurry.
34 **proper**: handsome, manly [N].   38 **nether**: lower.
39 **sycamore**: the fig-mulberry.

      Sing willow, willow, willow:
      The fresh streams ran by her, and murmur'd hei
         moans;
      Sing willow, willow, willow:
      Her salt tears fell from her, and soften'd the stones;—

Lay by these:—   46

      Sing willow, willow, willow:

Prithee, hie thee; he'll come anon.—

      Sing all a green willow must be my garland.
      Let nobody blame him, his scorn I approve,— 50

Nay, that's not next. Hark! who is it that knocks?
Emilia. It is the wind.
Desdemona
      I call'd my love false love; but what said he
         then?
      Sing willow, willow, willow:
      If I court moe women, you'll couch with moe men.
So, get thee gone; good night. Mine eyes do itch; 56
Doth that bode weeping?
Emilia.   'Tis neither here nor there.
Desdemona. I have heard it said so. O! these men, these
      men!
Dost thou in conscience think, tell me, Emilia,
That there be women do abuse their husbands 60
In such gross kind?
Emilia.   There be some such, no question.
Desdemona. Wouldst thou do such a deed for all the
      world?
Emilia. Why, would not you?

  46 **Lay by these**: put these clothes away.   48 **hie thee**:
hurry.   49 **garland**: here stressed gárlánd.   50 **approve**:
consider just.   55 **moe**: more [N].   **couch with**: lie with.
57 **bode**: foretell.   **'Tis . . . there**: it means nothing either way.
59 **in conscience**: honestly.   60 **abuse**: deceive.   61 **In
. . . kind**: so disgracefully.

Desdemona.   No, by this heavenly light!

Emilia. Nor I neither by this heavenly light;
I might do't as well i' the dark.   65

Desdemona. Wouldst thou do such a deed for all the
world?

Emilia. The world is a huge thing; 'tis a great price
For a small vice.

Desdemona.   In troth, I think thou wouldst not.

Emilia. In troth, I think I should, and undo't when
I had done. Marry, I would not do such a thing for   70
a joint-ring, nor measures of lawn, nor for gowns,
petticoats, nor caps, nor any petty exhibition; but
for the whole world, who would not make her husband a cuckold to make him a monarch? I should
venture purgatory for't.   75

Desdemona. Beshrew me, if I would do such a wrong
for the whole world.

Emilia. Why, the wrong is but a wrong i' the world; and
having the world for your labour, 'tis a wrong in your own
world, and you might quickly make it right.   80

Desdemona. I do not think there is any such woman.

Emilia. Yes, a dozen; and as many to the vantage, as
would store the world they played for.
But I do think it is their husbands' faults
If wives do fall. Say that they slack their duties,   85
And pour our treasures into foreign laps,
Or else break out in peevish jealousies,

67 price: reward.   **69 undo't**: make up for it [N].   **71
joint-ring**: ring made in two separate halves [N].   **measures**:
lengths.   **72 exhibition**: allowance, (perhaps) gift.   **79 for
your labour**: in return for your act.   **82 to the vantage**:
in addition.   **83 store ... played for**: people the world to win
which they committed adultery.   **85 Say that**: suppose
slack: neglect (as husbands).   **86** i.e. bestow on others the
love due to us (**foreign** = not their wives').   **87 peevish**:
unreasonable.

Throwing restraint upon us; or, say they strike us,
Or scant our former having in despite;
Why, we have galls, and though we have some grace,   90
Yet have we some revenge. Let husbands know
Their wives have sense like them; they see and smell,
And have their palates both for sweet and sour,
As husbands have. What is it that they do
When they change us for others? Is it sport?   95
I think it is; and doth affection breed it?
I think it doth; is't frailty that thus errs?
It is so too; and have not we affections,
Desires for sport, and frailty, as men have?
Then, let them use us well; else let them know,   100
The ills we do, their ills instruct us so.
    Desdemona. Good night, good night; heaven me such
        uses send,
Not to pick bad from bad, but by bad mend!   [*Exeunt.*

88 **Throwing . . . us :** interfering with our freedom.   89 **Or
. . . despite :** or cut down our former allowance out of spite.
90 **galls :** tempers, spirit to resent injuries.   **grace :** mercy, for-
giveness.   91 **revenge :** means to get our own back.   92
sense : feelings.   95 **sport :** sexual pleasure.   96 **affection :**
passion, desire.   97 **frailty :** the weakness of yielding to temptation (here sexual).   102 **uses :** habit, behaviour.   103 **pick
bad from bad :** imitate bad examples.   **by bad mend :** i.e. do
better from knowing them.

ACT V

Scene I. CYPRUS. A STREET

Enter IAGO *and* RODERIGO.

Iago. Here, stand behind this bulk; straight will he
    come:
Wear thy good rapier bare, and put it home.
Quick, quick; fear nothing; I'll be at thy elbow.
It makes us, or it mars us; think on that,
And fix most firm thy resolution.   5

Roderigo. Be near at hand; I may miscarry in't.

Iago. Here, at thy hand: be bold, and take thy stand.
                                   [Retires.

Roderigo. I have no great devotion to the deed;
And yet he has given me satisfying reasons:
'Tis but a man gone: forth, my sword; he dies.   10

Iago. I have rubb'd this young quat almost to the sense,
And he grows angry. Now, whether he kill Cassio,
Or Cassio him, or each do kill the other,
Every way makes my gain: live Roderigo,
He calls me to a restitution large   15
Of gold and jewels that I bobb'd from him,
As gifts to Desdemona;
It must not be: if Cassio do remain,
He hath a daily beauty in his life
That makes me ugly; and, besides, the Moor   20
May unfold me to him; there stand I in much peril.
No, he must die. But so; I hear him coming.

1 **bulk:** projecting part of a ship (cf. bulkhead) [*N*].   2 **home:**
to the vital spot.   11 **quat:** 'squirt' in slang sense (literally
a pimple).   **to the sense:** till he is raw, to the quick.   14 **live
Roderigo:** if Roderigo lives.   16 **bobb'd:** cheated.   21 **unfold:**
expose.   22 **But so:** enough!

Enter CASSIO.

Roderigo. I know his gait; 'tis he. Villain, thou diest!
        [*Makes a pass at* CASSIO.
Cassio. That thrust had been mine enemy indeed
But that my coat is better than thou know'st;   25
I will make proof of thine. [*Draws, and wounds* RODERIGO.
Roderigo.   O! I am slain.
   [IAGO *from behind wounds* CASSIO *in the leg, and exit.*
Cassio. I am maim'd for ever. Help, ho! murder!
 murder!   [*Falls.*
   Enter OTHELLO, *at a distance.*

Othello. The voice of Cassio: Iago keeps his word.
Roderigo. O! villain that I am!
Othello.   It is e'en so.
Cassio. O, help, ho! light! a surgeon!   30
Othello. 'Tis he: O brave Iago, honest and just!
That hast such noble sense of thy friend's wrong;
Thou teachest me. Minion, your dear lies dead,
And your unblest fate hies; strumpet, I come!
Forth of my heart those charms, thine eyes, are blotted; 35
Thy bed lust-stain'd shall with lust's blood be spotted.
              [*Exit.*
 Enter LODOVICO *and* GRATIANO, *at a distance.*

Cassio. What ho! no watch! no passage? murder!
 murder!
Gratiano. 'Tis some mischance; the cry is very direful.

23 *s.d.* **pass**: thrust.   25 **coat**: (probably) a leather jerkin (but possibly 'mail') [N].   26 **make proof of**: try.   28 **his word**: see IV. i. 209–10.   29 **e'en**: exactly [N].   32 **sense**: feeling.   33 **Minion**: hussy (properly 'darling' but often used contemptuously); said to Desdemona [N].   34 **unblest**: wretched, accursed.   **hies**: is near.   35 **Forth of**: out from.   36 **lust's blood**: my passionate revenge.   37 **watch**: watchman. **passage**: passers-by.   38 **direful**: dreadful.

Cassio. O, help!   40
Lodovico. Hark!
Roderigo. O wretched villain!
Lodovico. Two or three groan: it is a heavy night;
These may be counterfeits; let's think't unsafe
To come in to the cry without more help.
Roderigo. Nobody come? then shall I bleed to death.   45
Lodovico. Hark!

Re-enter IAGO, *with a light.*

Gratiano. Here's one comes in his shirt, with light and
weapons.
Iago. Who's there? whose noise is this that cries on
murder?
Lodovico. We do not know.
Iago.   Did not you hear a cry?
Cassio. Here, here! for heaven's sake, help me.
Iago.   What's the matter?   5C
Gratiano. This is Othello's ancient, as I take it.
Lodovico. The same indeed; a very valiant fellow.
Iago. What are you here that cry so grievously?
Cassio. Iago? O! I am spoil'd, undone by villains!
Give me some help.   55
Iago. O me, lieutenant! what villains have done this?
Cassio. I think that one of them is hereabout,
And cannot make away.
Iago.   O treacherous villains!
[*To* LODOVICO *and* GRATIANO.] What are you there? come
in, and give some help.
Roderigo. O! help me here.   60

41 **villain**: Roderigo means himself.   42 **heavy**: gloomy.
43 **counterfeits**: feigned appeals for help.   44 **come...cry**:
answer these cries.   45 **Nobody come**: Is there nobody to help?
47 **shirt**: night-shirt [N].   48 **cries on**: shouts.   53 **What**:
who.   54 **spoil'd**: very badly hurt.   **undone**: murdered.
58 **make away**: get away.

Cassio. That's one of them.

Iago.   O murderous slave! O villain!

                                [*Stabs* RODERIGO.

Roderigo. O damn'd Iago! O inhuman dog!

Iago. Kill men i' the dark! Where be these bloody thieves?

How silent is this town! Ho! murder! murder!

What may you be? are you of good or evil?   65

Lodovico. As you shall prove us, praise us.

Iago. Signior Lodovico?

Lodovico. He, sir.

Iago. I cry you mercy. Here's Cassio hurt by villains.

Gratiano. Cassio!   70

Iago. How is it, brother?

Cassio. My leg is cut in two.

Iago.   Marry, heaven forbid,

Light, gentlemen; I'll bind it with my shirt.

Enter BIANCA.

Bianca. What is the matter, ho? who is't that cried?

Iago. Who is't that cried!   75

Bianca. O my dear Cassio! my sweet Cassio!

O Cassio, Cassio, Cassio!

Iago. O notable strumpet! Cassio, may you suspect

Who they should be that have thus mangled you?

Cassio. No.

                                                 80

Gratiano. I am sorry to find you thus; I have been to seek you.

Iago. Lend me a garter. So. O! for a chair,

To bear him easily hence!

Bianca. Alas! he faints! O Cassio, Cassio, Cassio!

65 of good or evil: of the good or evil party, honest men or villains.   **66 As ... praise us:** judge us on the way we behave. **69 I ... mercy:** I beg your pardon.   **78 notable:** notorious. **may you suspect:** have you any idea.   **82 chair:** i.e. a sedan-chair, *or* a litter.

Iago. Gentlemen all, I do suspect this trash   85
To be a party in this injury.
Patience awhile, good Cassio. Come, come.
Lend me a light. Know we this face, or no?
Alas! my friend and my dear countryman,
Roderigo? no: yes, sure, O heaven! Roderigo.   90
  Gratiano. What! of Venice?
Iago. Even he, sir: did you know him?
  Gratiano.   Know him! ay.
Iago. Signior Gratiano? I cry you gentle pardon;
These bloody accidents must excuse my manners,
That so neglected you.
  Gratiano.   I am glad to see you.   95
Iago. How do you, Cassio? O! a chair, a chair!
  Gratiano. Roderigo!   [*A chair brought in.*
Iago. He, he, 'tis he.—O! that's well said; the chair:
Some good men bear him carefully from hence;
I'll fetch the general's surgeon. [*To* BIANCA.] For you,
    mistress,   100
Save you your labour. He that lies slain here, Cassio,
Was my dear friend. What malice was between you?
  Cassio. None in the world; nor do I know the man.
Iago. [*To* BIANCA.] What! look you pale? O! bear him
    out o' the air—   [CASSIO *and* RODERIGO *are borne off.*
Stay you, good gentlemen. Look you pale, mistress?—
Do you perceive the gastness of her eye?   106
Nay, if you stare, we shall hear more anon.
Behold her well; I pray you, look upon her:
Do you see, gentlemen? nay, guiltiness will speak
Though tongues were out of use.   110

   85 **trash**: worthless person (Bianca).   86 i.e. to be involved in
this attack [*N*].   94 **accidents**: happenings.   98 **well said**:
well done.   101 **Save . . . labour**: don't bother (ironical) [*N*].
102 **malice**: hatred, ill-feeling.   106 **gastness**: terror, horror.
107 **stare**: i.e. with horror.   109 cf. the proverb 'murder will out' [*N*].

Enter EMILIA.

Emilia. 'Las! what's the matter? what's the matter,
    husband?
Iago. Cassio hath here been set on in the dark
By Roderigo and fellows that are 'scap'd:
He's almost slain, and Roderigo dead.
Emilia. Alas! good gentleman; alas! good Cassio!   115
Iago. This is the fruit of whoring. Prithee, Emilia,
Go know of Cassio where he supp'd to-night.
What! do you shake at that?
Bianca. He supp'd at my house; but I therefore shake
    not.
Iago. O! did he so? I charge you, go with me.   120
Emilia. Fie, fie upon thee, strumpet!
Bianca. I am no strumpet, but of life as honest
As you that thus abuse me.
Emilia.   As I! foh! fie upon thee!
Iago. Kind gentlemen, let's go see poor Cassio dress'd.
Come, mistress, you must tell's another tale.   125
Emilia, run you to the citadel,
And tell my lord and lady what hath happ'd.
Will you go on afore? [*Aside.*] This is the night
That either makes me or fordoes me quite.   [*Exeunt.*

Scene II. A BEDCHAMBER IN THE CASTLE. DESDE-
MONA IN BED ASLEEP. A LIGHT BURNING

Enter OTHELLO.

Othello. It is the cause, it is the cause, my soul;
Let me not name it to you, you chaste stars!

117 **know of**: find out from.   118 **shake**: tremble (to Bianca).
122 **honest**: respectable [*N*].   124 **dress'd**: have his wounds
dressed.   128 **you**: i.e. Gratiano and Lodovico.   129 **fordoes**:
ruins.   1 **It ... cause**: the charge, i.e. her offence is adultery [*N*].

It is the cause. Yet I'll not shed her blood,
Nor scar that whiter skin of hers than snow,
And smooth as monumental alabaster.   5
Yet she must die, else she'll betray more men.
Put out the light, and then put out the light:
If I quench thee, thou flaming minister,
I can again thy former light restore,
Should I repent me; but once put out thy light,   10
Thou cunning'st pattern of excelling nature,
I know not where is that Promethean heat
That can thy light relume. When I have pluck'd the rose,
I cannot give it vital growth again,
It needs must wither: I'll smell it on the tree.   15
                                        [*Kisses her.*

O balmy breath, that dost almost persuade
Justice to break her sword! One more, one more.
Be thus when thou art dead, and I will kill thee,
And love thee after. One more, and this the last:
So sweet was ne'er so fatal. I must weep,   20
But they are cruel tears; this sorrow's heavenly,
It strikes where it doth love. She wakes.
    Desdemona. Who's there? Othello?
    Othello.   Ay, Desdemona.
    Desdemona. Will you come to bed, my lord?
    Othello. Have you pray'd to-night, Desdemona?
    Desdemona.   Ay, my lord.   25

5 **monumental alabaster**: alabaster (a substance like marble)
used for tombs.   6 **betray**: lead astray, seduce.   7 **the light**:
first means the 'light burning' (*s.d.*), then Desdemona's life [*N*].
8 **flaming minister**: agent of flame (light), i.e. the candle [*N*].   10
Should ... me: if I should change my mind.   11 **cunning'st**:
most skilfully wrought.   **pattern**: model, masterpiece.   **excelling**
nature: nature at her most excellent [*N*].   12 **Promethean**:
accent on second syllable [*N*].   13 **relume**: rekindle [*N*].   15
on the tree: while it is still living.   18 **Be thus**: i.e. look thus.
20 **So ... fatal**: nothing so sweet (as Desdemona) was ever so deadly.

Othello. If you bethink yourself of any crime
Unreconcil'd as yet to heaven and grace,
Solicit for it straight.

   Desdemona. Alas! my lord, what may you mean by that?

   Othello. Well, do it, and be brief; I will walk by: 30
I would not kill thy unprepared spirit;
No; heaven forfend! I would not kill thy soul.

   Desdemona. Talk you of killing?

   Othello.   Ay, I do.

   Desdemona.   Then heaven
Have mercy on me!

   Othello.   Amen! with all my heart.

   Desdemona. If you say so, I hope you will not kill me.   35

   Othello. Hum!

   Desdemona. And yet I fear you; for you are fatal then
When your eyes roll so. Why I should fear I know not,
Since guiltiness I know not; but yet I feel I fear.

   Othello. Think on thy sins.

   Desdemona.   They are loves I bear to you.   40

   Othello. Ay, and for that thou diest.

   Desdemona. That death's unnatural that kills for loving.
Alas! why gnaw you so your nether lip?
Some bloody passion shakes your very frame;
These are portents, but yet, I hope, I hope   45
They do not point on me.

   Othello.   Peace, and be still!

   Desdemona. I will so. What's the matter?

   Othello. That handkerchief which I so lov'd and gave thee
Thou gav'st to Cassio.

---

26 **bethink yourself:** can remember.   27 **Unreconcil'd**
. . . grace: not yet forgiven by heavenly mercy.   28 **Solicit**
for it straight: ask pardon for it at once.   30 **by:** aside.
32 **forfend:** forbid [*N*].   37 **fatal:** deadly.   44 **bloody**
passion: murderous emotion.   46 **on:** at [*N*].   47 **the**
matter: i.e. of your charge against me [*N*].

Desdemona.   No, by my life and soul!
Send for the man and ask him.

   Othello.   Sweet soul, take heed,   50
Take heed of perjury; thou'rt on thy death-bed.

   Desdemona. Ay, but not yet to die.

   Othello.   Yes, presently;
Therefore confess thee freely of thy sin;
For to deny each article with oath
Cannot remove nor choke the strong conception   55
That I do groan withal. Thou art to die.

   Desdemona. Then Lord have mercy on me!

   Othello.   I say, amen.

   Desdemona. And have you mercy too! I never did
Offend you in my life; never lov'd Cassio
But with such general warranty of heaven   60
As I might love; I never gave him token.

   Othello. By heaven, I saw my handkerchief in's hand.
O perjur'd woman! thou dost stone my heart,
And mak'st me call what I intend to do
A murder, which I thought a sacrifice: 65
I saw the handkerchief.

   Desdemona.   He found it then;
I never gave it him. Send for him hither;
Let him confess a truth.

   Othello.   He hath confess'd.

   Desdemona. What, my lord?

   Othello. That he hath us'd thee.

   Desdemona.   How? unlawfully?   70

   Othello. Ay.

---

   52 **presently**: immediately.   54 **article**: particular item.
55–6 strong ... withal: the firm conviction (of your guilt) which
is the cause of my sorrow.   59 **Offend**: wrong.   60–1 **But
... love**: except with such a love as heaven allows us to entertain
for our fellow-men in general [*N*].   61 **token**: proof of love.
63 **stone**: make hard as stone [*N*].   70 **us'd**: had intercourse with.

Desdemona.   He will not say so.

Othello.   No; his mouth is stopp'd:
Honest Iago hath ta'en order for't.

Desdemona. O! my fear interprets. What! is he dead?

Othello. Had all his hairs been lives, my great revenge
Had stomach for them all.   75

Desdemona. Alas! he is betray'd and I undone.

Othello. Out, strumpet! Weep'st thou for him to my
    face?

Desdemona. O! banish me, my lord, but kill me not!

Othello. Down, strumpet!

Desdemona. Kill me to-morrow; let me live to-night!   80

Othello. Nay, if you strive,—

Desdemona. But half an hour!

Othello.   Being done, there is no pause.

Desdemona. But while I say one prayer!

Othello.   It is too late. [*He smothers her.*

Emilia. [*Within.*] My lord, my lord! what, ho! my lord,
    my lord!

Othello. What noise is this? Not dead? not yet quite
    dead?   85
I that am cruel am yet merciful;
I would not have thee linger in thy pain.
So, so.

Emilia. [*Within.*]   What, ho! my lord, my lord!

Othello.   Who's there?

Emilia. [*Within.*] O! good my lord, I would speak
    a word with you!

Othello. Yes; 'tis Emilia: by and by. She's dead.   90
'Tis like she comes to speak of Cassio's death;

72 **ta'en order for't**: taken steps to secure it.   73 **inter-**
prets: explains your meaning.   75 **stomach**: appetite.
82 **Being done ... pause**: (probably) since all is now settled,
there can be no delay.   88 **So, so**: That's that, it is over [*N*]
90 **by and by**: let her wait a minute (O. speaks to himself).

The noise was high. Ha! no more moving?
Still as the grave. Shall she come in? Were't good?
I think she stirs again: no. What's best to do?
If she come in she'll sure speak to my wife: 95
My wife! my wife! what wife? I have no wife:
O, insupportable! O heavy hour!
Methinks it should be now a huge eclipse
Of sun and moon, and that the affrighted globe
Should yawn at alteration.
   Emilia. [*Within.*]   I do beseech you   100
That I may speak with you, O! good my lord.
   Othello. I had forgot thee: O! come in, Emilia:
Soft, by and by: let me the curtains draw.
Where art thou?   [*Unlocks the door.*

         Enter EMILIA.

                 What's the matter with thee now?
   Emilia. O! my good lord, yonder's foul murder done. 105
   Othello. What! now?
   Emilia.   But now, my lord.
   Othello. It is the very error of the moon;
She comes more near the earth than she was wont,
And makes men mad.
   Emilia. Cassio, my lord, hath kill'd a young Venetian 110
Call'd Roderigo.
   Othello.   Roderigo kill'd!
And Cassio kill'd?
   Emilia.   No, Cassio is not kill'd.
   Othello. Not Cassio kill'd! then murder's out of tune, 113
And sweet revenge grows harsh.

---

   92 **high**: loud [*N*].   100 **yawn at alteration**: burst open
at the change [*N*].   103 **Soft**: wait.   **draw**: close (the curtains of the bed).   107 **It is ... moon**: this must be due to
the wandering of the moon from her true course [*N*].   113-14
murder's ... harsh: i.e. murder has missed its mark, and revenge
failed to gain its object [*N*].

Desdemona. O! falsely, falsely murder'd.

Emilia.   Alas! what cry is that?   115

Othello. That! what?

Emilia. Out, and alas! that was my lady's voice:
Help! Help, ho! help! O lady, speak again!
Sweet Desdemona! O! sweet mistress, speak.

Desdemona. A guiltless death I die.   120

Emilia. O! who hath done this deed?

Desdemona. Nobody; I myself; farewell:
Commend me to my kind lord. O! farewell!   [*Dies.*

Othello. Why, how should she be murder'd?

Emilia.   Alas! who knows?

Othello. You heard her say herself it was not I.   125

Emilia. She said so; I must needs report the truth.

Othello. She's like a liar gone to burning hell;
'Twas I that kill'd her.

Emilia.   O! the more angel she,
And you the blacker devil.

Othello. She turn'd to folly, and she was a whore.   130

Emilia. Thou dost belie her, and thou art a devil.

Othello. She was false as water.

Emilia.   Thou art rash as fire to say
That she was false: O! she was heavenly true.

Othello. Cassio did top her; ask thy husband else.
O! I were damn'd beneath all depth in hell   135
But that I did proceed upon just grounds
To this extremity. Thy husband knew it all.

Emilia. My husband!

Othello. Thy husband.

Emilia. That she was false to wedlock?   140

117 **Out**: an exclamation of horror [*N*].   123 **Commend me:**
remember me [*N*].   124 **should she**: can she have been.
130 **folly**: wantonness.   131 **belie**: tell lies about.
132 **rash**: reckless, hot-headed.   134 **top**: see III. iii. 397.
else: otherwise, i.e. if you don't believe me.   135 **were**: should be.

Othello. Ay, with Cassio. Nay, had she been true,
If heaven would make me such another world
Of one entire and perfect chrysolite,
I'd not have sold her for it.

 Emilia. My husband!

 Othello.   Ay, 'twas he that told me first: 145
An honest man he is, and hates the slime
That sticks on filthy deeds.

 Emilia.   My husband!

 Othello. What needs this iterance, woman? I say thy
  husband.

 Emilia. O mistress! villany hath made mocks with
  love.
My husband say that she was false!

 Othello.   He, woman; 150
I say, thy husband: dost understand the word?
My friend, thy husband, honest, honest Iago.

 Emilia. If he say so, may his pernicious soul
Rot half a grain a day! he lies to the heart:
She was too fond of her most filthy bargain. 155

 Othello. Ha!

 Emilia. Do thy worst:
This deed of thine is no more worthy heaven
Than thou wast worthy her.

 Othello.   Peace! you were best.

 Emilia. Thou hast not half the power to do me harm 160
As I have to be hurt. O gull! O dolt!
As ignorant as dirt! thou hast done a deed,—
I care not for thy sword; I'll make thee known,

---

142 **such another world**: a world like this [N]. 143 **chrysolite**: topaz [N]. 148 **iterance**: iteration [N]. 149
made mocks with: made game of. 154 **to the heart**:
abominably, utterly. 159 **Peace ... best**: you had better be
quiet. 160-1 **Thou ... hurt**: i.e. I can endure far more than
you can inflict on me [N]. 161 **gull**: fool, dupe. 163 **make
thee known**: i.e. reveal your deed.

Though I lost twenty lives. Help! help, ho! help!
The Moor has kill'd my mistress! Murder! murder!   165

Enter MONTANO, GRATIANO, IAGO, *and Others.*

Montano. What is the matter? How now, general!
Emilia. O! are you come, Iago? you have done well,
That men must lay their murders on your neck.
Gratiano. What is the matter?
Emilia. Disprove this villain if thou be'st a man: 170
He says thou told'st him that his wife was false.
I know thou didst not, thou'rt not such a villain.
Speak, for my heart is full.
Iago. I told him what I thought, and told no more
Than what he found himself was apt and true.   175
Emilia. But did you ever tell him she was false?
Iago. I did.
Emilia. You told a lie, an odious damned lie;
Upon my soul, a lie, a wicked lie.
She false with Cassio! Did you say with Cassio?   180
Iago. With Cassio, mistress. Go to, charm your tongue.
Emilia. I will not charm my tongue; I am bound to speak.
My mistress here lies murder'd in her bed.
All. O heavens forfend!
Emilia. And your reports have set the murder on.   185
Othello. Nay, stare not, masters; it is true, indeed.
Gratiano. 'Tis a strange truth.
Montano. O monstrous act!
Emilia.   Villany! villany! villany!
I think upon't, I think, I smell't; O villany!
I thought so then; I'll kill myself for grief.   190
O! villany, villany!

<hr>

168 **lay on your neck**: hold you responsible for.   170 **this villain**: i.e. Othello.   175 **apt**: likely.   181 **charm your tongue**:
hold your tongue [*N*].   185 **set ... on**: instigated.   189 **think
upon't**: remember it [*N*].   **I smell't**: i.e. it smells of Iago.

Iago. What! are you mad? I charge you, get you
  home.

Emilia. Good gentlemen, let me have leave to speak:
'Tis proper I obey him, but not now.

Perchance, Iago, I will ne'er go home.   195

  Othello. O! O! O!   [*Falls on the bed.*

  Emilia.   Nay, lay thee down and roar,
For thou hast kill'd the sweetest innocent
That e'er did lift up eye.

  Othello.   O! she was foul.
I scarce did know you, uncle. There lies your niece,
Whose breath, indeed, these hands have newly stopp'd: 200
I know this act shows terrible and grim.

  Gratiano. Poor Desdemona! I am glad thy father's dead.
Thy match was mortal to him, and pure grief
Shore his old thread in twain: did he live now,
This sight would make him do a desperate turn,   205
Yea, curse his better angel from his side,
And fall to reprobation.

  Othello. 'Tis pitiful; but yet Iago knows
That she with Cassio hath the act of shame
A thousand times committed; Cassio confess'd it: 210
And she did gratify his amorous works
With that recognizance and pledge of love
Which I first gave her. I saw it in his hand:
It was a handkerchief, an antique token
My father gave my mother.   215

  Emilia. O heaven! O heavenly powers!

  Iago.   Come, hold your peace.

  Emilia. 'Twill out, 'twill out: I hold my peace, sir? no;

---

199 **know**: recognize.   201 **shows**: looks.   **grim**: savage.
203 **mortal**: fatal.   204 **Shore**: cut.   **thread**: i.e. of life [*N*].
205 **do . . . turn**: take a desperate course, i.e. commit suicide.
207 **reprobation**: damnation [*N*].   211 **gratify**: reward.
works: deeds.   212 **recógnizance**: token.

No, I will speak as liberal as the north;
Let heaven and men and devils, let them all,
All, all, cry shame against me, yet I'll speak.   220
  Iago. Be wise, and get you home.
  Emilia.   I will not.

            [IAGO *offers to stab* EMILIA.
  Gratiano.   Fie!
Your sword upon a woman?
  Emilia. O thou dull Moor! that handkerchief thou
    speak'st of
I found by fortune and did give my husband;
For often, with a solemn earnestness,   225
More than, indeed, belong'd to such a trifle,
He begg'd of me to steal it.
  Iago.   Villanous whore!
  Emilia. She give it Cassio! no, alas! I found it,
And I did give't my husband.
  Iago.   Filth, thou liest!
  Emilia. By heaven, I do not, I do not, gentlemen.   230
O murderous coxcomb! what should such a fool
Do with so good a wife?
  Othello.   Are there no stones in heaven
But what serve for the thunder? Precious villain!

      [*He runs at* IAGO. IAGO *stabs* EMILIA, *and exit.*
  Gratiano. The woman falls: sure, he has kill'd his wife.
  Emilia. Ay, ay; O! lay me by my mistress' side.   235
  Gratiano. He's gone; but his wife's kill'd.
  Montano. 'Tis a notorious villain. Take you this weapon,
Which I have here recover'd from the Moor.

---

218 **as liberal . . . north:** as freely as the north wind blows [*N*].
221 *s.d.* **offers:** attempts.   224 **by fortune:** by chance.
225 **solemn:** serious.   226 **belong'd to:** suited.   231
coxcomb: fool (referring to Othello).   232 **stones:** thunderbolts [*N*].   233 **Precious:** arrant, vile.   237 **notorious:**
utter, complete [*N*].   238 **recover'd:** taken from (*not* back).

Come, guard the door without; let him not pass,
But kill him rather. I'll after that same villain,   240
For 'tis a damned slave.

                        [Exeunt MONTANO *and* GRATIANO.

   Othello.   I am not valiant neither,
But every puny whipster gets my sword.
But why should honour outlive honesty?
Let it go all.

   Emilia.   What did thy song bode, lady?
Hark, canst thou hear me? I will play the swan,   245
And die in music:—

               Willow, willow, willow.

Moor, she was chaste; she lov'd thee, cruel Moor;
So come my soul to bliss as I speak true;
So speaking as I think, I die, I die.   *[Dies.*

   Othello. I have another weapon in this chamber;   251
It is a sword of Spain, the ice brook's temper.
O! here it is. Uncle, I must come forth.

   Gratiano. [*Within.*] If thou attempt it, it will cost thee
     dear:
Thou hast no weapon, and perforce must suffer.   255

   Othello. Look in upon me then, and speak with me,
Or, naked as I am, I will assault thee.

              Re-enter GRATIANO.

   Gratiano. What is the matter?
   Othello.   Behold! I have a weapon;

---

241 **slave**: scoundrel.   **not . . . neither**: not even courageous.
242 **whipster**: whipper-snapper [*N*].   243 **But . . . honesty**:
but why should I care any longer about my reputation since I have
lost my integrity?   244 **bode**: foretell (see IV. iii. 39–50).
249 **So . . . bliss**: so may my soul go to heaven.   252 **the ice
brook's temper**: tempered (i.e. hardened) in ice-cold water [*N*].
255 **suffer**: get the worst of it.   257 **naked**: unarmed.

A better never did itself sustain
Upon a soldier's thigh: I have seen the day,   260
That with this little arm, and this good sword,
I have made my way through more impediments
Than twenty times your stop: but, O vain boast!
Who can control his fate? 'tis not so now.
Be not afraid, though you do see me weapon'd;   265
Here is my journey's end, here is my butt,
And very sea-mark of my utmost sail.
Do you go back dismay'd? 'tis a lost fear;
Man but a rush against Othello's breast,
And he retires. Where should Othello go?   270
Now how dost thou look now? O ill-starr'd wench!
Pale as thy smock! when we shall meet at compt,
This look of thine will hurl my soul from heaven,
And fiends will snatch at it. Cold, cold, my girl!
Even like thy chastity.   275
O! cursed, cursed slave. Whip me, ye devils,
From the possession of this heavenly sight!
Blow me about in winds! roast me in sulphur!
Wash me in steep-down gulfs of liquid fire!
O Desdemona! Desdemona! dead!   280
Oh! Oh! Oh!

Enter LODOVICO, MONTANO, CASSIO *carried in a chair, and*
Officers *with* IAGO, *prisoner.*

Lodovico. Where is this rash and most unfortunate man?
Othello. That's he that was Othello; here I am.

259 **itself sustain**: hold its place.   263 **your stop**: the opposition you offer.   266 **butt**: goal [*N*].   267 **sea-mark**
... **sail**: the furthest point to which I intend to sail ('sea-mark' =
beacon).   268 **lost**: unnecessary.   269 **Man** ... **rush**: arm
yourself only with a rush.   271 (turning to the body of D.)
272 **smock**: woman's undergarment.   **compt**: (literally) account,
i.e. the day of judgement.   276 **slave**: (cf. IV. ii. 132) probably
refers to himself.   279 **steep-down**: precipitous [*N*].

Lodovico. Where is that viper? bring the villain forth.

Othello. I look down towards his feet; but that's a fable.
If that thou be'st a devil, I cannot kill thee. [*Wounds* IAGO.

Lodovico. Wrench his sword from him.

Iago.   I bleed, sir; but not kill'd.

Othello. I am not sorry neither; I'd have thee live;
For, in my sense, 'tis happiness to die.

Lodovico. O thou Othello! that wert once so good,   290
Fall'n in the practice of a damned slave,
What shall be said to thee?

Othello.   Why, any thing:
An honourable murderer, if you will;
For nought did I in hate, but all in honour.

Lodovico. This wretch hath part confess'd his villany: 295
Did you and he consent in Cassio's death?

Othello. Ay.

Cassio. Dear general, I never gave you cause.

Othello. I do believe it, and I ask your pardon.
Will you, I pray, demand that demi-devil   300
Why he hath thus ensnar'd my soul and body?

Iago. Demand me nothing: what you know, you know:
From this time forth I never will speak word.

Lodovico. What! not to pray?

Gratiano.   Torments will ope your lips.

Othello. Well, thou dost best.   305

Lodovico. Sir, you shall understand what hath befall'n,
Which, as I think, you know not. Here is a letter
Found in the pocket of the slain Roderigo,
And here another; the one of them imports
The death of Cassio to be undertook   310
By Roderigo.

289 **in my sense**: in my opinion [*N*].   291 **Fall'n in the practice**: caught by the plot.   294 **in honour**: with honourable
intention, as a moral duty [*N*].   296 **consent in**: plot together,
agree to.   309 **imports**: has for purport, indicates.

Othello. O villain!

Cassio.   Most heathenish and most gross!

Lodovico. Now here's another discontented paper,
Found in his pocket too; and this, it seems,
Roderigo meant to have sent this damned villain,   315
But that, belike, Iago in the interim
Came in and satisfied him.

Othello.   O the pernicious caitiff!
How came you, Cassio, by that handkerchief
That was my wife's?

Cassio.   I found it in my chamber;
And he himself confess'd but even now   320
That there he dropp'd it for a special purpose
Which wrought to his desire.

Othello.   O fool! fool! fool!

Cassio. There is besides in Roderigo's letter
How he upbraids Iago that he made him
Brave me upon the watch; whereon it came   325
That I was cast; and even but now he spake,
After long seeming dead, Iago hurt him,
Iago set him on.

Lodovico. You must forsake this room and go with us;
Your power and your command is taken off,   330
And Cassio rules in Cyprus. For this slave,
If there be any cunning cruelty
That can torment him much and hold him long,
It shall be his. You shall close prisoner rest.

312 **heathenish** : villainous.   **gross** : monstrous.   313 **discontented paper** : letter expressing dissatisfaction.   317 **Came
in** : took action.   **satisfied him** : i.e. by killing him.   320 *see*
295.   **but even now** : just now.   322 **wrought ... desire** :
served his purpose.   **fool** (addressed to himself).   325 **Brave** :
defy.   326 **cast** : relieved of command.   326–7 **he spake ...
hurt him** : he (Roderigo) said Iago wounded him.   332 **cunning** : ingenious.   **cruelty** : torture.   333 **hold him long** :
keep him alive for a long time.   334 **close** : strictly guarded.

Till that the nature of your fault be known   335
To the Venetian state. Come, bring him away.
  Othello. Soft you; a word or two before you go.
I have done the state some service, and they know't;
No more of that. I pray you, in your letters,
When you shall these unlucky deeds relate,   340
Speak of me as I am; nothing extenuate,
Nor set down aught in malice: then, must you speak
Of one that lov'd not wisely but too well;
Of one not easily jealous, but, being wrought,
Perplex'd in the extreme; of one whose hand,   345
Like the base Indian, threw a pearl away
Richer than all his tribe; of one whose subdu'd eyes
Albeit unused to the melting mood,
Drop tears as fast as the Arabian trees
Their med'cinable gum. Set you down this;   350
And say besides, that in Aleppo once,
Where a malignant and a turban'd Turk
Beat a Venetian and traduc'd the state,
I took by the throat the circumcised dog,   354
And smote him thus.   *[Stabs himself.*
  Lodovico. O bloody period!
  Gratiano.   All that's spoke is marr'd.
  Othello. I kiss'd thee ere I kill'd thee; no way but this,
                   [Falling upon DESDEMONA.
Killing myself to die upon a kiss.   *[Dies.*

---

   336 bring him away: escort him (to the guard).   **337
Soft you:** not so fast.   **340 unlucky:** ill-fated, terrible.
341 extenuate: soften.   **344 wrought:** moved, worked
upon, wrought up.   **345 Perplex'd:** distracted [*N*].
346 base: ignorant [*N*].   **347 subdu'd:** overcome by
grief.   **350 med'cinable:** healing, medicinal [*N*].   **gum:**
aromatic resin.   **352 malignant:** rebellious against God,
evil.   **353 traduc'd:** slandered.   **356 period:** end.
All . . . marr'd: i.e. all that he has said is ruined by his
suicide [*N*].

Cassio. This did I fear, but thought he had no weapon;
For he was great of heart.

Lodovico.   [*To* IAGO.] O Spartan dog!   360
More fell than anguish, hunger, or the sea.
Look on the tragic loading of this bed;
This is thy work; the object poisons sight;
Let it be hid. Gratiano, keep the house,
And seize upon the fortunes of the Moor,   365
For they succeed on you. To you, lord governor,
Remains the censure of this hellish villain,
The time, the place, the torture; O! enforce it.
Myself will straight aboard, and to the state
This heavy act with heavy heart relate.   370
                    [*Exeunt.*

360 **Spartan**: relentless as a Spartan hound [*N*].'   361 **fell**:
cruel [*N*].   363 **the object**: that which is exposed to view.   364
keep: guard.   365 **seize upon**: take possession of.   **fortunes**:
belongings.   366 **succeed on**: pass to (as next of kin).   367
censure: judgement.   370 **heavy act**: the whole tragic
sequence of events.

COMMENTARY

ACT I, Scene I

Othello, like *Hamlet*, devotes the whole of the first Act to exposition, that is to the necessary foundation of character and situation on which the action is built. Its three scenes take place in Venice, and introduce all the main characters, except Cassio and Emilia. Though the Act is expository, it is full of excitement, with its torch-lit street scenes, the brutal awakening of Brabantio with 'dire yell', and the charge before the Senate.

Like the opening book of *Paradise Lost*, the first scene begins with the villain, and with the heavy threat to the hero's happiness that his character and philosophy imply. It is alive with malice and grudge; and Iago's language alone is enough to persuade us that we must not expect objective accounts of men and matters from him, and to prejudice us in favour of the absent Othello. Roderigo is the only person in whose presence he does not wear a moral disguise (though, of course, Roderigo is far from knowing all that there is to be known); and Iago's remarks to him present as much of his public face as he is ever prepared to show, and, from this point of view, are almost as important as his soliloquies. The fooling of Roderigo is apprentice work for Iago; he is too easy. Besides, he gulls him for money, and this is probably the least egocentric of his motives.

The masterly plunge into the action—'Tush! Never tell me'—is a mark of maturity. What 'this' in l. 3 is does not become specific until ll. 116–17, while Iago gives reasons for his hate of Othello and contempt for his lieutenant. All is dramatic, and nothing narrative. The whole of Act I takes place at night. So does much of Act II, and the great Act V is a night Act. Thus the time of much of the action fits the undercover activities of Iago, and suits also the violence of the play.

8 ff. Iago tells the story of his rebuff by Othello in order to convince Roderigo that he has no reason to love the Moor. One reason for his hatred of Othello and Cassio, the hurt to his professional pride, is thus introduced quite naturally. We also see, the more certainly because Iago unconsciously betrays it, that Othello is a person of some importance in Venice.

13 bombast means, literally, stuffed with cotton.
    Iago naturally takes an unfavourable view of Othello's mode of speech. Its dignity, quality, and content are unlike his own.

14 epithets, as well as having its present sense, could mean 'expressions, phrases'.

16. Nonsuits : a legal term meaning 'the stoppage of a suit by the judge when the plaintiff fails to make out a legal case'. There is no case for Iago, because Cassio has already been appointed.

19. arithmetician, like *bookish theoric, toged consuls, debitor-and-creditor,* and *counter-caster,* is expressive of the contempt felt by the ranker for the staff-officer. No one shares Iago's view of Cassio ; when the Senate orders Othello back to Venice, he is made Governor of Cyprus, though, it is true, of a Cyprus at peace.

20. a Florentine. Florence was a great commercial capital, and Iago may mean to link this injurious epithet to his other accusations of military book-keeping ; or, he may simply mean 'an outsider' (since he himself was a Venetian).

21. A fellow . . . wife : a difficult line, which has been much annotated. On the face of it, it looks as though Cassio is about to marry a beautiful woman, and is therefore already nearly damned ; the Italian proverb 'You have married a beauty ? Then you are damned' explains this cynicism (i.e. that female beauty is a mark of unchastity), which accords with Iago's cast of thought. Who the bride-to-be is, however, unless it is Bianca—an idea which Cassio finds ludicrous (IV. i)—the play does not tell us.

24. **spinster** means 'one who spins', not necessarily, though originally, feminine. Iago clearly means something derogatory, perhaps female, perhaps 'out of the active world'.

25. [**toged.** F has 'tongued', i.e. eloquent, which gives fair sense; but the stronger word of Q is more likely to be the original.]

30 **be-lee'd.** Bradley pointed out that Iago uses more nautical images and metaphors than is at all usual with Shakespeare's characters. After Act III these cease. 'Iago looks at the sea only from a professional point of view. In Othello's imagination, on the other hand, the sea lives in its whole breadth and adventurous power' (Clemen).

31. **counter-caster**: the old method of counting, or, as we should say, accounting, was by placing counters or discs on a counting-board. Iago paints a sarcastic picture of Cassio playing an indoor game, with counters for troops.

33. **Moorship's**: a sneering play on 'Worships' (which Q has), i.e. honourable gentlemen of standing or office, and J.P.s. Iago never again mentions his loss of promotion, nor does anyone else; which looks as if no one, including himself, expected his advancement.

    ancient: in full, 'ancient-bearer', i.e. 'standard-bearer'. The word 'ancient' is a corrupt form of 'ensign'.

36. **letter**: i.e. a letter from some great man, a letter of commendation. He forgets that, according to his own account, some 'great ones' have been soliciting for *him*, and that Cassio is Othello's free choice. He cannot describe anything objectively. 'One must constantly remember not to believe a syllable that Iago utters on any subject, including himself, until one has tested his statement' (Bradley).

49. **me**: an ethic dative, 'used to enliven the style by introducing a personal element where it is not really necessary for the thought' (Jespersen).

    honest: the first of very many instances of the word in the play. An essay could be, in fact has been, written on their occurrences with varied shades of meaning. It is often in the mouths of Othello and Iago; but Iago always uses it with a sneer or ironically, and it is clear that he is irked by it as his fixed epithet (see I. iii. 294, 405–7, and II. i. 199). The whole of the speech (41–65) is a statement of the 'enlightened' self-interest which passes with Iago for a philosophy.

57. Were I ... Iago. Iago often speaks in a cryptic way, perhaps, at least sometimes, as part of a mere habit of concealment. The simplest interpretation of this line is so banal that one hesitates to offer it, namely, that if he were in Othello's position he would not behave as he does now. Presumably his assumed character of anxious honesty would vanish.

61–5. 'When my outward actions show how I really think ; when how I behave to other people really expresses my nature ; then, the next thing you'll hear of me is that I am wearing my heart on my sleeve for jackdaws (i.e. fools) to peck at' (i.e. I should be a fool indeed).

65. I am not what I am. The complacency of this terrible remark (implying, perhaps : 'I am not what I appear to be') makes it worse. It has been suggested that it is a profane parody of God's revelation of Himself to Moses : 'I am that I am' (Exodus iii. 14).

66. thick-lips. GB says that this description of Othello as a negro is due to Roderigo's jealousy. But it is supported by Brabantio's reference to his 'sooty bosom' (I. ii. 70) ; and many would make it the key to Desdemona's words : 'I saw Othello's visage in his mind.'

70–1. The thought is that Venice is a pleasant place, not a dried-up country like Egypt, subject to such a plague of flies as is described in Exodus viii. 20.

78. Roderigo does not yell loudly enough for Iago, who has no gentlemanly inhibitions, at least in the dark, where he can be himself. Roderigo's speech is distinguished from Iago's, whenever they meet. One is flat, the other full of images and life. Roderigo's speech is decent and straight ; Iago's that of energy, however coarse.

88–91. A passage which illuminates Iago's imagination by its animalism. A tup is a ram, and *tupping* is a term from sheep-farming. A father could scarcely be aroused in a more shocking fashion.

117. You ... senator : suggests that Iago is biting back a coarse retort, or making 'senator' equivalent to an insult.

122. [odd-even. Onions takes this to mean 'about midnight'. *O.E.D.* does not record it. It may be suggested that it is a version of *Odd and even*, a 'game of chance' ; i.e. that it is a toss-up between night and morning.]

124. gondolier should be accented on first syllable only; but even then there are two extra syllables in the line.

150. stands. 'Wars' here is singular in meaning, and 'stands' is a sense construction, though grammatically a plural is needed.

157. Sagittary: probably a house of some sort, perhaps an inn. It has also been explained as (1) 'the residence at the Arsenal of the commanding officers of the Navy and Army' and (2) the Frezzaria, the 'street of the arrow-makers'.

160. despised time. Brabantio may mean by this something like 'I shall be the object of scorn for the rest of my life'. The sense given in the footnotes is derived from 'despised' = 'despicable' (the usual Shakespearian meaning), i.e. the time left to Brabantio is despicable in respect of its shortness.

168. treason . . . blood. In view of the following line, the meaning given in the footnote seems more probable than the other possible sense, 'treason arising from the natural impulses', i.e. Desdemona flies from a father to a husband, as girls do.

ACT I, Scene II

The first appearance of Othello is impressive. He is dignified and sure of himself. We learn that he is of royal descent, and, according to himself (and we have no reason throughout the play to doubt it), held in high esteem by the government of Venice. His speech is full and rounded, yet a moving simplicity. His command of himself and of the situation is beautifully seen in 'Keep up your bright swords, for the dew will rust them'—a line which Bradley called 'one of Shakespeare's miracles'. Anyone less like a probable victim for Iago could scarcely be imagined. This is Othello as he was before Iago played upon him.

Iago has now assumed his moral disguise of bluff, honest, uncomplicated loyalty. After his self-revelations in the first scene, this is nauseating, though his chameleon coloration gives great scope to any actor, who must show in the first two scenes of the play Iago as he is to Roderigo, and Iago as he is to Othello and the world. As Iago to Roderigo is almost the real Iago, but not quite, a nice shade of discrimination has to be made, and something held in reserve. The full depths of Iago are not plumbed in the first scene.

6. 'Tis better as it is. 'How well these words impress the truth of Othello's character of himself at the end upon us. He was not easily wrought' (Coleridge).

14. As double as the duke's. The meaning of this has been much debated. The Duke did not have a casting vote in the Council of Venice, though Shakespeare may have thought he did. Even so, this would not give Brabantio also a second vote. Steevens thought 'double' was used in the same way as we use it of liquors, 'double beer' meaning 'strong beer'. 'Brabantio had in his effect, though not by law, yet by *weight* and *influence*, a voice not *actual* and *formal*, but *potential* and operative, as *double*, that is, a voice that when a question was suspended, would turn the balance as effectually *as the Duke's*' (Johnson).

22. siege means 'seat', hence by specialization, 'seat of men of office and rank'.

   demerits has here the sense of Latin *demerita*, whose sense, like that of merit, was merely 'deserts', whether good or bad.

23. unbonneted. The general sense here requires that this should mean 'on equal terms (with those who have reached as high a rank as I have)'; and for this 'unbonneted' must mean 'without a bonnet', i.e. hatless, as showing easy familiarity, and *not* taking the hat off as a token of respect, which 'off-capp'd' meant in I. i. 10.

   [NS favours the conjecture 'e'en bonneted', i.e. even with the cap on. The evidence of 'bonneted' in *Coriolanus*, II. ii. 30 is indecisive.]

24–8. for know etc.: an important statement. Othello surrenders a life whose joy for him is best expressed in the famous lines beginning 'O! now, for ever' (III. iii. 348–58).

28. sea's worth. The sea is proverbially a store-house of treasure, both from its unknown richness, and from its innumerable wrecks.

33. Janus: 'There is great propriety in making the double Iago swear by Janus, who had two faces' (Warburton). Janus was a Roman god, represented with two faces; hence January, a month which looks before and after.

37. haste-post-haste: words written on urgent dispatches. Originally 'post' was a noun in the vocative case (= courier) and 'haste' the imperative of the verb; hence the unusual repetition of 'haste' here is quite intelligible.

50–1. Iago puts Othello's marriage with Desdemona in terms of piracy, and his is a *vulgar* version of Othello's view of Desdemona as treasure. A 'carrack' is a large merchant vessel, particularly one engaged in bringing back the wealth of the East and West Indies to Portugal and Spain. 'Prize' is not the same word as 'prize' = reward, but comes from French *prise* 'a capture, booty'.

52. We are told in III. iii. 70–2 that Cassio went wooing with Othello. Either his ignorance here is assumed, to keep his friend's affairs private, or he did not know of the elopement.

To who. We should expect 'whom' here, but the nominative instead is quite common in Shakespeare.

64. **things of sense.** (Cf. l. 72 'gross in sense'.) Brabantio's reaction is important, though not all-important, for our estimate of how Desdemona's choice might look to the common view. The common view is wrong, but it is one of Iago's weapons in his assault on Othello's happiness. To Brabantio it seems so incredible that he has to call in magic to explain it.

75. **motion:** besides meaning physical movement could also refer to mental and spiritual impulses (emotions). (See I. iii. 333.)

ACT I, Scene III

This scene completes the exposition with which the first Act is taken up. It gives the romantic, and, at the same time, charmingly domestic background of Othello's marriage, and brings out his and Desdemona's characters, as they are before they are played upon by Iago; it provides the ominous shadows cast by Brabantio, which Iago is to make use of later, though, without him, they would disappear; it reveals the Signiory's complete confidence in Othello; and it concludes with the first sinister sketch of Iago's plot, more deadly in its private nature than any of his public professions of hatred to Roderigo.

The preoccupation of the Signiory with State affairs is such that Brabantio's personal grief, when brought to their notice is, if not pushed aside, at least given second place.

We may note the flatness of the verse dealing with state affairs. Its business-like quality is in sharp contrast with that of the Brabantio–Desdemona–Othello matters. Similarly, the Duke's consolatory lines to Brabantio have an air of superficiality, which Brabantio bitterly resents.

1. **news,** derived from Latin *nova* = new things, is still felt as a plural here.

6. **aim.** There are other instances of its use in the sense of 'guess'.

9. **judgment** *may* here be used in a seventeenth-century sense of a 'competent critic' (Onions).

16. **Signior Angelo.** 'Luccicos' (44) is equally unknown. Such references give background, and no more, to the play.

52. **Good your grace.** The possessive adjectives, when unemphatic, are sometimes transposed, being really combined with nouns, as in 'milord' for 'my lord'.

64. **Sans.** This French word for 'without' was used in English from the fourteenth to sixteenth centuries; and the Q spelling 'saunce' shows at least one Anglicized pronunciation.

67. **bloody book** may refer to that part of the law which deals with capital offences.

76–94. Othello disdains eloquence, and there is no reason to doubt his belief in his own plainness. This speech has convincing, though formal simplicity. It is important dramatically for its statement of the kind of world in which Othello has lived until recently—not in the civilian world, but in the 'tented field'. We gather from l. 84 that he has been idle in Venice for nine months.

109. **modern.** The word had a depreciating sense in Elizabethan English, as, at least in undertone, it sometimes has today. The idea is that what has not been tested by time is likely to be shallow and fleeting.

134. 'All this', said the actor Booth, 'as modestly as possible—not a breath of bluster, and not declamatory.'

140. **antres vast** is the Latin phrase remembered by Shakespeare from Virgil (*Aen.* i. 52 *vasto antro*), and the noun does not recur till Keats, who doubtless recollected it from here.

144–5. **Anthropophagi** is a Greek word used by Herodotus, and then in Pliny's *Natural History*, known to Shakespeare. What follows is an old traveller's tale, revived by Elizabethan voyages of discovery.

158–66. Even if Desdemona's behaviour made her 'half the wooer' (176), she should not be regarded as unduly forward. Her situation required her to give Othello a masked invitation to propose to her. The beautiful simplicities of 167–8 ensure the right mood, and seem to favour the first interpretation of 162–3 given in the foot-note, rather then the second.

178. **gentle mistress**: used half-ironically, = 'Madam'. Brabantio is already beginning to fear that Desdemona has not been passive.

189. The two half-lines fall within the metrical pattern of one line if pronounced as 'Good bye! I've done'.

195. jewel: a bitter irony. Cf. *King Lear*, where Cordelia uses a similar irony of Goneril and Regan: 'The jewels of my father' (I. i. 271).

202–19. A series of rhymed aphorisms, with the Duke sententious, and Brabantio following on with an ironic echo. Perhaps the stiff couplets of the Duke's collection of maxims indicate his preoccupation with a matter of graver import, and irritate Brabantio into replying in a way which is frankly a parody. Proverbial wisdom in bulk is ill consolation; and Brabantio's *So* (l. 210) means that the Duke had better apply his maxims to the present affairs of state, and see where that gets him. Lines 212–13 are rude: they tell the Duke that he can well afford comfort from proverbs, since he has nothing to endure in this matter. In ll. 214–15, Brabantio means that a man who, like himself, has both to listen to sententious generalizations and endure sorrow, has to put up with both his sorrow and tedious gentlemen who generalize it. The Duke, after this display of temper, wisely carries on with State business; for which the prose of Brabantio's last line prepares the way.

219. [pierced: Q and F. Theobald emended to *pieced*, which NS adopted, meaning 'made whole', 'put together', 'mended'. However attractive this may be, it is not enough to outweigh the double authority of Q and F. 'Pierced' is merely a figurative expression, and means not 'wounded', but penetrated in a metaphorical sense: 'thoroughly affected' (Malone).]

225. more safer. Double comparatives are common in Elizabethan English.

231. thrice-driven. Feathers were selected for beds by driving or winnowing with a fan, lighter feathers being softer.

242–59. Desdemona now throws a quite different light on herself from Brabantio's earlier description (ll. 94–6). She is a girl of spirit and of spiritual courage, and knows well enough what she is doing. This is her first uninhibited speech, and of great dramatic significance. She is prepared for all, including Othello's warrior life. Had Othello remembered her fine line 'I saw Othello's visage in his mind' (252), Iago's insinuations might have found it more difficult to make way.

251. very quality. 'Quality' could mean both 'character' and 'profession' (i.e. in this case, 'military profession'). Perhaps Shakespeare means both here, and intended us to feel both.

256. **moth of peace** : a vivid image, meaning in general a parasite, in particular the 'fretting' or devouring clothes-moth. As this destroys hung-up and put-away garments, so Desdemona would eat her heart out in inaction.

257. [**rights** : both Q and F have *rites*, often interpreted as 'love's rites' or 'nuptial rites'. This is a perfectly possible meaning. The rest of the speech, however, lays a strong emphasis on a mental union, and so does Othello's speech which follows it. For this reason we take it to be an example of the common Elizabethan spelling for '*rights*' and its meaning as 'that which a wife may properly claim', i.e. a part in his whole life, and therefore going with him to war.]

261–4. A difficult passage, usually emended.

defunct (264). The modern sense of the word, 'dead' or 'done with', which is also the sense found elsewhere in Shakespeare, seems wholly unsuitable to the general picture of Othello in the play. The word is derived from the Latin verb *defungor* meaning 'to perform something', or 'to have finished with something'. Othello would then be saying that he does not desire to have Desdemona with him mainly for the physical satisfaction of marriage, already begun, however legitimate, but for such ends of marriage as companionship. 'Othello's marriage is important to him less as a sexual relationship than as a symbol of being loved and accepted as a person, a brother in the Venetian community' (W. H. Auden).

Lines I. i. 88–9 and 115–16 support the assumption that Othello consummated his marriage in Venice on the night of the elopement. Both come, however, from the contaminated imagination of Iago, and are automatically suspect. Roderigo, however, who, with all his faults, is not a liar, seems to believe this (I. i. 125).

Against this interpretation is (1) the strong evidence of II. iii. 8–10 and 15–16, unless these lines merely mean that this is the first undisturbed night that Othello and Desdemona have had; and (2) the fact that the past partic. *defunctus* and the English 'defunct' usually refer to something finished with.

[The reading adopted here is that of F and Q, which agree except in the matter of a comma. The usual emendation is

> Nor to comply with heat—the young affects
> In me defunct—and proper satisfaction.

This means : 'I do not ask for Desdemona to come with me to Cyprus for the purpose of my own sexual satisfaction, to satisfy hot desires, the passions of youth which I have now outlived'. Apart from the rejection of both Q and F which this emendation involves, it leaves 'and proper satisfaction' hanging in the air.]

291–4. A passage of foreshadowing irony. Brabantio's bitter warning is used to effect by Iago at III. iii. 206 ff.

302 ff. Prose is always a public statement with Iago, and part of his disguise. When alone, he speaks in verse.

  noble heart : a beautiful example of Iago's sardonic expression (missed, of course, by Roderigo).

309–10. Roderigo puns on *prescription* = (1) 'doctor's prescription', and (2) 'claim', 'right', and *physician* = (1) 'doctor', (2) 'cure'.

311–12. Iago's comparative youth makes him still more a psychological curiosity. His age is not given in the source, but he is described as of handsome presence.

319. virtue. The word is not here used in the modern sense as in 289 above, but rather as 'nature' or 'character'. Iago ridicules the notion that men's natures are pre-determined, and not subservient to their wills. For the modern use of 'virtue' see l. 289 above.

324. thyme. Perhaps Lyly's *Euphues* explains the connection of hyssop with thyme here: 'Good gardeneirs . . . mixe Hisoppe with Time, as ayders the one to the growth of the other; the one beeing drye, the other moyst.' Weeding up thyme and growing hyssop is just the kind of action that Iago's gardener, the will, might take, and illustrates his mastery of his argument.

335. It cannot be. Roderigo is something of a gentleman and, after his fashion, a romantic, though he intends adultery. He finds Iago's equation of love and lust difficult to follow.

345–8. In these lines Iago has ten recommendations to Roderigo to put money in his purse, whose strings, we know, he holds, and proposes to loose by pretending to get Desdemona for him.

350. locusts. Locust was a name for the sweet fruit of the carob-tree, sometimes called St. John's Bread, because it was thought John the Baptist ate it in the wilderness (Matthew iii. 4).

351. coloquintida, like locusts, is an Eastern and desert product.

357. sanctimony, and a frail vow. Iago refers to the sacrament and vows of marriage. 'Sanctimony' does not ascribe *pretended* holiness to Desdemona.

360–2. drowning . . . hanged : probably a reference to the saying 'He that is born to be hanged shall never be drowned'.

383–404. This is the first of Iago's eight soliloquies or asides, a larger number than is uttered by any other character in Shakespeare. There are two or three reasons for this : one is that Iago has both a public and a private character, and can only exhibit the latter, and then not fully, to Roderigo; another is the extraordinarily twisted quality of his nature and the need for its full revelation to the audience (a simple character like Othello needs only three soliloquies, and the first comes only after Iago has undermined him); and a third is that his plot only gradually shapes itself in its scope and detail (see note to l. 404) and the audience needs to be kept abreast of its growth.

393–4. plume up . . . knavery: the metaphor appears to be taken from the plumes on a helmet, the *panache* or swagger of a warrior. *Plume* does not elsewhere occur in Shakespeare as a verb. 'Will' might be taken as 'what I intend to do', 'my plan'. If it were so taken here, then the sense would be 'to trick out my plan, make it more splendid or elegant by making it serve two purposes' (i.e. revenge for his cuckolding and lack of promotion). *plume up* can be compared with the modern idiom *plume oneself on* = 'pride oneself on', where the reference is also to the idea of decking oneself with plumes. Bradley sees in this phrase Iago's one recognition of the real motives which drive him on—the heightening of the sense of power or superiority.

397. smooth dispose. Cassio's easy manner is shown in his courtliness with Desdemona in the next scene.

404. Of this soliloquy a certain W.N. (quoted by Furness) writes: 'Shakespeare has shown great judgment in the darkness which he makes to prevail in the first counsels of Iago. To the poet himself, all the succeeding events must have been clear and determined; but to bring himself again into the situation of one who sees them in embryo, to draw a mist over that which he had already cleared, must have required an exertion of genius peculiar to this author alone.'

ACT II, Scene I

This scene brings us to Cyprus, where the tragedy is to be enacted. It begins, appropriately enough, with a storm, which Shakespeare did not find in his source. Whether this is symbolic of the later course of events on the island, as those think who regard all storms in Shakespeare as symbolic, or whether it has a narrower dramatic purpose is for individual choice. It certainly provides a succession of arrivals, mounting in suspense: first, Cassio, who has lost his General 'on a dangerous sea'; then Desdemona and Iago; then, finally, the hero himself, and the splendid reunion of the lovers. It is the last moment where they know 'content so absolute', and is vital for an understanding of what might have been their lot without Iago. The time of waiting for Othello is beguiled by Iago's display of one of his public faces. The 'touch of roughness' in his public appearances is of course designed by him to show that he is too blunt to be subtle; but below this is a real 'innate brutality'; and perhaps the 'sex-jokes are a symptom of pathological obsession'. Anyway, the interchange between him and Desdemona and other characters is intended to be a display of 'honesty': to present the cynical but limited and honest Iago. It is very important that the social side of Iago should be seen: the audience might otherwise wonder why this coarse fellow is so universally liked.

In sharp contrast to his assumed character is the soliloquy which ends the scene. Here Iago invents or discovers a motive or two more for his villainy.

The scene gives a chance for a Cassio–Desdemona relationship to be shown, which, while it does not, *could* support Iago's plot. Cassio is inordinately courtly, but this very openness shows his feeling as innocent and idealistic.

14. **Bear**, i.e. the Great Bear. NS points out that the idea of the waves striking the stars was used in textbooks of rhetoric as an illustration of hyperbole. If the ocean here is high-wrought, so is the description.

15. **guards**: two stars called β and γ, part of Ursa Minor or the Little Bear, pointing to the Pole Star and objects of interest, particularly in Elizabethan days, for the purposes of navigation. They were sometimes called *Guardians*, according to an Elizabethan textbook of navigation, 'because they are diligently to be looked unto'.

20. **lads.** Q has 'lords'; but possibly excitement leads a mere Third Gentleman to address a company including the ex-Governor, as 'lads'.

26. **a Veronesa.** Since the ship has been already said to be 'of Venice' (22), this must mean *either* that it belongs to the inland city of Verona but is being used by Venice *or* that the F word 'Verennesa' describes a type of ship, perhaps a 'cutter' or fast ship. The latter interpretation (for details see Furness) gives better sense, but has no parallel.

50–1. surfeited, and **cure** in the next line, are connected as parts of a metaphor from medicine. However long Cassio has been hoping, hope has not yet died, as one might die of a surfeit; and because of Othello's stout ship and expert pilot, his hopes have reason behind them ('stand in bold cure' = 'have good reason to expect justification').

62. paragons. The word could mean simply 'match', 'equal', and perhaps does so here; but Cassio is in hyperbolical vein.

63. quirks: 'flourishes'; in writing, 'conceits'; perhaps, as 'blazoning' and the general sense suggest, a metaphor from heraldry.

64–5. And in . . . ingener: a difficult passage, which has received much comment. *Essential* is the adjective of *essence* and 'carries the full renaissance meaning of all that constitutes *being*' (NS). 'Vesture' in this context means not only the human body, as in *M.V.* v. i. 64 'this muddy vesture of decay', but also the best that nature could do spiritually. Character is often spoken of in metaphors from clothes in the Old Testament: e.g. 'clothed in righteousness'. 'Ingener' = 'inventor', here the poetic inventor, not the military engineer; and the phrase means that Desdemona in her actual person and in real life surpasses all that poets can imagine. 'Ingener' must be accented on the second syllable, not like the modern 'engineer'.

[F has *Ingeniuer*, a variant spelling of *ingener*; Q changes the phrase and has the tamer, but quite straightforward, *bear all excellency*. Whether the original version was this, perhaps altered, as Ridley suggests, to make Cassio's style more high-flown; or whether it is another example of Q's simplification, it is difficult to say. At all events, the F version sounds more like Shakespeare. See *Introduction, The Text.*]

83. riches . . . is. Riches, from French *richesse*, was still regarded as a singular noun in the sixteenth and seventeenth centuries.

98–9. It seems an odd thing for a gentleman either to extol his own manners, or to explain that it is only courtesy which makes him kiss a lady. It must be said lightly or laughingly. It has been called 'a little fatuity . . . endearing enough in its way'. As Heilman points out, 'Iago makes no comment, except for an entertainer's joke' (ll. 100–2).

109–75. The propriety of this passage has been questioned on the ground that no further display of Iago's vulgarity is needed, and that Desdemona's conduct in it is unnatural. But surely GB is right in seeing that it 'stimulates suspense'. More than this, it gives us Iago's jocular and social face. Finally, what the hearers regard as the comic exaggeration of an honest heart is Iago's true sexual philosophy.

109. pictures. It is not quite clear what Iago means. It may be a conventional satiric thrust at women who paint their faces (cf. *Hamlet*, III. i. 142); or mean that they put on a false face of demureness out of doors. The general meaning is clear: women present a prettier picture out of doors than they do at home, as we might say 'perfect pictures to look at' of children dressed for a party.

112. housewives ... beds. 'Housewife' could mean 'hussy', 'light woman' (cf. IV. i. 94). Line 115 seems to support this interpretation of l. 112: 'You don't take housekeeping seriously; you only put your heart into bed-work.'

120. Desdemona's inquiry shows that she is really thinking of Othello, and killing time by this badinage.

132–3. Iago's 'old fond paradoxes', as Desdemona rightly calls them in 138, ('old' = 'hackneyed' and 'fond' = foolish', are cast into the usual form of proverbial sayings in Shakespeare, i.e. closed couplets (cf. the Duke's speech of consolation to Brabantio).

136–7. She never ... heir. The play on *foolishness/folly* brings out the meaning of the couplet: 'If a woman is pretty and foolish, her foolishness (i.e. wantonness) will yet provide her with an heir.'

154. cod's head ... salmon's tail. The general meaning is probably that the wise woman would not exchange substantial fare—say, a dull husband—for an attractive titbit, such as, say, an attractive lover. 'Cod's head' was a common term for a fool, but appears to mean here only the humdrum, as Iago's 'To suckle fools', etc., indicates.

[Salmon's tails were the perquisites of the Queen's cooks at Court; but this does not necessarily mean that they were valuable. If they *are* to be taken as valuable 'change' would have to mean 'take in exchange'.]

159. chronicle small beer. Small beer is 'weak beer'; hence the phrase means 'to talk of trifles as if they were important'. Iago's 'most lame and impotent conclusion' is, of course, a designedly cynical anti-climax.

165–75. This aside betrays an envious sense of Cassio's elaborate courtesy, even while he despises it. Iago would like his part, though he plays another. He does not really understand loyalty, reverence, and manners. It should be added that Cassio's superfine manners might perhaps well provoke a better man than Iago. But his sense of inferiority comes out in contact with Cassio, whether over rank (Act I), manners (this passage), or moral beauty (v. i. 19–20).

Coleridge calls attention to 'the importance given to trifles, and made fertile by the villainy of the observer' in this speech.

166–7. It has been pointed out that Iago consistently describes himself in terms of hunting and trapping. Here he is the spider.

168–9. You say true, 'tis so indeed. These words refer to Cassio's last speech. Perhaps Iago means that if Cassio were more of a plain soldier and less courtly he would not be giving Iago the opportunity of getting him into trouble.

171. kissed . . . fingers. Kissing the fingers was a normal complimentary gesture to a lady.

180. A wonderful short passage of love and rejoicing begins here. It is an enacted statement of what Othello and Desdemona say about themselves before the Senate.

fair warrior is another tribute to Desdemona's spirit, recalling her speech at I. iii. 248, where she demands the hardships of a soldier's life. There is a sad echo of this at III. iv. 138 ff., where she tries to imagine Othello's behaviour towards her as part of the fortunes of war, and calls herself 'unhandsome warrior' for getting in the way of what she tries to think is military necessity.

188–91. There is irony in the situation, and suspense. Othello's content is absolute, but the audience know of the lurking devil, whose aside at l. 197 is threatening.

194–6. Othello means that his perfect contentment leaves him no more to say. In music to 'stop' is 'to press down a string (of a violin, lute, and the like) with the finger . . . in order to shorten its vibrating length, and thereby produce certain intermediate sounds' (*O.E.D.*). This word seems to have led Othello on to his musical metaphor in the next line, which Iago continues in l. 198. 'And this, and this' are his kisses, and since they are (presumably) silent, following his speech, which content has 'stopped', they are not discordant at all. Cf. *Lucrece*, l. 1124: 'My restless discord loves no stops nor rests', for a similar metaphor from music.

198. set down the pegs : literally, this means to slacken the strings of a musical instrument. Thus Iago means to spoil the Othello–Desdemona harmony.

199–210. A new kind of speech for Othello, the affable, which he does very well.

212. as they say: a revealing phrase. Iago knows, or claims to know, this only theoretically. The saying itself is a noble commonplace, which has been found in one form in Plato, and is attributed by Erasmus to Plutarch.

215. court of guard: an Elizabethan corruption of *corps de garde*, a French military term for the body of soldiers on duty at the guard-room, and hence the guard-room itself. (Cf. II. iii. 203.)

216–7. If Iago at present believes this to be a straight lie, he seems to have half-persuaded himself that it is true in l. 287, where he is motive-hunting.

225. devil: an allusion to Othello's colour. Devils were thought of as black.

248. found him: seen through him, in the sense that she has recognized him as one of her own kind.

249. Roderigo, who is more fool than villain, recognizes virtue when he sees it.

251. fig's end: a fig is something valueless and contemptible, 'fig's end' even worse. It is substituted here for some other expression, such as 'Rubbish'. Cf. 'blessed pudding' (l. 253), a similar expression of inexpressible contempt.

251–2. wine . . . grapes: i.e. she is as human as anybody else. As far as he can, Iago reduces everything to the physical, and acts as if the soul and will (at least, the will to be good) did not exist.

256–7. The image taken from books is carried through to 'history'. An Elizabethan index (literally, 'a pointer') was at the beginning of the book.

264. for the command . . . you. These words might be interpreted in the opposite sense, viz. 'I'll leave the matter to you'; but this is less suitable to the context. It is curious that most editors pass over the sentence in silence.

274. qualification: a word which means 'a detraction from the completeness of something' (as we speak of a 'qualified success'); hence, here, a falling off from their loyalty. The general sense is quite clear: 'whose loyalty will not be restored until Cassio is supplanted'.

286–312. Iago's second soliloquy provides some new motives for revenge. He suspects both Othello and Cassio of having cuckolded him. He never again mentions either his suspicion of Cassio with Emilia, or that he thinks Cassio and Desdemona love one another (except as a lie to Othello). Indeed he says in his next soliloquy that Cassio is an 'honest fool' (II. iii. 339). His own profession of love or lust for Desdemona is put into so ludicrous a form that it cannnot be taken seriously. The notion that Desdemona loves Cassio is present in his mind as a mere plausibility, something usable. Even the thought of personal reward (l. 308) is incidental.

291. A most dear husband. Beside the obvious sense of 'loved' and 'loving' there may be detected the ironical foretaste that Othello will prove an 'expensive' husband (cf. 'dear absence' = grievous absence, I. iii. 259). The two senses may have different roots.

296. leap'd ... seat: a metaphor from horse-riding, which reduces Emilia to a mare.

297. It is characteristic of Iago to speak in physical terms where another man would refer to his heart or mind.

303. trash: a hunting term, 'to check a dog that is too fast by attaching a weight to its neck'. Cf. *Tempest*, I. ii. 181: 'Who t'advance and who To trash for over-topping' (outstripping). Iago means that Roderigo is too eager in his pursuit of Desdemona.

> [**crush**, Q; **trace**, F. 'Trash' is Steeven's emendation, which has been commonly adopted. The emendation introduces a pun appropriate to both the poet and Iago.]

305. on the hip: a metaphor from wrestling meaning 'ready to be thrown', i.e. helpless.

306. in the rank garb. 'Garb' is not used of dress by Shakespeare. Iago means that he will accuse Cassio of adultery with Desdemona. **rank** (Q; F has the weaker **right**) is associated with sexual heat from its meanings of luxuriance, fertility, and reckless abundance. Iago intends to make Cassio seem like a goat.

ACT II, Scene II

This short scene is merely an indication that time will pass before the next scene. The proclamation is made at five of the afternoon. The next scene opens just before 10 p.m. It is one of the most careful indications of 'short' time in the play. (On 'Time in the play' see the passages in *Select Criticism*.)

ACT II, Scene III

This is a scene in which Iago's plot first comes to action. It is consummately managed and brilliantly acted. It is impossible to find fault with Iago in any of his roles, from that of the boon companion singing tavern songs to the grieved friend, reluctantly reporting the events of the night to Othello, or acting as the counsellor to the disgraced Cassio, and the consoler of Roderigo. A peculiar beauty of the plot is Iago's apparent honesty of speech and action, and the extreme economy he employs in serving several purposes. The scene ends with a soliloquy expounding the 'divinity of hell', and showing that the plot and some of its means are now clear to him.

1. **Michael.** The use of the Christian name shows the relationship of trust and affection between the general and his lieutenant. Othello uses it for the last time in 'How comes it, Michael, you are thus forgot?' (l. 175). Thereafter he is 'Cassio'. Friendship is lost in the responsibilities of command.

16–25. Iago speaks throughout in sensual and prurient terms of the marriage; Cassio, without being rude, tries to turn him to Desdemona's qualities as a person. Iago thinks of sheets (and it is difficult not to see that, among other things, he is maliciously plaguing and probing the idealistic Cassio), and Cassio thinks of love. Cassio is obviously uneasy, Iago obviously enjoying himself. He cuts this indulgence in his native climate short at l. 25, and proceeds to business, namely the temptation to Cassio to drink. The drunken scene, like that on the quay in the previous scene, is essential for showing the audience how Iago appears to others, and how good his social disguise is. His subsequent advice to Cassio reinforces the same point.

63–7. Iago's stanza is either an old drinking-song, or one made up on old models.

66. **span**: no doubt a quasi-proverbial version of Psalm xxxix, verse 6, in the Prayer Book: 'Thou hast made my days as it were a span long'.

70. Drunkenness is a common accusation against Englishmen; whether exaggerated by moralists and humorists, or objectively true, it is difficult to say. At all events, this would be safe to raise a laugh in an audience of Englishmen who like their habits flattered.

71. **your Dane**: an example of what has been called 'a generalizing

possessive pronoun'; like 'my young mistress' in 46. The 'you' of 75 ('he drinks you with facility') is a similar colloquialism equivalent to 'let me tell you' or 'believe me', called by commentators on the classics an 'ethic dative'.

77-8. **gives . . . filled.** The sense of this depends on the idiom *gives you*, which seems to employ the terminology of sports and handicaps, e.g. 'give you ten yards' (in a race). The Dutchman (and the Dutch were said to be notable drinkers) gets so drunk that he vomits, while the Englishman remains untouched. Thus the Dutchman has the advantage of starting the next round with an empty stomach.

82-9. Lines of a popular song. The earliest known version of it belongs to the eighteenth century; but references to King Stephen and his breeches occur in the sixteenth century, and, we may take it, had been set to song.

93-111. Cassio is now maudlin, and the fit takes him solemnly, morally, and religiously. What he says is inspired drunken nonsense. The famous actor, Kean, said of this scene, 'the great secret of delineating intoxication is the endeavour to stand straight when it is impossible to do so'; and Booth said, 'Whatever you do here, do it delicately and with great seriousness, and show a readiness to fight any one who *thinks* you're drunk. The more dignified your manner, the more absurd and yet correct your performance will be.'

113 ff. Iago sows suspicion wherever it is safe to do so. This speech is part of his foundation-laying. This direct lie seems safe enough.

116. **equinox.** Day and night are equal at the equinox, i.e. the time when the sun crosses the equator. Iago means that Cassio is as much a man of integrity as he is a drunkard.

121. **the prologue to his sleep:** i.e. Cassio always goes to sleep drunk, and cannot sleep without drink.

139. **twiggen bottle:** means a bottle surrounded by wicker-work, or raffia, like a Chianti flask. Cassio may mean that he will drive him into a bottle, that is, therefore, into retreat or a bolt-hole; or he may mean that he will cut him into a network.

145. Iago's assumption of honest concern is masterly. So his speech of anxious zealousness (153-5) shows how he made himself trusted.

157-8. **Turks, Ottomites.** Othello's awareness of the chaos of the barbarian and the civility of the Christian life comes out here: 'in attacking one another, we are doing the Turks' work for them, although Heaven has already destroyed them.'

160. **carve . . . rage**: an ingenious metaphor, whereby carving with swords is compared with carving food (to satisfy, in this case, not hunger, but anger).

164. Iago's acting is not confined to speech.

169. **planet**: a reference to the belief that men's lives were affected by the benign or malign influence of the planets; e.g. that the moon produced lunacy.

176. **I cannot speak**: not from drunkenness, but from shame. He speaks well enough when he is alone with Iago.

181. **unlace** seems to have the natural connotation of 'be slack, careless, about'. It has been suggested, however, that it is a concealed metaphor from the purse (loosing the purse-strings) which the 'rich opinion' of the following line supports.

191–204. Othello should speak 'with restrained anger—not loud' (Booth). This is the first hint that passion lies behind Othello's calm and dignity. 'The thing most apt to break Othello's normal calm is failure to get a straight answer to a straight question. Iago knows this and later uses his knowledge (Ridley).

Cassio cannot speak, and Iago and Montano are evasive. A General, called out in the middle of his marriage night (in a state of affairs which must have been like Cyprus in 1958) on this sort of brawl, can scarcely be other than exasperated. The incident here cannot be used to demonstrate Othello's shortness of temper, nor does his speech suggest a barbaric passion, as some critics have suggested, beneath a Western veneer. On the contrary, what he says is good military sense.

193. **collied**: *to colly* meant 'to make black'. Cf. 'Brief as the lightning in the collied night' (*M.N.D.* I. i. 145).

203. **court and guard** may well be a mistake for 'court of guard' (Fr. *corps de garde* = guard-room).

253 ff. Nothing could be more convincing than Iago's consolation, partly because he believes the cynicism about reputation, and partly because the course he recommends to Cassio is not only sensible, but fits in with his plot.

261–2. **as one would beat . . . imperious lion.** The expression 'to beat the dog before the lion' is proverbial. Iago means that Othello had to punish Cassio for the sake of appearances.

292. Hydra. In Greek mythology Hydra had nine heads. It was one of Hercules' tasks to destroy this monster; but for each head that he struck off, two grew in its place.

296. familiar. Cassio's use of 'devil' provokes this ironic reply. Iago plays on 'familiar', the noun for a demon attending and obeying a witch or wizard. Shakespeare had already punned on this in *L.L.L.* I. ii. 177: 'Love is a familiar: Love is a devil.'

304. denotement: should from the use of the verb 'denote' mean 'indication' (and so Onions explains the word here); but from the context it clearly has a different shade of meaning, viz. 'noting'.

[Q and F have **deuotement** = devotement, and there is some reason for sticking to it and its meaning, 'devotion', 'worship', 'dedication to'. But the word should be the last of three parallel terms, and this *denotement* is, and *devotement* is not. Even apart from this, Theobald's objection is valid: 'I cannot persuade myself that our Poet would ever have said any one *devoted* himself to the *devotement* of anything.']

321. Cassio's 'honest' is picked up again by Iago in his following soliloquy, where he once more shows a cynical but irritated sense of his label. It gives him cover, but he hates it.

322 ff. It would be difficult to parallel this soliloquy in literature for its appreciation of goodness and its determination to ruin it. The nearest likeness is Satan in *Paradise Lost*. Iago is beginning to see himself more clearly as 'of the devil's party', and no longer indulges in the nonsense of motives. None is suggested here, and the whole soliloquy is concerned with the use of goodness against goodness.

328. elements. The Elizabethans, like the medieval and ancient philosophers, thought of these as earth, water, air, and fire. Since they make up all bodies, to be as 'fruitful' as they are is indeed to be generous.

329–30. Othello is a baptized Christian. Baptism is a sacrament which is 'the outward and visible sign of an inward and spiritual grace'.

333–4. her appetite: probably an objective use of the possessive, meaning Othello's appetite for her, and not hers for him.

function: glossed by Schmidt as 'the operation of the mental faculties' and by Onions similarly: 'operation . . . of intellectual or moral powers'.

335. parallel. It is not easy to see what the parallel is with. As well as the meaning given in the footnote, the parallel could be with Iago's own design, as Johnson thought: 'that is *level, and even with his design*'.

336. Divinity of hell: 'a favourite theme of Shakespeare's and other sixteenth-century writers, based on the Devil's citation of Scripture during the Temptation' (Matthew iv. 6) (NS). Cf. *M.V.* I. iii. 99: 'The devil can cite Scripture for his purpose.'

339 ff. 'All this with a quiet chuckle, and increasing intensity' (Booth).

362–3. These lines are of somewhat doubtful interpretation. The paraphrase in the footnote takes 'against the sun' as 'exposed to', and does not attempt to find a strong antithesis in the two lines.

364. 'tis morning. The scene had begun just before 10 o'clock on the previous evening (l. 13). The time both of its opening and close is marked; and the next act begins where this leaves off, with the *aubade* or dawn-song to the married couple. All this illustrates the concentrated or 'short-time' aspect of the play, as opposed to the longer time required to make Desdemona's infidelity plausible.

ACT III, Scene I

Half this short scene is taken up by the poor bawdy and other puns of the clown; but it is important as beginning Cassio's importuning of Desdemona for his pardon and the second stage of Iago's plot. We gather from it that not only Desdemona and Emilia, but Othello himself, are desirous of rehabilitating Cassio at the first opportunity.

Inept as the Clown is, he helps to make up a feeling of ordinariness, or the usual, in the life of Othello and Desdemona, lacking until now.

1–2. Such morning greetings with music, particularly on the morning of a marriage, were customary. They give poor Cassio some cover for his pathetic attempt to regain favour; but it is promptly stopped by Othello, either because of the quality of the music, or because he suspects its purpose.

3–10. The Clown, who is clearly either Othello's batman, or a domestic of his billet, is the dreariest of all Shakespeare's clowns. Most of his remarks are either conventional bawdy, with one remark, perhaps, of some wit (see 16–17); and one is simply the old gag of 'mistaking the word' or the punctuation (22). The puns on 'instruments', and on 'tail': 'tale' are obvious. A kind of syphilis was sometimes called the Neapolitan disease, hence

'Naples'. 'Speak it in the nose' because the disease attacks the nose and the music of bagpipes is nasal.

28. **seem** : originally an impersonal verb with indirect object, as in 'meseems' = it seems to me. The indirect object was early converted into the subject, here *I*, and the sense 'think', later 'think fit', arose. The Clown will 'think fit' or 'make it his business', to tell her.

> [Judging by those who use this idiom in Shakespeare, e.g. Launcelot in *M.V.* (II. iv. 11) and Bottom in *M.N.D.* (III. i. 16), it is a vulgarism. Notify is rather a high-flown companion for it: the clown is no doubt mimicking Cassio's cultured speech.]

36. **mean** was used in the singular as well as the plural in Elizabethan English.

40. **Florentine.** Cassio comes from Florence, Iago from Venice, so that this is a high compliment!

41–50. Emilia is a comfortable soul, and is also tactful in giving Cassio his old title.

49. **front.** In a Latin schoolbook that Shakespeare could have read, and Bacon quoted in his essay *Of Delays*, Opportunity (*Occasio*) is represented with hair in front of her head, but bald behind.

> [**saf'st**: If Shakespeare wrote this (the line is absent from F), he must have meant the first occasion on which Othello could decently reinstate Cassio. Johnson boldly read 'first'!]

ACT III, Scene II

This is probably the shortest scene in Shakespeare. It serves the purpose of indicating a passage of time, and of showing Othello in his job. It also draws Othello away, so that Cassio has a chance to intercede with Desdemona, and be found sneaking away in so guilty a fashion in the next scene. It seems from l. 36 of the previous scene that Iago might have arranged this; but it is more probably one of those likely chances on which he relies, since there is no indication in the scene itself that he has done anything.

ACT III, Scene III

This very long scene, of nearly 500 lines, is the most important in the play from the point of view of plot. It is mainly a long study in temptation and damnation; but it covers perhaps the widest range of feeling in Shakespeare, from happiness, innocence, and trust to torment and revenge. It begins with Desdemona's well-meaning assurances to Cassio, and ends with Othello's determination

> To furnish me with some swift means of death
> For the fair devil.

This shocking transformation could not be tolerated by either audience or reader without the most careful plan of progression, that is, mainly, the subtle movements of Iago from suggestion to statement.

It has been pointed out by Herford that there are six sub-scenes within the scene.

(i) The first is that between Desdemona and Cassio, the openness and innocence of whom are, ironically enough, the opportunity for Iago. Desdemona's frankness and Cassio's natural diffidence are psychologically sound to the audience in the know; but they can be interpreted otherwise by a malicious mind. Iago strikes the first blow—or, rather, begins on the merest tap—with his 'Ha! I like not that', though Othello scarcely notices it at the time.

(ii) The second sub-scene is Desdemona's guileless, and, though frank and warm-hearted, tactless pleading with Othello for Cassio. Othello dismisses her courteously but with some impatience. His mind is apparently full of military matters, as the previous scene indicates, but he forgets both these and Iago, in rapt meditation on his love ('Excellent wretch!').

(iii) Iago, therefore, having miscalculated on the movements of love, has to start again at l. 92, when he breaks in on Othello's reverie with 'My noble lord'. This sub-scene stretches to Desdemona's re-entry at l. 279. It begins with insinuation so smooth that it is scarcely perceptible, and words so harmless and hesitant that Iago could withdraw at any sign of danger. By l. 167, he has managed to introduce the infuriating word 'cuckold', but still only as a part of a generalization, so that its application at this point is to be made by Othello, not himself. During this episode, every circumstance capable of a malicious interpretation is used to shake Othello: the fading away of Cassio at their approach; his part in Othello's wooing; and, after some generalizing remarks (in which Iago specializes, and to which Othello, by virtue of character, is particularly susceptible) on 'good name', 'jealousy', and the sophistication of Venetian women (of whom Othello knows less than the average man of Chinese), he makes specific links with Othello's own situation, by reference to Desdemona's deception of her own father, and the sinister nature of her choice of a black man. The real devilry of the episode is Iago's first-class simulation of the honest friend and the reluctant witness.

(iv) The sight of Desdemona revives, but in a modified form, his faith in her. All intuition speaks for her. It is at this point, through a kindly wifely act, that the handkerchief is lost.

(v) In the fifth episode, Iago takes the handkerchief from Emilia, who, at this point, seems to be completely dominated by him. It seems that Iago had foreseen the possible use it could be put to, for he had wooed his wife 'a hundred times' to steal it. It is to be noted that Emilia neither knows nor cares why.

(vi) In the last and sixth episode Othello returns out of control. This means that Iago can be bold. His language is now brutal, and he brings in two pictures, one of Cassio's dream, the other of Cassio's 'wiping his beard' with the handkerchief. These seem conclusive with Othello and he ends with the command to kill Cassio and the intention to kill Desdemona.

Theatrically speaking, the seduction of Othello takes much time. Coghill compares it with the forty-eight lines it takes King John to persuade Hubert to murder Arthur (*King John*, III. iii. 19–66), and the ninety lines in which Antonio persuades Sebastian to murder Alonzo in *The Tempest* (II. i. 195–286).

16. [**circumstance.** F has the plural' which is clearer but introduces an extra syllable. The paraphrase in the footnote gives 'out of' the ordinary sense of 'arising from'; but it would be possible by taking it as 'away from' to make Cassio say that policy may become an end in itself, forgetful of what has caused it in the first place, and that he will go on being cashiered because he *has* been cashiered.]

23. **watch him tame:** a metaphor from the training of hawks. 'Hawks and other birds are tamed by keeping them from sleep' (Steevens). 'watch' is used in Shakespeare intransitively meaning 'to be or lie awake', or, transitively, as here, 'to keep (someone) awake'.

   Desdemona's innocent confidence in herself and Othello—she talks as if they were intimate and trusting friends—is made more distressing by the outcome. The next hawk-image is used by Othello himself—'If I do prove her haggard' (i.e. a wild female hawk) (III. iii. 260).

24. **shrift.** The idea of penance following a confession is implied.

35. **Ha ! . . . that.** 'Don't growl this,—let it barely be heard by the audience' (Booth). Othello is preoccupied, either mentally or with dispatches and letters. Owing to this, Iago has to make a second start.

39. [Q has **sneak** for F's **steal**, but this might be thought too strong a word for Iago at this stage. He moves, and must move, by catlike steps.]

43. For Desdemona, there is nothing to conceal, and her openness and sincerity could have defeated Iago's plots, as this defeats his first insinuation here, if she had had more chance to speak.

56. Some critics have seen in the short evasive sentences beginning here evidence that Othello has in fact been already disturbed by Iago's remarks. The sequence rather means that Othello, in his experience, has decided, in policy, that the matter must wait a while; but that ultimately (see l. 75), he will recall him. His wish not to be further importuned is clear in l. 85, but this shows not so much suspicion as business, as is evinced in his ll. 90–2.

76. Desdemona in her enthusiasm and innocence does not know when to stop. Othello has already yielded.

79. [**peculiar**: Q and F have 'a peculiar', which is unmetrical; 'a' is omitted by Pope and NS.]

90. **wretch.** Playful depreciation is often affectionate: cf. 'You young rascal', 'you little rogue', and so on.

Of ll. 90–2 Booth writes 'With joyousness,—yet there should be an undertone of sadness—as at their first embrace in Cyprus. Iago, at the back of the stage, watches him with a sneering smile.'

92. **Chaos is come again.** Othello is, of course, thinking of a future he does not envisage as possible, not of a present in which he does not love Desdemona. 'He has so totally forgotten Iago's "Ha! I like not that", that the tempter has to begin all over again' (Bradley). Othello refers to primal chaos, before the world was made and out of which it was made.

95–116. A masterpiece of apparently reluctant *suggestio falsi*. 'It is one of the artifices of Iago to make his victim draw every conclusion from premises that are put before him, so that, in event of detection he can say "I said nothing, I made no accusation"' (Lewes, quoted by Furness).

106. **echoes.** Iago's 'echo' technique is designed to arouse suspicion and imply reluctance; and much is to be conveyed by tone of voice and quality of manner, as is indicated by Othello's description in the speech, ll. 112–15.

123. **dilations**: derived probably from the common Latin word *dilatio* meaning a delay; hence 'pauses', 'hesitations'. The word

appears in a French–English dictionary of 1611 a few years later than the acting date of *Othello*, with the same sense. The lines may be paraphrased 'in an honest man who is not the slave of his passions these hesitations are due to the hidden ('close') motions of a heart that cannot suppress its feelings'.

This involves supposing an awkward inversion of order making 'passion' the object of 'rule'. (Contrast 'whom passion could not shake' at IV. i. 262.) If this is not acceptable, the sense would have to be 'a heart not ruled by its passions' (cf. 'a man that's just') which rather contradicts the suggestion of uncontrollable spontaneity.

[Most modern editors accept Johnson's emendation 'delations' meaning 'accusations'; but there is only one earlier occurrence of this Latin sense in English. Q's harmless 'denotements' = 'indications' avoids the difficulty, and might be preferred here.]

126. Men . . . seem. It is ironic in the extreme that Shakespeare's greatest master of dissimulation should state what has been called 'an obsessive theme' of Shakespeare's: the difference between seeming and being. It is also ironic that the same man should speak so truly of his own character in 146–7.

140. leets and law days: a tautologous phrase. Both refer to courts of law, the first special, held once or twice yearly, the second general. Iago says: 'Who has so pure a mind but that some improper thoughts will not sometimes enter it, and sit on the bench together with lawful and just thoughts.' The metaphor is from courts of session, as in the beautiful Sonnet XXX:

> When to the sessions of sweet silent thought
> I summon up remembrance of things past.

[145–8. This is a vexed passage in logic and syntax with variant readings in F, Q, and Q². Our text allows 'vicious' to have its ordinary meaning and not a special meaning of 'wrong'.]

166–7. It is . . . feeds on. Jealousy is thought of as a power outside the man, a monstrous power. The argument seems to be that jealousy feeds on love, but, at the same time, is a mockery of love. Once a man knows that he is a cuckold, and no longer loves his unfaithful wife, he lives (comparatively) in bliss, and is no longer tortured but indifferent.

By warning Othello against what he scarcely entertains, Iago induces it.

Two references, neither of which is exactly parallel, may,

nevertheless, illuminate the lines. One is from Daniel's *Rosamond* (1592):

>   O, jealousy . . .
> Feeding upon suspect [i.e. suspicion] that doth renew thee,
> Happy were lovers if they never knew thee.

The other is from Emilia's mouth at III. iv. 158–60.

green-ey'd is almost a stock epithet for jealousy (e.g. *M.V.* III. ii. 110). It was the colour of unfaithfulness in Chaucer's *Squire's Tale* (F. 646).

171. O misery: spoken perhaps as a general reflection on Iago's description of the state of the jealous man, and not yet applied by Othello to himself. But it could be an exclamation of dawning pain.

172–4. Iago compares the state of anticipating poverty all the time with that of a man doubtful of his wife's love.

176–92. Why, why is this? Othello partly does Iago's own work for him by applying his generalizations to his own case. 'Why are you saying this to me, who would settle the matter one way or another once and for all?' This gives Iago his cue to proceed to directer hints (193 ff.).

180. Is . . . resolved: not, as Schmidt explains, and some critics appear to understand, 'to be fixed in a determination'. This does injustice to Othello.

182. exsufflicate: not found elsewhere, but in both Qq and Ff (spelt *exufflicate*). It comes from Latin *exsufflare*, 'blow up'. **blown** has the same sense, so that this is a double-barrelled expression for 'windy guesses'.

184. feeds well: a curious detail, not usually reckoned among the attributes of attractive women, and probably an interpolation in the text since it is hypermetrical.

191–2. Othello means that he will either prove his jealousy unfounded and dismiss it, or, if he finds it justified, give up his love.

197. Iago now moves on to specific insinuations.

202. In Venice. Venice was celebrated for its wantons, but this is irrelevant in the world of the play. We have no evidence (unless we count Bianca) other than Iago's, that Venice is a city of sexual looseness. Emilia is worldly, but not wanton.

Iago plays here on Othello's ignorance of fashionable society. Othello's trade has been war, and he first sees what civilized life is as a generalization from Iago, who himself really has no more notion of what it is like than the Man in the Moon. Desdemona and Emilia both show that his suspicions are wrong.

205. As in l. 165 above, Iago works on general rules about human conduct, and his simplified version of humanity is sufficiently impressive to convert Othello, as 258 ff. finally shows.

In this scene he moves from easy generalities to particular instances. 'The plurals, the generic singulars, the abstraction *jealousy* all subtly imply universal experience' (Heilman). Othello is lost once he accepts this in his soliloquy, one of the few places where he utters his private thoughts. This is not a realm where he has any experience, or even wisdom; the 'tented field' *might* be after all very different from the sexual customs of Venice. Iago is not merely a practical corrupter, but a philosophic corrupter.

206. Iago echoes Brabantio's parting words to Othello (I. iii. 292–3), and thus uses a father's prejudice (which, there is every sign, left Othello unmoved at the time) to support his suggestions.

209–11. The broken syntax is that of speech. In l. 210 the metaphor from falconry (*seel*, cf. I. iii. 269) passes into a simile from the close texture of oak.

222. **success** in Elizabethan English is often closer to its Latin origin than it is now, and could mean 'what follows as the result of an action, . . . result' (Onions). Thus one could talk of *bad success*, i.e. 'poor result'.

226. The exclamation implies 'The more fool you!'

227. Othello again starts Iago up by a generalization which the latter brings to the particular, Desdemona. He is encouraged to do so by the fact that the generalization itself betrays a softening of Othello's position. The gist of Othello's interrupted thought, which Iago so eagerly breaks into, is that no human being is always true to his nature.

Iago once more echoes Brabantio—'for nature so preposterously to err' (I. iii. 62). The curse of the situation is that Iago has so much apparent circumstantial evidence, and Othello apparently none.

232–5. Iago is becoming grosser, but, though he speaks of 'her', he pretends he is speaking generally.

235–8. Othello is now too distracted to resent the gross insult that Desdemona's 'better judgment' would never have accepted him.

240. Othello has now fallen far enough to ask Iago to set Emilia to spy upon his wife.

248. A very cunning stroke, as it is certain that Desdemona will plead further for Cassio if he is 'held off'.

250. **entertainment**: used of maintaining a person in one's service or company.

261. **jesses . . . heart-strings.** Jesses were left attached to the hawk when it flew, unless it were being dismissed.

262. **whistle her off.** Hawks are controlled by whistling.
    down the wind. Hawks are always let fly against the wind; if they fly with the wind behind them, they seldom return. A dismissed bird was therefore 'let down the wind' (cf. Cotgrove's French–English *Dictionarie* (1611): 'To cast, or whistle off, a hawke; to let her goe, let her flie'). Untameable hawks (haggards) were thus sent packing and left to shift for themselves.

263–6. This is the first time that Othello has shown any consciousness of the colour-bar, or expressed lack of confidence in himself.

265. **chamberers**: cf. I. ii. 67–8, where Brabantio tells Othello that Desdemona   shunn'd
        The wealthy curled darlings of our nation.

It is clear that some of Brabantio's remarks are coming back in force to Othello's memory. By derivation the word means those who frequent indoors rooms, especially ladies' *chambers*, as opposed to soldiers, etc.

267. **my relief**: with reference, no doubt, to Iago's remark in 167–8, that the conscious cuckold who no longer loves his wife is comparatively happy.

274. Elsewhere (*A.Y.L.I.* III. iii. 59) Touchstone claims that cuckoldom is common to all men, poor and noble alike. It is not clear why Othello thinks the 'plague' attacks the great ones more than the humble; possibly because they belong to the leisured and more free-thinking classes.

276. **forked**: Cuckolds were fancifully said to wear horns on the brow (cf. 284).

278. **If . . . itself.** 'If she is false, then God in making her so like heavenly beauty, derides his own creation.' Othello's intuitions are better than his cogitations. Desdemona's appearance, her 'seeming', is in fact true.

285. 'Desdemona's tender response' is 'a proof of her unconscious innocence' (Furness).

287. It is a sad irony that Desdemona lost the handkerchief which was to prove so fatal to her through solicitude for Othello.

288. **Let it alone** might refer *either* to the handkerchief (which Desdemona could have made a movement to pick up), *or* to the headache.

292. **wayward**: a curiously light word to use of Iago; but Emilia knows him very little better than do the other innocent characters of the play.

    a hundred times: one of several references which indicate a considerable lapse of time. Other indications contradict this.

296. **the work ta'en out.** Handkerchiefs were delicate and expensive things, part of the rich dress of people of fashion. The interest taken in the embroidery of the handkerchief Othello gave to Desdemona (apart from the magic Othello attributed to it) indicates a piece of rare workmanship. It is no common handkerchief, and ought not to be, in view of the part it plays in the accidents which aid Iago.

299. This line is usually interpreted as in the footnote, or somewhat similarly, e.g. 'I only know how to humour his whim;' Emilia's indifference here indicates both a lazy mind and lack of suspicion of her husband. She does, however, mean to return the handkerchief to Desdemona, and merely hand Iago a copy. The soliloquy and the subsequent exchange between them reveal much about the nature of their relationship.

302–5. Iago grossly and gratuitously insults Emilia by suggesting that she is sexually open to all; when she bristles (*Ha!*—an exclamation of indignation) he changes his sentence to form a minor insult, which she accepts good-humouredly enough. ('thing' is a common euphemism for a sexual organ.)

320. **acknown** is the p.p. of *acknow* 'to confess to', and is a word not found elsewhere in Shakespeare.

330. **mines of sulphur.** Holland's translation of Pliny, which Shakespeare had read, has: 'Sulphur ... is engendered within the Islands Aeolia, which lie between Italy and Sicily ... which do always burn by reason thereof.'

    I did say so. Othello shows in his face the truth of what Iago has just been saying.

331–4. Some of the most beautiful lines in *Othello*, or, indeed, of their kind, in Shakespeare. Possibly, in that age, when they would more directly suggest drugs to the mind, 'poppy', 'mandragora', and 'drowsy syrups' would have had a less romantic appeal; but the sound of the words and their rhythm must have been as magical and mysterious as they are now.

Indeed, Iago is more than Iago here: he is the mouthpiece of the tragic and pathetic fate of Othello. He has been said to be 'deliberately parodying the ceremonial love-idiom of Othello' (J. Bayley).

334. i.e. is Desdemona false to me? Othello does not notice Iago until l. 336.

347. Pioners: usually manual labourers, who worked under the direction of engineers, but had no skill themselves. Soldiers were sometimes degraded to their ranks for misdemeanours. Hence Othello is saying, in effect, that the dregs of the army might have enjoyed Desdemona, so long as he knew nothing of it.

348–58. This moving lament for the loss of life's happiness depended on a sense, now perhaps lost, of military glory, by which Othello lived. This explains why the lines are apparently not about Desdemona at all, but about war. 'In *Othello* . . . love [is] shown as part of social morality, its firm substance allied with the no less firm one of reputation. Both are "jewels"' (Bayley).

357. immortal Jove . . . counterfeit. In classical mythology, Jove caused thunder and hurled thunderbolts.

359. Is it possible. Iago assumes concern that Othello should have been so affected by what he had said to him.

360. my love: the last time Othello calls her so before her death.

364. Is't come to this? i.e. is this how my loyalty to you is to be repaid (i.e. by abuse and threatened violence)? At l. 361 Rowe added a stage-direction: *Catching hold on him.* This is a probable interpretation of the situation. Iago's plot has at last led him into danger.

366–7. hinge . . . doubt on. This appears to be one of Shakespeare's mixed metaphors. 'Hinge' is here taken as the kind of pivot on which a door hangs, and therefore on which a doubt could turn: 'loop' much as we use 'loop-hole' metaphorically to imply the possibility of evasion or escape. The rapidity of Shakespeare's imagination has combined and compressed two images: one the

idea of a door working this way or that on its hinge; the other an
opening (i.e. for doubt).

[The present editors do not accept Onions's suggestion that 'loop' is
here used in a Northern dialectal sense, namely 'part of a hinge'.]

370. **abandon all remorse,** i.e. 'throw aside all the restraints that
pity lays upon one'. Remorse usually means in Shakespeare 'pity',
'compassion', and does not possess the modern sense of regret for
past action.

385. **I think . . . is not.** Othello is in a state in which he does not
know what to believe. 'Be' is subjunctive, i.e. 'may be'.

392. Iago encourages Othello's agitation by opposing it. This is one
of his techniques.

397. Iago's descent into coarse terms and references before his
General is an indication of his sense of growing mastery, and also
of his willingness to torture.

414. **I lay with Cassio.** 'This custom, which now appears so strange
and unseemly to us, continued to the middle of the seventeenth
century. Cromwell obtained much of his intelligence during the
Civil Wars from the mean men [i.e. men of much lower rank]
with whom he slept' (Malone). In fact it went on longer than the
seventeenth century.
    'In the fiction of Cassio's dream, Iago can satisfy almost every
motive: he can madden Othello, vilify Cassio and Desdemona, and
snatch vicariously at the unattainable—in his savouring of bodily
delight' (Heilman).

417. **There are a kind of men:** a common construction, where *kind
of* is treated as an attributive or adjectival phrase, qualifying the
noun. Hence the plural verb *are* goes with *men*, not *kind*.
    loose of soul. The contemptuous phrase is itself revealing of the
close and plotting Iago.

446. **thus.** No doubt here Othello makes some appropriate
gesture, such as blowing away something imaginary from his
open hand.

448. **thy hollow cell.** Revenge was thought of as dwelling in a
cave or lair, hence the force of 'hollow'. Shakespeare speaks of
'Revenge's cave' in *Titus Andronicus,* III. i. 270, and in *Henry IV*,
Part II, v. v. 40 he has 'Rouse up revenge from ebon den'.

449. A grand and moving line, made terrible in its context.

450–1. Swell, i.e. with poison. Cf. 'The poison of asp is under their lips' (Romans iii. 13).

452. blood. Is Othello only thinking of a bloody vengeance, or also of faults of blood, i.e. passion ?

454–7. Like to the Pontick sea . . . Hellespont. These lines probably have behind them a passage in Philemon Holland's translation of Pliny (1601): 'And the sea Pontus evermore floweth and runneth out into Propontis, but the sea never retireth backe againe within Pontus.' Bradley points out that 'the reminiscence here is of *precisely the same character* as the reminiscences of the Arabian trees and the base Indian in Othello's final speech'.

461. marble. The main sense is 'white', 'shining', but no doubt the sense of 'hardness', 'enduring for ever' is also present. The first sense is classical; *marmoreus* is an epithet of the sea in Virgil, and of the air in Milton's 'pure marble air' (*P.L.* iii. 564).

465. elements, i.e. the four elements, earth, water, air, fire, or all our natural and physical surroundings; a proper oath for Iago, who is a follower of naturalism. Othello's oath gives some notion of the supernatural ('heaven', 'sacred').

469. [The meaning given in the footnote to **remorse** here is that assigned by Onions and the *O.E.D.*; but it is suggested to suit this context only, and not paralleled elsewhere (for it is not needed in 370). Hence some would emend the text here to 'without remorse'.]

476. But let her live. Presumably he says this because he knows there is no chance that Othello will agree.

480. I am . . . for ever. In these terrible words there is perhaps a hint of the familiar spirit (see note to II. iii. 296) who appears to be the servant of his victim, but only to destroy him.

ACT III, Scene IV

Desdemona, as yet unaware of the changed Othello, is still busy with her innocent plans for restoring Cassio. The handkerchief now becomes magical, sewn in 'prophetic fury' from silk of hallowed worms, and linked with lost or preserved love. It is thus a powerful symbol for Othello and a frightening loss for Desdemona. Her brave white lie (l. 85), joined with her persistence for Cassio, makes the scene so dangerous for her and maddening for Othello—the one ignorant, the other corrupted—that the passage between them (ll. 36–96) reaches great heights of dramatic intensity, where only the audience knows all and aches at the incomprehensions and risks.

Emilia must not be blamed too hardly for denying knowledge of the handkerchief. She is not yet aware of the issues involved, and, in a sense, *expects* Othello's behaviour from her worldly knowledge of men—

> 'They eat us hungerly, and when they are full
> They belch us' (103–4).

12–13. lie ... throat. '"To lie in the teeth" was less intentional, and gave less offence' (Hunter). The gradations of the lie in *Books of Honour* ranged from teeth to entrails.

14–15. edified by report. Desdemona humours the Clown by talking in his own affected way, and perhaps punning on 'edify', as 'lodging' requires an edifice.

16–17. catechize ... answer. 'The Clown picks up the religious associations of edify' (NS). The Catechism is a treatise for instruction in the elements of the Christian religion, done in the form of question and answer. The Clown makes this droll by promising to answer through his questions, i.e. to tell Desdemona where Cassio lodges from the answers he receives to his questions.

24. Emilia's lie is perhaps pardonable, since she has no notion of the use her husband intends to make of the handkerchief, and is obeying his command (III. iii. 320) to know nothing of it. The dialogue here is reassuring for her, since Desdemona is so confident of Othello's freedom from jealousy.

26. cruzadoes were worth about three shillings in Elizabethan money. The name is derived from the cross (L. *crux*, Sp. *cruz*) stamped on them.

30–1. A fine specimen of tragic irony, in view of what precedes and follows it!

31. humours. The original sense of *humour* is 'moisture' (L. *humor*), and Desdemona has this in mind in referring to the sun; but it also means 'mood', 'disposition', 'inclination', and this is the primary sense of her remark.

34. my good lady. Othello has not addressed her so formally before.

36. moist. A moist (and **hot**, l. 39) hand, was taken as a sign of amorousness. Throughout this and the following lines Othello's innuendoes pass over Desdemona's head.

37. A most pathetic line, in the circumstances! Age and sorrow have not dried her skin, but the latter is imminent.

43. rebels : often used by Shakespeare of the rebellion of the senses and instincts against the will.

46–47. Othello follows up Desdemona's remark (l. 45) by reversing her order of words (with a secret meaning unknown to her), and by saying that in the past the hand gave the heart, either in marriage or greeting, i.e. that the giving of the hand was motivated by love or friendship, but that nowadays it is fashionable for people to give their hands without their hearts.

[The precise force of *heraldry* is difficult to ascertain. Many editors since Warburton think that a topical allusion is concealed here, and that the lines refer to the new order of baronets, instituted by King James in 1612, of which the badge was a hand gules (i.e. red), added to the coat of arms. There are some difficulties about this explanation. First, in the context, it would be satirical, and it might seem to be an artistic blunder to introduce a topical satirical sneer, of some ingenuity, at this point. Second, it means an interpolation at least eight years after the play was written. It might be replied that an interpolation of a topical kind would not be repugnant to Shakespeare, if it fitted in with his purpose (and it can be so fitted). Such a reflection is not really alien to Othello's thought and method in this passage. He is quibbling all through it.

Nevertheless it seems better on the whole to reject the topical allusion and follow NS in taking *heraldry* as simply 'mark of honour': 'it is now a mark of honour for marriage to be no assurance of love' (taking 'heraldry' as associated with, and therefore meaning, fashion and gentry).]

48. Possibly Desdemona's most innocent remark. She does not know what Othello is talking about, and presses on with her kindly purpose.

55 ff. Othello's account of the handkerchief fits his and Desdemona's circumstances, as he supposes them to be, so pat, that it sounds like an *ad hoc* invention—possibly to frighten her into confessing. He has not previously talked of its magical quality, or of his attachment to it but merely mentioned that it was his first gift to Desdemona. In Act I he rejects notions of magic; and one can only suppose that his present account is a romantic version of what his first gift to his love means. If this is not so, then Othello has retained more superstition from his past than he is commonly supposed to have done. It has been suggested that Othello produces this account here 'to cover up the real reason for his disproportionate passion over such a trifle'.

56. Egyptian : probably a real Egyptian, as the mention of mummy (l. 74) suggests; otherwise, the word was often used of gipsies, whose name is derived from Egypt.

70. **A Sibyl** was one of the women who in ancient times at various places acted as a mouthpiece of the gods, and made prophecies.

71. **The sun . . . compasses**: 'to course' is equivalent to 'to run', as we say of a clock. In this case the 'course' is round the earth. Shakespeare used the Ptolemaic view of the Universe, in which the sun went round the earth.

75. **Indeed ! is't true ?** Desdemona is terrified out of her wits by this description, and the following dialogue is a result. She feels she has mislaid, not lost, the handkerchief and tries to divert the terrifying intensity with which Othello pursues it.

91–5. Othello's threefold repetition of **The handkerchief**, while Desdemona evades the demand, is frightening. Desdemona is not tactless but puzzled, as she well may be. Every word she utters, innocent as it is, confirms Iago's story and Othello's suspicions.

97. **Is . . . jealous ?** Emilia harks back to Desdemona's happy assurance of her husband's nature in 30–1. She still does not speak out because she expects husbands to be jealous, and the interchange has not shown her how serious the matter is.

101–4. Emilia is not a refined woman, and the image she uses here is coarse but powerful : 'every one of them is a stomach, for which every one of us is merely food', i.e. we merely serve their bodily appetites.

109. **virtuous** is used most frequently in the moral sense, but also, as here, meaning 'of powerful properties'. Cf. *M.N.D.* of the flower 'Whose liquor hath this virtuous property' (III. ii. 367).

110. **Exist** : i.e. without his office as lieutenant he is nothing, and is dragging out an aimless existence.

111. **all . . . heart** : i.e. all that a heart should do—its proper action— is devoted to Othello (L. *officium* = duty).

119. **shut . . . up in** gives the sense of constriction and difficulty he would find in any other job.

126. **blank** : the white spot in the centre of a target (Fr. *blanc*) ; hence, anything aimed at or within range.

134. **like the devil** : i.e. as the devil may take our next-door neighbour in his snares. But there is a primary sense of devilish fury.

135. **and can he be angry ?** i.e. if he is indeed angry then it must be a matter of great moment ; for he remained cool while his soldiers were shot to pieces.

148. **as fits the bridal**: another suggestion of 'long time', and a brave attempt to put the best face on it.

149. 'A lovely reminiscence of her husband's having called her "my fair warrior" [II. i. 180] in the joy of his first meeting, on arrival' (Cowden-Clarke, quoted by Furness); and also perhaps of her own brave speech before the Signiory where she chooses to follow Othello to the wars. She says in effect: 'I am not showing the stuff of which soldiers are made.'

150-2. **Arraigning . . . falsely**: the imagery is legal, and refers to the offence of 'subornation of perjury', i.e. of procuring false witness. The court is Desdemona's soul, before which she cites Othello to appear; but she has unlawfully procured the witnesses (her own thoughts) to give false evidence, because she did not understand the case, so that Othello has been falsely charged.

156. **Alas the day**: a common expression of dismay or regret, meaning no more than 'Alas!', though originally 'Oh, sad day!'

   I never gave him cause: almost reduplicated in Cassio's 'Dear general, I never gave you cause' (v. ii. 298); and cf. Othello's 'It is the cause' (v. ii. 1).

159-60. **monster . . . on itself**. Emilia echoes Iago's thoughts on jealousy (III. iii. 165-7).

164-5. In spite of her own trouble, Desdemona is still concerned with Cassio.

167. *s.d.* **Enter Bianca**. Bianca's part is small but, from the point of view of plot, important. This entry is really the prelude to her next appearance in IV. i, where she throws the handkerchief at Cassio in sight of Othello. Shakespeare has brought to life the anonymous wife who copies the handkerchief in his source.

172. **Eight score eight**, i.e. eight score and eight, 168 hours, or a week.

ACT IV, Scene I

Othello is now Iago's creature and can be handled with increasing boldness. His sufferings can be measured in intensity by his falling in a fit, and his fury by his striking Desdemona in public. It is now safe for Iago to produce a fake confession of Cassio's. As usual his luck holds with the arrival of Bianca and the handkerchief, which provides the 'ocular proof' Othello had demanded in III. iii. 361. The opening of the scene shows Iago in a role most likely to bemuse and infuriate Othello, namely that of the man who knows the

Venetian sophisticated world, to which Othello believes Desdemona belongs, and accepts its sexual pranks with cynical matter-of-factness. Othello's 'unbookish jealousy'—the thought of this repulsive unknown world he has married into—infuriates him.

The most impudent performance conducted by Iago is the over-seen (*not* over-heard) interview with Cassio. The most painful moment (perhaps in the whole of Shakespeare) is the striking of Desdemona. A report of a performance at Stratford says: 'Five seconds of horror-struck silence followed the blow, and then Desdemona's control cracked suddenly in outraged sobbing . . .; and her agony was unbearably prolonged by allowing her to climb to the top of the staircase, before Othello, maliciously misinterpreting the ambassador's words, calls her back for further humiliation.'

Lodovico, a kinsman of Brabantio and therefore of Desdemona, brings back for a moment the pre-Cyprus world, the Venetian world of Othello's honour and Desdemona's girlhood. 'This Lodovico is a proper man', says Desdemona later; not because she regrets her choice but because of the happy past and a revival of courteous conduct. He gives occasion for the blow because of the mandate he brings, which, while it elevates Cassio, also allows Desdemona's innocent pleasure, which Othello misconstrues.

1–8. We should no doubt suppose that Iago had, before they appeared in this scene, been giving reasons for false comfort to Othello; 'as that, though the parties had even been found in bed together, there might be no harm done; it might be only for the trial of their virtue' (Warburton).

In the context **Will you think so?** (l. 1) should probably be understood as in the footnotes. Iago means 'Are you determined to think that kissing in private or lying in bed naked together must be sinful?'. *But* it could imply 'Won't you agree with me that such things are venial?' In either case **What! to kiss in private?** is an exclamation of feigned incredulity that anyone could be so simple as to regard this as something to be concerned about.

Iago is playing on Othello's ignorance of Venetian customs, as in III. iii. 201–4.

6. **hypocrisy against the devil**: 'As common hypocrites cheat men by seeming good, and yet living wickedly, these men would cheat the devil, by giving him flattering hopes, and at last avoiding the crime he thinks them ready to commit' (Johnson).

10–13. Hitherto, Iago has talked about generalities, in this case, Venetian behaviour. At this point he brings in the handkerchief, which becomes part of his 'concrete proof' as distinct from theorizing about sexual relationships. This is really Iago's trump card: if Desdemona and Cassio are guilty, they will certainly lie. In 12–13 Iago says, of course, the opposite of what he desires to insinuate.

16. essence ... seen. Iago's cynicism about all but material values comes out here, as it had with Roderigo on virtue—'Virtue ? a fig' (I. iii. 321) and with Cassio on reputation (II. iii. 255, etc.).

32. he ... what he did. Iago employs his trick of coy refusal to give the blunt facts, to make Othello more insistent.

34. Othello's euphemism, 'with', is given a coarser expression with 'on', and is the last straw.

Cassio's supposed confession is Iago's boldest stroke so far. But there is no chance now of Othello's confronting Cassio.

Furness points out, quoting Abbott, that here, as in *Lear*, IV. vi. 127, the highest passion of all (i.e. madness, or next door to it) is expressed in prose.

35–6. lie on her ... belie her. Othello's play on words is the product of misery; 'the very verbal play leads him to the doorstep of truth' (Heilman). But we cannot expect to be sure of the train of thought in the distracted outburst of this speech.

38. confess, and be hanged: a proverbial remark, perhaps arising from the confessions of criminals before hanging (see *O.E.D.*, *Confess* 10).

38–9. First...confess. Presumably there is a mad irony in Othello's remark. If Cassio is hanged before he confesses, his next confessor and judge will be God. Othello, then, means him to be damned. (Cf. Hamlet's desire to damn his uncle's soul.)

40–1. Nature ... instruction. 'Othello feels all his faculties failing him on the sudden, and a cloudy or misty darkness creeping very fast upon him. This circumstance suggests to him the thought that his very nature, which sympathizes with him in his present agony, must have received some secret mysterious instruction, intimation, or instinctive knowledge of the reality of that calamity which so deeply presses him, otherwise she would never have spontaneously invested herself in that horrid darkness which he now felt overwhelming him' (Heath, quoted by Furness). This elucidation seems to be one of the clearest on this sentence. In it, *nature* must be taken as both external Nature, 'the order of nature and of life', and Othello's own personal nature. Nature is, as it were,

casting a shadow over him, and the darkness which falls upon him
is his and hers, premonitory and actual. Nature herself is taking
part in the drama, as Othello thinks.

51. **yesterday.** 'Iago is so solid a liar that this cannot be taken
literally; but it aids to give the effect of long dramatic time'
(Cowden-Clarke).

60. **mock me:** i.e. 'are you referring to cuckolds' horns?'

64. **civil monster.** In his pun on 'civil' Iago means in his secondary
sense those who are well-bred enough to bear their cuckoldom
patiently. This refers back to his instruction to Othello on
Venetian customs (III. iii. 201–4). This indoctrination continues
in 66–9.

68. **unproper** is coined as the opposite of 'proper' = 'one's own'
(L. *proprius*), which is common in Shakespeare.

79. **ecstasy:** the word implies either unconsciousness, and can be
rendered as 'swoon', 'fit', 'trance', or 'a state of being beside oneself with some emotion, even to the extent of madness'.

81. **encave:** i.e. hide where you can see. A box-hedge on the apron
stage will serve for this; or possibly the pillars supporting the
penthouse (see v. i. 1).

88. **spleen:** an abdominal organ, regarded by the Elizabethans as
the source of emotions, including, as here, rashness and anger.

93–9. The shortest of Iago's soliloquies, which would be better
described as an aside, giving something which the audience should
know in advance. The scene which follows is difficult on the stage,
with a lurking, watching, but not hearing Othello, and the
ridiculousness of his interpretation of what he sees. Nevertheless,
the scene is cleverly contrived.

101. **unbookish.** Curiously enough, the word appears here to mean
'unversed in the ways of the world', which might normally be
described as 'bookish'! But the book that Iago is talking about is
the world of practical experience, in which he fancies himself so
learned.

107–8. **Now ... speed:** a clumsy but effective way of getting Cassio
on to the necessary subject, Bianca.

118. **Do you . . . Roman.** Othello calls him 'Roman' ironically.
'*Triumph*, which was a Roman ceremony, brought *Roman* into
his thoughts' (Johnson). Perhaps Othello has also in mind his own
race, as contrasted with that of Cassio, the Italian (though not

from Rome). Iago has injected some bitterness about his own alien quality into him.

119. **customer** : one of numerous euphemisms for prostitute, arising from the sense 'a person one has dealings with'.

126. 'score' can mean 'cut', 'slash', 'wound', and also, from the method of recording debts by means of notches on a stick or tally, 'to write down as a debt'. (Most editors think a reference to reckoning is intended here.) Othello would then be saying ironically, 'Have you made me your debtor for your attentions to my wife ?' **Well** implies an ironical acceptance of the situation, but also its later reversal—colloquially, 'that's fine ; but you wait'.

    The meaning might also, perhaps, be 'Have you squared the account with me for cashiering you ?'

132-9. Cassio does not come well out of this interview either in his sensibility or choice of language (see also 'fitchew', 145). It is, however, the only place where he offends ; and Iago's envious tribute, 'he hath a daily beauty in his life', must be regarded as true.

141-2. **nose of yours . . . throw it to.** Othello's revenge is in the future, like the dog. The remark is one of bitter ferocity. 'I see your nose which I shall soon cut off, and fling to the first dog that comes in my way' (Deighton). 'Noses' had been singled out in 42.

144. **Before me** : a mild oath 'modelled on *before (my) God!*' (Onions).

145. **'Tis such another** : 'she's no better than . . .', a kindly contemptuous phrase. **fitchew** : used figuratively for 'prostitute'. The polecat was noted both for its smell and its lechery. **perfumed one** : Bianca is presumably preceded by a strong wave of scent.

154. **hobby-horse** : 'a figure of a horse, made of wicker work, or the like, fastened about the waist of one of the performers in a morris-dance, or on the stage, who executed various antics in the character of a horse' (*Shorter O.E.D.*). It was a sixteenth-century colloquialism for a loose woman.

163-6. **Will you sup there ?** It is important for Iago's plans that he should know where Cassio is to be that night. **speak with you** is a delicate euphemism that the audience would not miss (see 209).

185-90. Othello's recurrent fits of pity and admiration are dangerous to Iago's intentions. Strongly pursued, they would wreck them,
so that he has to come out as the direct prompter of hate ('She's
the worse for all this'; 'Ay, too gentle').

192. gentle a condition: i.e. goodness and kindness of nature.
Iago's 'too gentle' makes Othello see her gentleness as 'the inability
to resist temptation' (Mrs. Jameson, who also points out that the
sweetness of Desdemona's disposition never produces an effect of
feebleness).

195. O ! Iago, the pity of it, Iago ! The heart-rending repetition
(omitted in Q, which is an instance of its inferiority to F) will remind some readers of David's lament over Absalom (2 Sam. 18: 33).

206. Do it not with poison. Iago refers poisoning minds to poisoning
bodies. The plan he proposes involves no risk of his being impli-
cated or being thought of as an accomplice. Othello accepts his
suggestion because 'the justice of it pleases', with none of the prudential considerations that actuate the Moor of his source (see
Appendix, The Source).

217. cousin. Lodovico is simply called 'a noble Venetian' in F's list
of *Dramatis Personae*. The evidence for his kinship with Brabantio
is derived from this passage. *Cousin*, as Shakespeare used it,
could mean anyone not in the first degree of relationship.

226. *This fail you . . . will*: the opening of a formal diplomatic
command from a high authority, which could continue 'as you
will keep our love and authority', etc.

231. wise. Othello is astonished at Desdemona's open pressing for
Cassio at this point, and her innocence must seem like boldness
to him.

232-4. It would have been natural enough for the state to recall its
great general when the danger from the Turkish fleet had been
removed. Perhaps the 'mov'd' only represents some disappoint-
ment at recall to a quieter life.

235. I am glad on't. Desdemona can only be glad that Othello is
to be recalled from a job where his talents are now wasted, and to
home. But she also rejoices in Cassio's promotion.

   Oth. **Indeed !** *Des.* **My lord ?** Desdemona is perhaps shocked
by his vehemence and demeanour. Othello is beside himself at
what seems to him her brazen impudence, and the implication
that he is blind and complaisant. The moment is the height of
cross-purposes, and is followed by the blow. Desdemona's

bewilderment is indicated, as well as in other ways, by her thrice repeated query 'My Lord ?', and by her 'Why, sweet Othello ?'.

236. I am glad to see you mad. Presumably by *mad* Othello means so infatuated that she is recklessly imprudent. I think he is also savagely playing on her *glad*, and the sounds of the two words, *mad, glad*. This is not very bright; but bitter anger does not make for witty remarks.

241–2. If that ... crocodile. 'If the earth could be made pregnant by means of woman's tears, each drop she (Desdemona) lets fall would produce a crocodile.' The crocodile was fabled to weep hypocritically or with a malicious purpose; hence the expression 'crocodile's tears', i.e. feigned tears. Mandeville (*Travels, c.* 1360) writes, 'These serpents slay men and eat them while weeping.'

246. Mistress: a formal, and, here, unfriendly address = 'Madam'.
    What ... sir ? Othello feigns to suppose that Lodovico (much to his surprise—l. 247) wishes Desdemona to come back for his own purposes, and implies that she is any man's game.

249–50. Sir, . . . turn again. Othello is bitterly quibbling on (1) 'turn round', (2) 'transfer her affections easily', perhaps even 'turn in the arms of men'.

257. 'With Desdemona's exit, Othello recovers himself, and for a moment becomes the servant of the state and the courteous host, though the control is brief, and breaks again on his own exit' (Ridley).

259. Goats and monkeys. Othello's mind is dwelling on lust, and recalling Iago's words at III. iii. 404—'Were they as prime as goats, as hot as monkeys'.

265. Lodovico has a small part to play, but shows humanity and feeling in the unknown situation where he finds himself. He speaks like a gentleman, and is shocked by what he sees and hears (cf. 278). Iago pours poison into his ears also. Lodovico is prepared to think that Othello is disturbed by his recall (271–2), but Iago insinuates, in his creeping way, otherwise.

267–8. What he might be . . . he were: one of Iago's cryptic remarks which betray nothing to speak of, but insinuate more. The obscurity of his utterance is intended to suggest that he could say more, but loyalty restrains him (cf. 273–4). This was his first method with Othello.

269–70. Iago seems to be preparing the way in official circles for
    Desdemona's murder.

273–4. 'The archetypal technique of the ambiguous statement that
    encourages inferences which are half-right and hence more difficult
    to deal with than if they were all wrong' (Heilman).

ACT IV, Scene II

The brothel scene (as this is called), like the striking of Desdemona in
the previous scene, is brutal, but more extended in brutality. The
brutality is less direct in not being physical but psychological; but
its pain lies in the incomprehension of Desdemona as to what it is
about, her near-ignorance of the very terms in which Othello
accuses her. Othello is never less sympathetic to us; yet he weeps—
and the world of disorder in which he now lives is movingly portrayed
(l. 42). Bewilderment is the key of this scene: two sensitive people
in love, but at odds, neither giving the other the information on
which understanding could be made. Othello is so poisoned that he
can scarcely attend to what she says; she is so bewildered that she
can only say something as weak as 'I hope my noble lord esteems me
honest'. But she is still spirited, and rejects as much as she under-
stands of his charge.

Emilia now begins to emerge as a sympathetic character. She lays
many shrewd blows upon the unknown villain, enough to provoke
Iago. Some stage representations give him a moment of remorse in
his gestures at l. 148, but this is unwarranted by the text. The
moment therefore is ironic; Desdemona's appeal is made to egoistic
flint. (See note to the lines.)

The final passage of this scene belongs only outwardly to it.
Roderigo is now dangerous, and Iago lays plans to dispose of him
and (or) Cassio at once. The height of action for Iago is now reached,
and all depends on how it goes.

3. **she,** nominative, might be used for the accusative 'her' at this
    period. There are other instances in Shakespeare.

8. **mask :** a covering for the face worn by women out of doors to
    keep their complexion, and for concealment and the preservation
    of modesty at theatres, balls, and other public occasions.
    nor nothing : a double negative, used for emphasis, such as may
    still be found in dialect speakers today.

15. **the serpent's curse :** i.e. God's curse on the serpent for seducing
    Eve (see Genesis iii. 14)—an appropriate penalty for the snake-like

Iago. It is ironical that Emilia still does not suspect him. (For another snake-reference see V. ii. 283—when Lodovico says, 'where is that viper?')

19-20. yet ... as much. Othello is now almost incapable of judging any witness other than Iago, and the patent honesty in Emilia's words seems to him only an extension of her mistress's hypocrisy, and one of the tricks of the trade.

26-9. Othello speaks to Emilia as if she were the keeper of a brothel. How much of his meaning Desdemona grasps it is difficult to say.

28. 'hem': a vocalized representation of the sound made in clearing the throat, often exaggeratedly, to give warning, express hesitation, etc.

46-52. Othello may be thinking of the afflictions of Job, but, if so, goes on to argue that Job was a figure of affliction, not of scorn.

53-4. The fixed figure ... finger at. The image seems clearly to be taken from the face of a sundial. Othello thinks of himself as being the figure on this, to which the hand will always point, or seem to point. The hand is the *time of scorn*, which we may take, with Onions, to mean 'the scornful world', time here being thought of in the sense of 'the age in which one lives' (hence) the 'world', 'society', 'mankind'. This is a sense of which there are several examples in Shakespeare. Cf. *Macbeth*, I. v. 64, 'beguile the time', or *Richard III*, V. iii. 93, 'deceive the time'. Othello may, and probably does, mean, however, that *all* time will point at him.

[The reading adopted in this text is that of Q, which seems illogical, but psychologically more powerful than F's 'and moving'. Othello means that scorn will go on pointing at him, as if time could never move. Cf. Sonnet 104:

> Ah! yet doth beauty, like a dial-hand,
> Steal from his figure, and no pace perceived;
> So your sweet hue, which methinks still doth stand,
> Hath motion, and mine eye may be deceived.

Compare also *Antony and Cleopatra*, III. iii. 18–19, where the gait of Octavia is described: 'She creeps; her motion and her station are as one.']

58-61. The *language* 'reflects Proverbs v. 15–18, and the note in the Geneva version . . . which (exhorting to refrain from whoredom) speaks of a wife as a man's "whole cistern" and "well", and of children born in wedlock as "rivers" therefrom' (NS). But the *thought* rests on a contrast between the fountain and the running current on the one hand, symbols of freshness and life, and the stagnant cistern on the other.

61–3. Turn thy complexion . . . grim as hell: Johnson's para-phrase, given in the footnote, seems the best interpretation of this much-disputed passage. Othello says that the picture he has conjured up is beyond all patience to endure. Patience is pictured as young and fresh because of her cheerful acceptance of sorrow; but her cherubic beauty is perhaps the reflection of Desdemona's physical beauty in Othello's mind.

[The text is that of F, interpreting 'I' as 'Ay' (a not uncommon spell-ing). 'Cherubin' is properly plural, but was taken as a singular at the time.]

64. Desdemona's prim reply is an indication of her ignorance of the cause of the fury.

66–8. A beautiful expression of his sense both of her beauty and her worthlessness, coming on top of what is possibly the most degrad-ing image he uses.

'Once more (as at v. ii. 15), Othello's invincible love for Desde-mona surges like a tide over his conviction of her guilt, not diminishing it a tittle, but changing its complexion for a moment from ferocity to anguish' (Herford).

73–4. forges . . . modesty: a compressed image, in which a blush (the product of modest feeling) is seen as the fire of a forge, which destroys its own fuel (modesty). Blush and its origin are here conflated.

77. bawdy: because the wind penetrates everywhere and embraces all. Cf. *strumpet wind*, *M.V.* II. vi. 16.

82. vessel. This expression is borrowed from the Bible: 'to possess his vessel in sanctification' (1 Thessalonians iv. 4).

90. That . . . Peter. Peter's office is to keep the gates of Heaven.

92–3. In this speech, Othello enacts the part of a customer of a brothel and pays his wife's own gentlewoman as he leaves her bedchamber; 'not', as White observed, 'either to reward or offend Emilia, but that he may torment his own soul by carrying out his supposition to its most revolting consequences'.

96. Faith, half asleep: a splendid simplicity, of fine imaginative insight. It is both surprising and inevitable. There is actually nothing so exhausting as a scene of tense emotion. 'This sudden revelation of ordinary womanhood in Desdemona engages the audience's sympathy when it is particularly needed, and also points a contrast between her sensible normality and the emotional exaggeration of Othello' (S. L. Bethell, *Shakespeare and the*

Dramatic Tradition; he is discussing the sudden switch to naturalism after the emotional tone of the preceding episode).

103–4. Prithee ... remember: perhaps a pathetic device to remind Othello of the love they began with, or to comfort herself with the same thought.

108. [F has **The small'st opinion on my least misuse**, which it is difficult to make sense of, though editors have tried to do so. The Q reading is therefore adopted in this text.]

124. Do not weep. Is it just possible that Iago feels a twinge at watching the sorrow of his victim ? Bradley says, 'there is not the least sign of his enjoying the distress of Desdemona'; but he also remarks elsewhere on Iago's 'extraordinary deadness of feeling'. Her destruction may be incidental to his purpose, but his purpose is more important than she is. She is a useful implement to torture Othello with, and to ruin Cassio.

130 ff. One never *likes* Emilia more (except in the last scene, where one *admires* her) than when she abuses with such heartiness the unknown villain who has got at Othello. She has a remarkably pungent style, and says for the audience what needs saying at this painful stage. Even Iago seems uncomfortable (144 and 148), no doubt because she is getting near the truth. This is a prime piece of dramatic irony.

131. insinuating. The word in Shakespeare rarely if ever meant suggestion or innuendo, but commonly 'ingratiate oneself with'. Line 132 shows this is the sense here—'to get some office'. Emilia hits on at least one of Iago's motives; she also knows, though Desdemona does not, that it is Cassio who is suspected (see l. 3 of this scene). Yet she does not put two and two together. Line 190 of v. ii—'I thought so then'—implies that she had her suspicions (see note to the line).

Why does Othello not mention Cassio to Desdemona, but only accuse her of general whoredom ? Ridley asks this interesting question, and replies: 'The answer I think, is that Shakespeare dared not allow him to. The specific accusation would have provoked from Desdemona such a flaming denial . . . that even Othello's confidence must have been shaken, and he might "send for the man and ask him".'

138. Shakespeare is bold enough to raise the question of time in a play in which he has played tricks with it. It is clear, however, that Emilia here is less occupied with time than with circumstance.

In her time-scheme, the events could have been possible; her 'what time' means not 'how much time', but 'when'.

151. Here I kneel: a touching parallel to the evil kneeling of Othello and Iago in III. iii. 'That she, as well as he, should be brought to her knees before their trusted tormentor is a stroke of stage-craft of great visual force and point ... an image the eye will retain for her utter innocence, as it retains that of Othello kneeling as the image of his resolved vengeance' (Coghill).

162. abhor. This seems a queer place to find a quibble, but Shakespeare could hardly resist one (cf. v. ii. 7). Literary tastes change: Milton puns in serious passages of *Paradise Lost*.

175. daff'st: a variant of *doff*, 'do off, put off one's clothes', hence, figuratively, 'to put off with an excuse'.

189–90. expectations ... respect: 'and brought me back hope and encouragement of immediate consideration (*or* favour)'. Roderigo does not, of course, want Desdemona's *respect*. Cf. 'I have a widow aunt ... And she respects me as her only son' (*M.N.D.* I. i. 157).

acquaintance. Although Desdemona shows no knowledge of Roderigo, it is impossible in view of I. i. 96, where Brabantio says he has told him 'not to haunt about my doors', and l. 176 ('O! that you had had her') that they are unacquainted. The word may mean here something like 'recognition' (of his suit), and the giving him her company.

193–5. Very well ... fopped in it. Roderigo has spoken sensibly and forthrightly enough up till now; but his expressions of anger here are in petulant and petty terms, the asseverations of a weak man.

195. fopped: a verb, very rare, and not found elsewhere in Shakespeare, from *fop*, 'fool'. The word 'fobbed', which some editors substitute for Q and F here, is from the same root.

197–8. make ... Desdemona: perhaps a reference to the disguise he was told to assume (I. iii. 342).

225. Mauritania: the northern coast of Africa, towards the west, inhabited by Moors. Ridley points out that 'Iago seldom tells a direct lie, on a matter of fact which can be readily checked'; but Iago must, in the first place, stampede Roderigo, and, in the second, trusts that the night's events will settle him. See his soliloquy, v. i. 12–18.

243-4. supper-time: then about 5.30 p.m. This makes it clear that the sense sometimes given to the phrase 'grows to waste' of 'is wasting fast' or 'approaching its end' cannot be correct here.

ACT IV, Scene III

This is a static scene, almost a pause in the action, whose main business is to show Desdemona's innocence and sorrow. GB calls it 'A scene of ordered calm; of action of every sort, and of violence and distress of speech, we have had plenty. This prepares us, in its still-ness, and in the gentle melancholy of the song, for the worse violence and the horror to come, and is . . . a setting against which no shade of Desdemona's quiet beauty can be lost.'

The song that her unhappiness recalls to her comes from her child-hood; it is an old pathetic ballad of a deserted girl. It ends with a cynical jeer from the betrayer that women are as loose as men. This is outside Desdemona's experience; hence her ensuing dialogue with Emilia, who confirms in worldly experience the last stanza of the ballad. Emilia sees the marriage bond as a contract, whose breaking by the husband (which she seems to take for granted) justifies similar action by the wife. We see Emilia as a worldly person here for the last time: her purpose as foil to Desdemona is finished, and she joins her in kindred spirit in the last act.

Bradley has pointed out Shakespeare's fondness for introducing a new emotion, usually of pathos, at this stage of a tragedy: it is a constant constructional device with him. *Lear* IV. vii, and *Hamlet* IV. v, are famous examples, and *Macbeth* IV. ii a miniature instance of this. Bradley thought that pathos of a beautiful and moving kind reached its height in this scene, and was only surpassed by the greatness of the moment when Lear wakes up to find Cordelia bending over him.

7-10. Othello's curt requirements—GB notes 'the dry anonymity of the "your attendant there"'—are in ironic contrast with Emilia's hopeful 'he looks gentler than he did'.

22. how foolish are our minds: either in reference to her change of mind (only apparent, however) about the wedding-sheets ('All's one'); or meaning 'how foolish are women in caring about such trifles' or, most probably, in reference to what seems to her a morbid thought of death. She has no reason to fear death at Othello's hands; but the audience, knowing better, finds her fancy grimly appropriate.

27. willow: a traditional symbol of grief for unrequited love or the loss of a mate; cf. 'weeping willow', so called for its drooping shape (*OED*).

30–51. 'Desdemona can at first hardly forbear to sing the song [i.e. abstain from singing it]; she endeavours to change her train of thoughts, but her imagination at last prevails, and she sings it' (Johnson). The passage is absent from Q, but it is difficult to imagine the scene without it.

34. Lodovico. The sudden transition to Lodovico is a masterly stroke of psychology. It is clear from the whole course of the play, and from its end, that Desdemona never repents of her 'bargain'; but she has been touched by his kindness and courtesy, and he recalls happier days for her.

39. The poor soul. Desdemona sings a version of an earlier song or ballad; the earliest known music for it is for the lute, about 1572. Originally, it was meant to be sung by a man who has been rejected, not by a woman forsaken; but it has been altered to bring it into line with Desdemona's situation. In the original our l. 50 had 'her' for 'him' and 'his' and did not follow l. 49, but 'Let nobody blame him, his scorn I approve' is 'a line so perfectly expressive of Desdemona's own feelings' that it 'comes to her mind by sheer force of aptness, out of its context; an exquisite trait' (Herford).

55. This line appears to have been invented by Shakespeare, as part of his adaptation of the song for the scene.

56–8. GB has noted the fine detail of these lines, the light reference to the saying that this *bodes weeping*, and the half-humorous way in which she 'shakes her head over

... *these men ! these men !*'

It is a brave effort to assume normality and worldly-wiseness on her part; and artistically speaking, a most imaginative creation.

63–5. Emilia pretends to misunderstand Desdemona's words, which are merely an exclamation, and to take them as meaning 'I would not commit such a sin in daylight'.

69–70. undo't when I had done. Emilia seems to mean that she would console herself or her husband for her fault by making him monarch of the whole world (74). Q's 'done it' perhaps makes this clearer. Heilman points out that Emilia's jocular treatment of the matter is a foil to Desdemona's girlish seriousness; also that her 'logical frolic' is no doubt kindly intended to distract Desdemona's thoughts.

71. joint-ring. Such split rings, joined by hands at the lock, were common love-tokens of the sixteenth and seventeenth centuries.

84–101. A change to verse marks the change to seriousness. Here Emilia speaks forcibly on a matter of interest to her and rejects the double standard, one for husband, one for wife. Her plea for women's sensibilities is like Shylock's plea for the common humanity of Jews and Christians. There is suppressed passion here, which throws light on her experience with Iago, and on him. The threat, plea, and warning are clinched by a couplet, as if in part directed at the audience.

ACT V, SCENE I

This scene plunges straight into action: 'Wear thy good rapier bare, and put it home' is the second line. Iago's plot reaches its climax. His 'puppets are turning dangerous'. He hopes that one victim, Roderigo, will kill the other, Cassio, or, at the best, that they will kill each other; but he resolves to finish off either survivor. It does not seem to have occurred to him that both might live. But it is a very dark night and his plan goes wrong: Cassio is not even injured, and Roderigo only wounded. At this point he is swift in action; he improvises brilliantly, gains further credit for honesty and valour, wounds Cassio, 'kills' Roderigo, and smears Bianca, both because he is vicious, and because she may later serve his purpose.

Whether because of haste or because his nerve is shaken by the plot going awry, he makes a bad job of both his attempted assassinations. Roderigo revives for a moment (v. ii. 326–8) to throw light on the conspiracy (though the papers in his pocket do this almost sufficiently), and Cassio is borne in to testify both his love for Othello and his innocence ('Dear General, I never gave you cause').

But all this fails to halt the smooth progress of his main plot. Othello, deceived as ever, hurries away to execute his own justice; and all that this scene may be said to do, apart from its intrinsic excitement, is to provide sad material in the last scene for the revelation of Iago's villainy and Othello's blindness.

1. bulk: On the Elizabethan stage the 'bulk' could be represented by one of the two pillars supporting the penthouse (cf. IV. i. 81).

19–20. This is the only *open* admission by Iago that he envies virtue. He seems for this brief moment to be aware of a beauty that he cannot reach, and must destroy (cf. Satan in *Paradise Lost*, Bk. iv). He may, of course, mean that his *public* face is discredited. GB calls it 'that strange involuntary' remark, wrung from him by the crisis, and quickly obliterated by practical considerations (20–1).

26–7. [*s.d.* Iago either wounds Cassio in the leg because he now knows he is wearing a body-protection (which would indicate 'mail' as the meaning of *coat*), or makes an awkward stroke owing to the necessity of concealing his identity. As it is pitch-dark the former explanation seems more probable. In the Source, the blow is intended to make him fall, and Iago leaps upon him to finish him off; but Cassio, though badly wounded, fights him off and brings up aid by shouting. In the play, Iago has no time to make more than one attempt.]

27–8. [*s.d.* F has simply *Enter Othello.* Rowe changed to *Enter Othello above at a window.* This would mean that he appeared, like Brabantio in the first scene, on the centre balcony, and the action would be imagined as taking place before his own lodgings. Otherwise, he can be thought of as lurking in the distance, i.e. at the side or back of the stage.]

29. e'en so. We ought to assume that Othello hears only the voice and not the words. He is correct in recognizing Cassio's voice at l. 28; but mistakes Roderigo's for his in this line.

33–6. One of the ugliest of Othello's speeches. There is an ironic contrast between it and the tribute to Iago which precedes it— the 'perennial infatuate refrain' as GB calls it.

47. Iago has made a quick change, and now appears in his night-shirt from his innocent bed. The stage-craft here is interesting. He flies after wounding Cassio, at l. 26. Then comes a brief appearance of Othello (some nine lines), necessary for his priming for his own task, followed by a few lines from Lodovico and Gratiano. It is very economically and skilfully managed.

63. Kill men i' the dark : a fine simulation of virtuous indignation that there are men base enough to kill in the dark. If said loudly enough, as indignation demands, it serves the dual purpose of covering up Roderigo's exclamation, and enhancing his reputation with Lodovico and Gratiano.

75. who . . . cried : a scornful repetition of what Bianca has said, leading up to his accusation in l. 85. Bianca shows deep concern, and takes some risks for Cassio's sake. She is indeed the strumpet that Othello thought Desdemona to be; but she has some share in the gift of loving that Desdemona has.

82. **garter.** Iago is asking one of the gentlemen (not Bianca) for the loan of a garter, in order to bind up Cassio's wound. The garter was a broad band of silk or velvet used by men to tie the hose to the stockings.

85–6. Iago implicates Bianca in the attack (see 104–10), not out of motiveless malice, though he is quite capable of this, but because he is turning her unexpected appearance to his own safety. In l. 117, though he knew where Cassio had supped, he sends Emilia to inquire. He does not wish to be suspected of this knowledge. He takes risks, but is as careful of his own skin as he can be. His performance in this scene is worthy of admiration for its speed and adroitness, and of abhorrence for its ruthlessness. The anxious, fussy, bustling impersonation (93–9) he assumes here is masterly.

101. **Save . . . labour.** Iago here apparently pushes aside Bianca' who is hanging over Cassio, perhaps, as GB suggests, in order to find out whether Cassio knows anything of his assailants.

104. **out o' the air.** Fresh air was thought to be bad for wounds and sickness.

105. Iago stops Bianca from moving off with Cassio. He explains her 'gastness' and 'stare' as terror arising from guilt, and not as what they are, horror arising from concern.

109–10. **guiltiness . . . speak.** Guilt will manifest itself in behaviour though the guilty keep silent. Cf. *Hamlet*, II. ii. 630–1:

> For murder, though it have no tongue, will speak
> With most miraculous organ.

121, 123. It is amusing to see Emilia's shocked repudiation of Bianca. In spite of what she says in the previous scene with Desdemona she is a respectable soul; and although she says, no doubt playfully, that she is prepared to cuckold her husband for the world, when she meets a really loose woman in Bianca, she assumes the garb of virtuous womanhood.

ACT V, SCENE II

This great scene, intolerably moving, and exciting in so many ways, is also a marvel of stage-craft. Only a few minutes before (v. i. 33–6) Othello had hurried away with savage words ('Minion', 'strumpet') to murder Desdemona. He speaks very differently, though not less inexorably, when he next enters. The scene, as GB points out, falls into three parts: the first, that of Desdemona's murder, pathetic and

terrible; the second, the gallant disclaim of Iago's villainy by Emilia,
and her death; the third, Othello's despairing agony and his determination on suicide. The handkerchief comes in again twice,
once as clinching evidence for Othello of Desdemona's guilt and of her
lies, which turn his heart to stone; and then immediately afterwards
the simple truth about the magic handkerchief is revealed by Emilia.
Desdemona, frightened but courageous, must both feel momentary
relief and think she is dealing with a madman when she finds that
the handkerchief is the 'matter' she asks him about (47). The
reader or spectator must ask himself at this poignant moment why
her simple solution—'Send for the man and ask him'—is not followed; but we are in the tragic world where the obvious is not
perceived, and a fatal course must be followed.

The death-bed dominates the scene, although in the background
of the stage, until Lodovico commands it to be hidden: 'the object
poisons sight'. GB comments on the more or less passive role taken
by Othello after the murder: 'It eddies about him; but he has lost
all purpose, and even the attack on Iago is half-hearted. . . . So the
bulk of the scene is given to a survey of the spiritual devastation
that has been wrought in him.' But not a pang of this is withheld;
and a vindictive but truly tragic satisfaction is given by Emilia's
exposure of his horrible mistake and Iago's guilt. She speaks too
late; but she speaks splendidly.

Structurally, the scene ends, in a sense, where it began. Othello's
first 'justice' is on Desdemona; his last, on himself, so that false and
true justice respectively begin and end the scene. Each justice is
accompanied by a kiss of love, the first reluctant, the second penitent, as if the scene were an expanded ballad, or, at least, of poetic
construction.

1. The soliloquy opens abruptly, as sometimes elsewhere in Shakespeare, with the argument concluded. Othello has persuaded himself that he must be the minister of justice to put the adulteress
to death, as the O.T. commanded (Leviticus xx. 10). But his
mysterious language with its repetition is infinitely more powerful
than a prose paraphrase.

Cause is a legal term meaning 'the subject of an action at law'.
Here it is used generally for 'offence' or 'nature of offence', and
the nature of that offence here is adultery. The association of
'cause' and 'adultery' in the poet's mind is probably due to the
N.T. connection between cause and adultery (Matthew xix. 3–10),
as was first pointed out by Whiter in 1794. Cf. *Lear*, IV. vi. 112:
'What was thy cause? Adultery?'

The *cause* is particularly abhorrent to Othello; he refuses to name it to the chaste stars. The imagery and references here are cold and pure—'stars', 'snow', 'monumental alabaster'—but kindles to life with 'light', 'flaming minister', 'rose', 'vital', i.e. where Othello is most disturbed, as minister of justice, at the sight of Desdemona's innocent-seeming beauty. The calm and coherence of this great speech are broken from time to time by tears, and by reflections that Justice must not entertain.

2. chaste. 'In classical poetry, the Moon is Diana, the goddess of *chastity*, and the stars are the train of *virgins* attending on her' (Hudson). The stars naturally suggest chastity by their remote, cold, light.

7. Put out ... the light. Many editors emend 'the' to 'thy' in the second clause, or else italicize the second *the*. This is unnecessary; 'the second phrase half-veils, by the comparison with an innocent act, the deadlier extinction he has in view'. Lines 8–13 clarify the point.

It is not probable, although it has been suggested, that he intends to put out the light of the candle, because he cannot trust himself to look upon her while he does it, and then to put out the light of life in her. He plays on the ease with which life can be extinguished, as if it were a candle's light. 'To me it is the despairing utterance of utter love' (White, quoted by Furness).

8. minister: used in its Latin sense of 'servant'. The candle acts as the source of light for the man, i.e. as his servant in this respect. But the word also suggests a minister of religion, the Puritan equivalent of the Anglican 'priest', and Othello conceives himself as sacrificing like a priest (cf. 65).

11. cunning'st ... nature: cf. II. i. 61–5, where Cassio, in different words, sees Desdemona as the finest product of creative power. Part of Othello's pain is owing to the difference he finds between her appearance and her reality, as if Nature herself had lied.

12. Promethean. Prometheus, in Greek myth, stole fire from heaven, and bestowed the gift upon men. Othello is still holding to the fancy of candle-light versus Desdemona's life.

13–15. The artificial 'flaming minister' lies in man's power; but none can call back the life either of roses or of Desdemona. Othello is thinking of what is irrevocable and what is not. The candle by Desdemona's bed makes him think that he can put it out or light it at will; Desdemona's beauty sends him to the rose, a living thing, which he cannot restore if he plucks it. Finally, the abstract rose becomes the Desdemona rose.

17. **Justice**: the sword and scales are emblems of Justice.

21–2. By **cruel tears,** Othello means that he cannot refrain from weeping, but that he cannot relent.

This **sorrow's heavenly** may be an echo of 'For whom the Lord loveth, he chasteneth' (Hebrews xii. 6). Johnson said: 'I wish these two lines could be honestly ejected', and GB thought the words blasphemy; but perhaps those in sympathy with the lines that lead up to them, and with Othello's mistaken sense of his duty, will not think them so, but find them pathetic.

31–2. Othello is not acting as revenger, and wishes to save her soul, not damn it. Contrast the opposite sentiment in *Hamlet*, III. iii. 94, where Hamlet decides not to kill his uncle *because* he is at prayer.

36–46. **Hum:** a menacing exclamation, no doubt of a stock type. 'These outward displays of passion would appear to have been usual in the time of Shakespeare. . . . Expressions such as "gnaw the lip" (43), or "bite the thumb" or "nails till the blood came" are so common that they must have reference to actual practices' (Hart). R. Watkins, however, pointing out how common it is for an actor's facial expressions to be described by another actor, as here, concludes that in a theatre where there was no artificial lighting, such expressions were less visible than in modern acting, and [the descriptions] had something of the effect of a cinema 'close-up'.

40. **loves I bear to you:** i.e. I love you too much for my soul's welfare. NS compares Colossians iii. 2—'Set your affection on things above, not on things on the earth.'

45–6. **portents . . . point on:** a concealed metaphor, drawn from the supposed influences of heavenly bodies on human life. 'Portent' foretells something about to happen, especially of a grievous nature; 'point on' is used with special reference to the influence of planets.

47–9. Othello's answer must seem to her so preposterous that she must think she is about to be murdered by a jealous lunatic. The audience, however, know what she does not know, the other 'evidence' Iago has given Othello, which he cannot recapitulate here. The handkerchief is apparently the only tangible 'proof' he has.

The peculiar painfulness of the scene here lies in Desdemona's

bewilderment and Othello's obduracy. GB points out that the
fact that this 'ridiculous trifle' (the handkerchief) should outweigh
Desdemona's denials sharpens the play's tragic irony 'to its keenest
point'.

58–61. It is in this scene that Desdemona first learns that she is
accused with Cassio. Her concise and forthright denial, when she
knows what she is accused of, is too late.

60–1. general warranty . . . love, i.e. not in sexual love, but in
what we should now call friendship (the *agape*, as opposed to *eros*,
of the N.T.).

63 ff. Desdemona's 'perjury' arouses Othello's indignation, first
because it contradicts the bit of 'ocular proof' that he had asked
Iago for, and secondly because it is beginning to destroy his conception of himself as the minister of justice. His rage is mounting
(cf. 77) at what he thinks is an outrageous lie. His argument here
is disgraceful. His heart, he says, is only soft if she admits her
guilt.

66–83. More critics than Johnson have found this dialogue intolerably painful. The brave frank words of Desdemona, unable
to make way against the blindness of Othello, her pitiful appeals
for time ('But half an hour'), the truth half-known to her and fully
to the audience must make the passage quite the most unendurable
in Shakespeare. Furness speaks of the 'unutterable agony' of it,
and goes so far as to write, 'I wish this tragedy had never been
written'. Nowhere does Shakespeare sail so near the wind, in the
matter of sympathy with the hero, as in this play.

76. Alas . . . undone: taken as a confession of guilt by Othello;
but Desdemona means not only that she has lost a friend, but that
her last chance of being cleared by Cassio has gone. 'Betrayed'
may be only general in its meaning, but perhaps Desdemona now
guesses that Iago is the traitor.

88. So, so: presumably Othello's exclamation of satisfaction that
further applications of the pillow are successful in smothering
Desdemona; but see note to l. 115.

92. It is not quite certain what the 'high' noise is. The noise involved
by the attack on Cassio is most likely in view of the preceding line:
Othello thinks that Emilia must have heard it, and have been
called out by it. See l. 105.

99–100. i.e. Nature herself should be convulsed at this frightful
change, just as earthquakes occur when eclipses of the sun and

moon take place. (The current belief was that earthquakes occurred at eclipses.) 'Alteration' in one sense is the eclipse; in the other, Othello's wifeless condition.

Theobald thought it obvious that the allusion was grounded on the events which took place at the Crucifixion, when 'darkness' is said to have 'covered the whole face of the land'; when 'rocks' were rent; and 'graves opened'. This is quite likely; it would be in character, since Othello has a Christian and Biblical imagination.

102. **I had ... forgot thee.** He had been thinking of his wife, and not of external consequences. This is very different from the source.

106. **What! now:** Othello is startled into thinking that Emilia knows of his own murder. Otherwise, if he were thinking of Cassio, his surprise would be simulated, since he believes him to have been settled.

107. The moon's influence was held to produce lunacy (hence the name, L. *luna*), and if she were nearer the earth her effect would be more deadly.

113–14. Othello regards the murder of Desdemona and of Cassio as complementary revenges. If one has escaped, then the death of the other is only half the contemplated extinction of the guilty.

115. Desdemona's temporary recovery, especially after Othello's 'So, so' (88), has naturally caused difficulty. A full discussion, mainly from the medical point of view, can be found in the *Variorum* edition of Furness, pp. 202–7. But she revives because Shakespeare thought it dramatically effective—and this every spectator and reader can judge for himself.

117. 'Emilia rushes to the bed and throws back the curtains' (Booth).

122–3. **Nobody ... farewell.** Desdemona gives the supreme proof of her love in this most moving effort to proclaim her murderer's innocence along with her own. The nearest parallel that comes to mind is Pompilia pardoning her husband and murderer, Guido, in *The Ring and the Book* of Browning.

127. The savagery of these words is perhaps best understood as Othello's attempt to silence the emotions which Desdemona's dying words must have roused in him.

128 ff. Emilia says what needs to be said to Othello at this time. She channels splendidly, like a lightning conductor, the audience's

or reader's anger with Othello, and averts, or releases (whichever way one looks at it) the charged emotion so dangerous to the necessary sympathy with Othello. Her love for Desdemona, and her unquestioning belief in her innocence—she needs no 'proofs'—produce some home-truths of splendid directness—'She was too fond of her most filthy bargain' (155).

141–4. Just as Desdemona would not cuckold Othello for the whole world (IV. iii. 76), so Othello would not exchange her for all its riches if she were chaste.

143. chrysolite: a name given formerly to various greenish-coloured gems. By derivation from Greek the word means 'golden stone', and topaz is probably meant here. Othello habitually speaks of love and Desdemona in terms of things of great price.

148. iterance. Emilia's threefold exclamation 'My husband', which so irritates Othello, shows how dumbfounded she is, and her dawning suspicion. How much she suspects Iago at this point is not clear, but her 'villany' in l. 149 is significant (cf. l. 188) and her words in ll. 153–5 almost conclusive.

152. Honest, honest. The irony of 'honest' Iago appears here for the last time. Othello doubles the word as if to quell his own rising doubts.

156. Ha: an exclamation of anger at what he may take to be a reference to his colour.

160–1. The explanation in the footnote fits the words well enough; but it is also possible that Emilia means that Othello cannot hurt her as much as the fate of Desdemona has hurt her.

181. Shakespeare speaks several times of charming the tongue, i.e. keeping it silent as if by a spell.

Iago is becoming uneasy at the vigour of this new wife. He 'can calculate, but takes no account of self-forgetful passions' (Raleigh). He is always dull upon affections, except sexual appetite.

190. then. To what point 'then' refers, is dubious. When Iago is about to take the handkerchief from her (III. iii. 314), she asks 'What will you do with it?' It has also been thought that she has Iago in mind at IV. ii. 130, but perhaps this does injustice to Emilia.

196. Othello's threefold 'roar', as Emilia calls it, indicates that in spite of his later words to Gratiano (l. 198) he suspects the truth—perhaps, indeed, unwillingly already knows it.

202. **Poor Desdemona**: touching in its simplicity. So Brabantio's anger and grief had been no momentary thing; and the event has apparently justified him.

204. The allusion is to the thread of life which the three Fates, or Parcae, in Roman myth, were supposed to spin and cut.

206. **better angel.** Human beings were commonly supposed to be accompanied on their way through life by two angels, one good and one evil, one from God and the other from the Devil. In Marlowe's *Dr. Faustus* they appear and take part in the action.

207. Suicide was commonly considered a mortal sin, endangering the soul after death.

210. **a thousand times**: indefinite for 'many times'. An extreme indication of 'long time'.

215. **mother.** In III. iv. 55–75, Othello tells Desdemona that an Egyptian gave it to his mother as a charm to hold his father. Is it true, as Steevens thought, that Othello's first account of the handkerchief 'was purposely ostentatious in order to alarm his wife the more', or is it just a slip ?

216 [There is a strong case for restoring the Q text, 'O God'—altered by F, together with other oaths, because of the 1606 Act against swearing on the stage. The emasculated version of F does not bring out Emilia's agony at the realization of what has happened.]

218. **liberal . . . north.** The north wind was proverbially rough, and no respecter of persons.

227. **Villanous whore !** Iago's philosophy has broken down. His indignation shows that he expects loyalty to himself, though he owes none.

232–3. **stones . . . thunder.** In classical mythology, thunderbolts were imagined as the missiles hurled by angry Jove. Othello is challenging divine dispensation by asking why Jove (= God) does not destroy such villains as Iago with them.

237. **notorious**: not, as in modern usage, 'well known for villainy'. The adjective is again used, as in IV. ii. 140, as an intensifier— 'arrant', 'thorough'.

242. Othello refers to Montano; he wonders dully about the loss of his fighting virtue, and we are reminded of the great Othello of the past ('Keep up your bright swords, for the dew will rust them' (I. ii. 59), and 'If I once stir' (II. iii. 194)). With the revelation of what he has done his heart has gone.

245–6. swan . . . music : alluding to the superstition that the mute swan sings just before it dies ; it is a most appropriate image for Emilia, whose great final moment this is.

251. Othello's true note, 'the Othello music' as it has been called, starts again here. He has taken the resolution, not to live, but to die.

252. the ice brook's temper. This has given rise to much comment. Spanish swords, particularly from Toledo, which lies on the river Tagus, had a great reputation from the excellent temper of their steel. This was held to be due to the ice-cold streams into which the Spaniards plunged their weapons hot from the forge. This reputation came from classical times, being referred to by Martial.

260 ff. Almost the last touch of Othello the great soldier, pathetic in its sad reminiscence, and for the flash of pride which he realizes has no place now ('but, O vain boast!'). For the sea-imagery of 266–7, the beautiful last speech of Romeo (*R. and J.*, v. iii) may be compared :

> Thou desperate pilot, now at once run on
> The dashing rocks thy sea-sick weary bark!

266. butt : This word first meant an end or terminal point in general, and then a mark for archery practice, a place where the target was set up.

271. O ill-starr'd wench. 'Wench' could be a term of endearing and familiar address, like 'my girl' (274).

'Ill-starred' need not have any precise belief in stellar influence behind it. In the Prologue to Act I of *Romeo and Juliet* the lovers are called 'star-crossed', and theirs is partly, though not entirely, a tragedy of destiny, which they can do as little to avert as Desdemona can.

276–81. Othello would prefer the tortures conventionally associated with Hell to the present agony of his remorse.

281. Order resumes its sway with Lodovico's entrance. He is compassionate ('most unfortunate man'), but judicial ('rash'). Shakespeare's tragedies always end with the assumption that the normal course of events must go on, but with grief that they have been interrupted. Lodovico's part is delicately and accurately expressed.

283. That's he . . . Othello. He means that the former Othello is gone, not only as far as his jealous passion is concerned, but as to most of his personality.

285. fable: refers to the belief that devils have cloven feet.

287. The diabolical nature of Iago and his impudence is enhanced by this, though it has its naturalistic explanation in the weakness of Othello's attack. Iago, even at this moment, seems to be teasing Othello about his previous remark, and to be saying, 'Yes, I *am* the devil you think me.'

289. Cf. II. i. 187–8: 'If it were now to die, 'Twere now to be most happy.' 'The refrain first heard in the very heaven of his happiness [recurs] now in his hell of misery' (Booth).

293–4. honourable . . . honour. This was the mood in which he began, as minister of justice, even if baser passion crept in later. He means that he intended to vindicate the moral order of things, to act as champion of the chastity that Desdemona had outraged.

298–9. 'One is sure Cassio had never used that adjective before. It tells us that his hero is no longer unapproachably above him' (Bradley). Or does it rather tell us of a love which disregards rank and feels for pain?

300–1. Will you . . . body? Bradley remarks 'this is *the* question about Iago, just as the question "Why did Hamlet delay?" is *the* question about Hamlet.' Whether Iago could have answered the question is doubtful. At all events, such motives as he thinks he has are revealed in the text, and their implications, while not analysed in the play, point to a much darker underworld of the spirit than is common among men.

302–3. Demand . . . word. Iago has confessed something as we see from ll. 295 and 320; but we hear no more from him after these words. He remains inscrutable, and the threat of torture leaves him unmoved. The vicious brawler of the play's opening ends in silence.

304. Lodovico's remark is either shocked (Iago is in need of prayer for his soul's salvation) or satirical (Iago is not a praying man).

305. thou dost best: i.e. in keeping silent; because, perhaps, Othello thinks his villainy is beyond words, or because Othello himself finds explanations so little to the point now he has determined on his course.

306–11. Nevertheless, Lodovico gives him the details of the plot in a number of discovered letters, a dying confession by Roderigo, and Iago's own confession. Lodovico clearly feels that justice demands that Othello should know how he was tricked. Lodovico of course does not know of Othello's intention.

339. **No more of that.** Othello recalls his service to the state to arrest for a moment the execution of Lodovico's order, and to get a hearing for himself. He does not plead any extenuation of his deed.

345. A good example of the much stronger sense of *perplex'd* here than it usually carries is quoted from another Elizabethan writer where the lover, seeing his beloved at the very point of being ravished, says 'I, seeing my love in perplexed plight', etc., where 'desperate' would be the best rendering. A stronger sense is also found in Milton where Juno's wrath 'perplex'd the Greek' (*P.L.* ix. 18), i.e. pursued him almost to ruin.

346. **Indian.** We can be pretty sure that some familiar fable lies behind Othello's lines, as the use of the definite article *the* (marking a thing already known) and the past tense *threw* imply. No such story is known; but Jonson appears to be pointing to one in his *Discoveries* (first published in 1641, but written before that) where he speaks of that which 'perisheth and is passed by, like the pearl in the fable'. The American Indian was almost proverbial even at this date for his ignorance of precious metals and objects prized in Europe. Drayton's *Legend of Matilda* (1594) has:

> The wretched Indian spurns the golden ore.

The point of the reference is the rejection of value through ignorance.

[**Indian** is Q; F has **Iudean**, i.e. Judean. Hart remarks that, judging by the space taken up in notes by commentators, this passage stands fourth in the list of difficult passages in *Othello*. Indeed, F's *Iudean* (which is accented on the first syllable) has a couple of attractive arguments in its favour. It would seem to refer to Judas, who betrayed Jesus with a kiss, as Othello kissed Desdemona before he killed her. Again, both Judas and Othello destroy themselves in remorse. However, Judas did not betray through ignorance of the value of his victim, nor did he throw his 'pearl' away, but received thirty pieces of silver. Nor did Othello betray Desdemona in intention, but only in fact.]

350. Othello is talking of fast-falling tears, but perhaps the word 'med'cinable' of the simile reflects back on the plain meaning. His tears are also in some sense 'healing', for they come from bitter sorrow and are penitential.

352–4. The turban and circumcision marked the Moslem, as against the Christian Othello.

354–8. Some critics, judging by strict theological tenets, consider that Othello damned himself by his suicide (although Donne was shortly to argue in *Biathanatos* that suicide was lawful). But in the world of the play his action seems the only *amende* he can make (cf. 'For he was great of heart', 360). Brutus and Antony commit suicide, Horatio contemplates it, and Kent looks as though he were in search of it at the end of *Lear*. Attempts to consider the tragedies of Shakespeare too closely from the point of view of Christian dogma usually result in misinterpretation.

[The present editors would not agree to 'the profoundly theological structures' found in *Othello* by S. L. Bethell, in spite of all the references and imagery drawn from heaven, hell, and damnation; see his article in *Shakespeare Survey* 5 (1952).]

360. Spartan dog. These were reckoned to be fierce, savage, and excellent hunters. But Spartan warriors were renowned for their silence under suffering, and their general power of endurance. This looks like an example of Shakespeare's frequent conflation of two ideas: Iago is a dog of savage persistent quality; in his present position, he is a silent Spartan: he means to say nothing.

361. This final comment on Iago and his work is a splendid line, completely expressive of Iago's activity. Lodovico's repudiation of Iago is also the repudiation of him by civilization.

362. [The editor of the new Arden edition is the first to print Q's *lodging* for F's *loading*. He points out that 'lodge' occurs three times in Shakespeare as a verb meaning to 'beat down', always of corn; but he does not remark that it is not the bed which has been beaten down but the corpses upon it.]

SELECT LITERARY CRITICISM

General Impression of the Play

THERE is not another of Shakespeare's plays which is so white-hot with imagination, so free from doubtful or extraneous matter, and so perfectly welded, as *Othello*.

RALEIGH, Shakespeare, 1907

IN *Othello* we are faced with the vividly particular rather than the vague and universal. The play as a whole has a distinct formal beauty: within it we are ever confronted with beautiful and solid forms. The persons tend to appear as warmly human, concrete. They are neither vaguely universalised, as in *King Lear* or *Macbeth*, nor deliberately mechanised, and vitalised by the poet's philosophic plan, as in *Measure for Measure* and *Timon of Athens*, wherein the significance of the dramatic person is dependent almost wholly on our understanding of the allegorical or symbolical meaning. It is true that Iago is here a mysterious, inhuman creature of unlimited cynicism: but the very presence of the concrete creations around, in differentiating him sharply from the rest, limits and defines him. *Othello* is a story of intrigue, rather than a visionary statement.

G. WILSON KNIGHT, The Wheel of Fire, 1930

IN reading *Othello* the mind . . . is more bound down to the spectacle of noble beings caught in the toils from which there is no escape; while the prominence of the intrigue diminishes the sense of the dependence of the catastrophe on character, and the part played by accident in this catastrophe accentuates the feeling of fate. . . . In *Othello*, after the temptation has begun, it is incessant and terrible. The skill of Iago was extraordinary, but so was his good fortune. Again and again, a chance word from Desdemona, a chance meeting of Othello and Cassio, a question which starts to our lips, and which anyone but Othello would have asked, would have destroyed

Iago's plot and ended his life. In their stead, Desdemona drops her handkerchief at the moment most favourable to him, Cassio blunders into the presence of Othello only to find him in a swoon, Bianca arrives precisely when she is wanted to complete Othello's deception and incense his anger to fury. All this, and much more seems to us quite natural, so potent is the art of the dramatist; but it confounds us with a feeling . . . that for these star-crossed mortals . . . there is no escape from fate, and even with a feeling . . . that fate has taken sides with villainy.   A. C. BRADLEY, *Shakespearean Tragedy*, 1904

THE generally recognised peculiarity of *Othello* among the tragedies may be indicated by saying that it lends itself as no other of them does to the approach classically associated with Bradley's name: even *Othello* (it will be necessary to insist) is poetic drama, a dramatic poem, and not a psychological novel written in dramatic form and draped in poetry, but relevant discussion of its tragic significance will nevertheless be mainly a matter of character-analysis. It would, that is, have lent itself uniquely well to Bradley's approach if Bradley had made his approach consistently and with moderate intelligence. Actually, however, the section on *Othello* in *Shakespearean Tragedy* is more extravagant in misdirected scrupulosity than any of the others; it is, with a concentration of Bradley's comical solemnity, completely wrong-headed—grossly and palpably false to the evidence it offers to weigh. Grossly and palpably?—yet Bradley's *Othello* is substantially that of common acceptance. And here is the reason for dealing with it, even though not only Bradley but, in its turn, disrespect for Bradley (one gathers) has gone out of fashion (as a matter of fact he is still a very potent and mischievous influence).

According to the version of *Othello* elaborated by Bradley the tragedy is the undoing of the noble Moor by the devilish cunning of Iago. Othello we are to see as a nearly faultless hero whose strength and virtue are turned against him. Othello and Desdemona, so far as their fate depended on their characters and untampered-with mutual relations, had every ground for expecting the happiness that romantic courtship had promised. It was external evil, the malice of the demi-devil that turned a happy story of romantic love . . . into a tragedy. This . . . is to sentimentalize Shakespeare's tragedy and to displace its centre. . . . It is as extraordinary a history of triumphant sentimental perversity as literary history can show. . . . It is the vindication of Othello's perfect nobility that Bradley is preoccupied with, and we are to see the immediate surrender to Iago as part of that nobility. But to make absolute trust in Iago—trust at Desdemona's expense—a manifestation of perfect nobility is (even if we ignore what it makes of Desdemona) to make Iago a very remarkable person indeed. . . . And it is plain that what we should see in Iago's prompt success is not so much Iago's diabolic intellect as Othello's readiness to respond. Iago's power, in fact, in the temptation-scene is that he represents something that is in Othello—in Othello the husband of Desdemona: the traitor is within the gates. . . . As for the justice of this view that Othello yields with extraordinary promptness to suggestion, with such promptness as to make it plain that the mind that undoes him is not Iago's but his own, it does not seem to need arguing. . . . It is plain, then, that his love is composed very largely of ignorance of self as well as of ignorance of her: however nobly he may feel about it, it isn't altogether what he, and Bradley with him, thinks it is. It may be love, but it can only be in an oddly qualified sense love of her: it must be much more a matter of self-regarding satisfactions—pride, sensual possessiveness, appetite, love of loving—than he suspects. . . .

Contemplating the spectacle of himself, Othello is overcome with the pathos of it. But this is not the part to die in: drawing himself proudly up, he speaks his last words as the stern fighting man who has done the state some service [v. ii. 351–5 quoted]. It is a superb *coup de théâtre*. As, with that double force, a *coup de théâtre*, it is a peculiarly right ending to the tragedy of Othello. . . . However he is likely to remain for many admirers the entirely noble hero, object of a sympathy poignant and complete as he succumbs to the machinations of diabolic intellect.

F. R. LEAVIS, Diabolic Intellect and the Noble Hero
in Scrutiny, Dec. 1937

[This vigorous article has had to be very much abbreviated, but no intentional injustice has been done to the point of view, although it is not that of either of the editors of this edition, who might prefer to turn against Mr. Leavis what he says of Bradley: 'With obtuseness to the tragic significance of Shakespeare's play goes insensibility to his poetry.' Two other extracts, from T. S. Eliot and A. P. Rossiter, on the character of Othello, represent a somewhat similar point of view.]

AMONG the tragedies of Shakespeare *Othello* is supreme in one quality: beauty. Much of its poetry, in imagery, perfection of phrase, and steadiness of rhythm, soaring, yet firm, enchants the sensuous imagination. This kind of beauty *Othello* shares with *Romeo and Juliet* and *Antony and Cleopatra*; it is a corollary of the theme which it shares with them. But *Othello* is also remarkable for another kind of beauty. Except for the trivial scene with the clown, all is immediately relevant to the central issue; no scene requires critical justification. The play has a rare intellectual beauty, satisfying the desire of the imagination for order and harmony between the parts and the whole. Finally, the play has intense moral beauty. It makes an immediate appeal to the moral imagination, in its presentation in the figure of Desdemona of a love which does not alter 'when it alteration finds', but 'bears it out even to the edge of doom'. These three kinds of beauty are interdependent, since all arise from the nature of the hero. Othello's vision of the world expresses itself in what Mr. Wilson Knight has called the 'Othello music'; the 'compulsive course' of his nature dominates the action, driving it straight on to its conclusion; Othello arouses in Desdemona unshakeable love. I am unable, therefore, to accept some recent attempts to find meaning in a play, which has to more than one critic seemed to lack meaning, in its progressive revelation of the inadequacy of the hero's nobility. Such an interpretation disregards the play's most distinctive quality. It contradicts that immediate and overwhelming first impression to which it is a prime rule of literary criticism that all further analysis must conform.

H. GARDNER, *The Noble Moor* (Annual Shakespeare
Lecture of the British Academy, 1955)

Time in the Play

TIME . . . is contracted and expanded like a concertina. For the play's opening and closing the time of the action is the time of its acting; and such an extent of 'natural' time (so to call it) is unusual. But minutes stand for hours over the sighting, docking and discharging—with a storm raging, too!—of the three ships which have carried the characters to Cyprus; the entire night of Cassio's undoing passes uninterruptedly in the speaking space of four hundred lines: and we have, of course, Othello murdering Desdemona within twenty-four hours of the consummation of their marriage, when, if Shakespeare lets us—or let Othello himself—pause to consider, she plainly *cannot* be guilty of adultery.

Freedom with time is, of course, one of the recognized freedoms of Shakespeare's stage; he is expected only to give his exercise of it the slightest dash of plausibility. But in the maturity of his art he learns how to draw positive dramatic profit from it. For this play's beginning he does not, as we have noted, contract time at all. Moreover, he allows seven hundred lines to the three first scenes when he could well have done their business in half the space or less, could even, as Johnson suggests, have left it to be 'occasionally related' afterwards. The profit is made evident when later, by contrast, we find him using contraction of time, and the heightening of tension so facilitated, to disguise the incongruities of the action. For he can do this more easily if he has already familiarised us with the play's characters. And he has done that more easily by presenting them to us in the unconstraint of uncontracted time, asking us for no special effort of make-believe. Accepting what they *are*, we the more readily accept what they *do*.

H. GRANVILLE-BARKER, *Prefaces to Shakespeare*, Fourth Series, 1945

THE chronological contradictions which *Othello* displays when considered realistically go in point of strangeness beyond anything similar in Shakespeare. . . . It comes to this: that Iago's plot can pass undetected only in the press of rapid action, but other elements in the story are plausible only if there is the contrary impression of a considerable efflux of time; and therefore Shakespeare juggles skilfully with his two clocks. But it strikes me that there is something inward about the oddity of the time-scheme in *Othello*. It is as if Iago only wins out because of something fundamentally treacherous in time, some flux and reflux in it which is inimical to life and love. Mr. Middleton Murry has a fine perception here when he sees that *Iago* and *time* are in some sort of imaginative balance. This is one of the things that Iago *is*: an imaginative device for making visible something in the operation of time.

J. I. M. STEWART, *Character and Motive in Shakespeare, c.* 1950

BUT he must have been aware of the contrasts he was creating between the story he had borrowed and the play that would burst upon his audience. The time problem he overrides by putting a paralysing speed and force into the impact of the plot and its *dénouement*—(the *novella*, naturally enough, lingers into weeks and months)—while leaving a *sense* of time to work quite openly in the minds and reactions of the characters. As Bradley observed, this doubleness of time is evident to any spectator who reflects on the action of the play. Physically there is neither time nor occasion for adultery; but this does not stop Othello being convinced that Desdemona 'has the act of shame a thousand times committed', nor Iago asserting that Cassio has talked in his sleep about it. These are apprehensions that only the novel, with its unremittingly quotidian effect, could produce, and Shakespeare has retained them.

JOHN BAYLEY, *The Characters of Love,* 1960

The Characters

Othello

OTHELLO is, in one sense of the word, by far the most romantic figure among Shakespeare's heroes; and he is so partly from the strange life of war and adventure which he has lived from childhood. He does not belong to our world, and he seems to enter it we know not whence—almost as if from wonderland. There is something mysterious in his descent from 'men of royal siege'; in his wanderings in vast deserts and among marvellous peoples; in his tales of magic handkerchiefs and prophetic Sibyls; in the sudden vague glimpses we get of numberless battles and sieges in which he has played the hero and has borne a charmed life; even in chance references to his baptism, his being sold to slavery, his sojourn in Aleppo. . . . There is no love, not that of Romeo in his youth, more steeped in imagination than Othello's. . . .

The sources of danger in this character are revealed but too clearly by the story. In the first place, Othello's mind, for all its poetry, is very simple. He is not observant. His nature tends outward. He is quite free from introspection, and is not given to reflection. Emotion excites his imagination, but it confuses and dulls his intellect. On this side he is the very opposite of Hamlet, with whom, however, he shares a great openness and trustfulness of nature. In addition, he has little experience of the corrupt products of civilised life, and is ignorant of European women.

In the second place, for all his dignity and massive calm (and he has greater dignity than any other of Shakespeare's men), he is by nature full of the most vehement passion. Shakespeare emphasises his self-control, not only by the wonderful pictures of the First Act, but by references to the past. Lodovico, amazed at his violence, exclaims [IV. i. 260–4 quoted]. Iago, who has here no motive for lying, asks [III. iv. 132–5 quoted]. This and other aspects of his character are best exhibited by a single line—one of Shakespeare's miracles—the words by which Othello silences in a moment the night-brawl between his attendants and those of Brabantio:

Keep up your bright swords, for the dew will rust them.

And the same self-control is strikingly shown where Othello endeavours to elicit some explanation of the fight between Cassio and Montano. . . .

Lastly, Othello's nature is all of one piece. His trust, where he trusts, is absolute. Hesitation is almost impossible to him. He is extremely self-reliant, and decides and acts instantaneously. If stirred to indignation, as 'in Aleppo once', he answers with one lightning stroke. Love, if he loves, must be to him the heaven where either he must live or bear no life. If such a passion as jealousy seizes him, it will swell into a well-nigh incontrollable flood.   BRADLEY, op. cit.

How wise it is in Shakespeare not to let Othello alone go blindly into Iago's snares; that all are equally ready to be deceived by him makes Othello's confidence in him not only probable but even excusable. Othello thereby loses the look of folly which would otherwise have been the case.

        OTTO LUDWIG, *Shakespeare-Studien*, 1872

THERE is, in some of the great tragedies of Shakespeare, a new attitude. It is not the attitude of Seneca, but it derived from Seneca; it is slightly different from anything that can be found in French tragedy, in Corneille or in Racine; it is modern, and it culminates, if there is ever any culmination, in the attitude of Nietzsche. I cannot say that it is Shakespeare's 'philosophy'. Yet many people have lived by it; though it may only have been Shakespeare's instinctive recognition of something of theatrical utility. It is the attitude of self-dramatisation assumed by some of Shakespeare's heroes at moments of tragic intensity. . . . But Shakespeare, of course, does it very much better than any of the others, and makes it somehow more integral with the human nature of his characters. It is less verbal, more real. I have always felt that I have never read a more terrible exposure of human weakness—of universal human weakness—than the last great speech of Othello . . . [v. ii. 337–55 quoted]. What Othello seems to me to be doing in making this speech is *cheering himself up*. He is endeavouring to escape reality, he has ceased to think about Desdemona, and is thinking about himself. . . . I do not believe that any writer has ever exposed this *bovarysme*, the human will to see things as they are not, more clearly than Shakespeare.

        T. S. ELIOT, *Shakespeare and the Stoicism of Seneca*, 1927

THESE ten lines [IV. i. 199–208, from 'Cuckold me!' to 'the justice of it pleases'] epitomize the transition from self-pity (mingled with a sense of the pitifulness of his plight) through wounded self-esteem, turning the knife of insult in the wound, to insane self-love taking vengeance and calling it justice. However we read here, we shall carry forward our reading to the interpretation of 'It is the cause, it is the cause . . .'.

The ambivalence of feeling in envy, and even more in sex-jealousy, is too obvious to need demonstration. It is a feeling with an ambiguity like that of the Elizabethan word 'jealous': i.e. it combines desire of owning (called 'love') with aversion, or hatred or loathing, all antitheses of love or attraction. But the ambivalence can be resolved, as jealous people *do* resolve it, by making a virtue of the hatred. Iago does this with *envy*: presenting himself as an honest-spoken undeluded mind, in a self-deceiving hypocritical world. In this he exactly parallels Othello as agent of justice.

[Rossiter has previously distinguished the two senses of 'jealous' in Shakespeare as 'suspicious' in general and sexually jealous, remarking that Othello is 'markedly unsuspicious in listening, while being as markedly apt by nature to jealousy'.]

A. P. ROSSITER, *Angel with Horns*, 1961 (ch. x)

THIS character [Leontes in *The Winter's Tale*] Mr. Coleridge contrasted with that of Othello, whom Shakespeare had portrayed the very opposite to a jealous man: he was noble, generous, open-hearted; unsuspicious and unsuspecting; and who, even after the exhibition of the handkerchief as evidence of his wife's guilt, bursts out in her praise.

From a report of Coleridge's lectures
at Bristol, 1813–14

ALL men that are ruined, are ruined on the side of their natural propensities. There they are unguarded. Above all, good men do not suspect that their destruction is attempted through their virtues.   BURKE

Iago

CONTEMPT is never attributed in Shakespeare but to characters
deep in villainy, as Edmund, Iago, Antonio and Sebastian.

COLERIDGE, *Lectures on Shakespeare*, 1818

PSYCHOLOGICALLY, Iago is a slighted man, powerfully possessed
by hatred against a master who (as he thinks) has kept him
down, and by envy for a man he despises who has been pro-
moted over him. All this comes out in the first fifty lines of the
play. Such a man will naturally have a fantasy life in which
he can hate those enemies the more, that he may revenge himself upon them the more. The fantasy that comes most easily
to him is that of crude copulation; it is his theme-song. In the
opening scene his language to Brabantio is all stallion, and now
his first thought is

> to abuse Othello's ear
> That he is too familiar with his wife.

His next idea is to diet his revenge on Desdemona herself, 'not
out of absolute lust', as he says; but in order to spite Othello,
whom (of course) he now fancies to have 'leap't into his seat'
and debauched Emilia. So strong with him is this vulgar
fantasy that he extends it to Cassio as well,

> For I fear Cassio with my night-cap too.

He indulges these imaginings as a sadist will conjure up whole
histories of imaginary crimes committed by the victim he is
about to chain up and whip, so that he may 'punish' them.
He may not exactly 'believe' in the imputed guilt, but he
pretends to because it gives relish to his performance.

N. COGHILL, *Shakespeare's Professional Skills*, 1964

IAGO has not a point of view at all. He is no realist. In any
sense which matters he is incapable of speaking truth, because
he is incapable of disinterestedness. He can express a high
view or a low view to taste. The world and other people exist
for him only to be used. His definition of growing up is an
interesting one. Maturity to him is knowing how to 'distinguish
between a benefit and an injury'. His famous 'gain'd knowledge' is all generalisations, information docketed and filed.
He is monstrous because, faced with the manifold richness of

experience, his only reaction is calculation and the desire to manipulate. If we try to find in him a view of life, we find in the end only an intolerable levity, a power of being 'all things to all men' in a very unapostolic sense, and an incessant activity. Iago is the man of action in this play, incapable of contemplation, and wholly insusceptible to the holiness of fact. He has, in one sense, plenty of motives. His immediate motives for embarking on the whole scheme are financial, the need to keep Roderigo sweet, and his desire for the lieutenancy. His general motive is detestation of superiority in itself and as recognised by others; he is past master of the sneer. Coleridge has been much criticised for speaking of his 'motiveless malignity', yet the note of glee in Iago confirms Coleridge's moral insight. Ultimately, whatever its proximate motives, malice is motiveless; that is the secret of its power and its horror, why it can go unsuspected, and why its revelation always shocks. H. GARDNER, op. cit.

WHEN Coleridge speaks of 'the motive-hunting of a motiveless malignity' . . . he means really that Iago's malignity does not spring from the causes to which Iago himself refers it, nor from any 'motive' in the sense of an idea present to consciousness.

BRADLEY, op. cit.

Desdemona

DESDEMONA . . . is warmly human. There is a certain domestic femininity about her. She is 'a maiden never bold'. We hear that 'the house affairs' (had Cordelia any?) drew her often from Othello's narrative. But she asks to hear the whole history [I. iii. 155–66 quoted]. The same domesticity, and gentleness is apparent throughout. She talks of 'to-night at supper', or 'to-morrow dinner'; she is typically feminine in her attempt to help Cassio, and her pity for him. This is how she describes her suit to Othello [III. iii. 76–80 quoted]—a speech reflecting a world of sex-contrast. She would bind Othello's head with her handkerchief—that handkerchief which is to become a terrific symbol of Othello's jealousy. The *Othello* world is eminently domestic and Desdemona expressly feminine. We hear of her needlework, her fan, gloves, mask. In the exquisite willow-song scene, we see her with her maid,

Emilia. Emilia gives her 'her nightly wearing'. Emilia says she has laid on her bed the 'wedding-sheets' Desdemona asked for. Then there is the willow-song, whilst Emilia 'unpins' Desdemona's dress. . . . The extreme beauty and pathos of this scene are largely dependent on the domesticity of it. *Othello* is eminently a *domestic tragedy*. But this element in the play is yet to be related to another more universal element. Othello is concretely human, so is Desdemona. Othello . . . is also . . . a symbol of human—especially masculine—'purpose, courage, and valour,' and, in a final judgement, is seen to represent the idea of human faith and value in a very wide sense. Now Desdemona, also very human, with an individual domestic charm and simplicity, is yet also a symbol of woman in general, daring the unknown seas of marriage with the mystery of man. Beyond this, in the far flight of a transcendental interpretation, it is clear that she becomes a symbol of man's ideal, the supreme value of love.

G. WILSON KNIGHT, op. cit.

Love is not love
Which alters when it alteration finds,
Or bends with the remover to remove:
O, no! it is an ever-fixed mark (etc.).

SHAKESPEARE, Sonnet CXVI

THIS unconquerable love . . . is apparent in a slight, thoroughly Shakespearian touch, than which nothing can be more beautiful. When the Willow Song of poor Barbara occurs to her, when her heart is full to overflowing of suffering, she suddenly remarks, apparently without connection, 'Lodovico is a proper man'. The whole scene of her ill-treatment at the hand of her husband, the coming of her relative, like a true knight, to her defence,—all is present to her again and to us. But she will not complain of her loved husband, who has done the worst to her, who has *struck* her. She thinks, as the memory of the bitter scene fills her mind with grief and her eyes with tears, only of him who had so kindly taken her part, 'He is a proper man!' 'And he speaks well!' she adds.

MRS. JAMESON, Characteristics of Women, 1832

Cassio

CASSIO is a handsome, light-hearted, good-natured young fellow, who takes life gaily, and is evidently very attractive and popular. Othello, who calls him by his Christian name, is fond of him; Desdemona likes him much; Emilia at once interests herself on his behalf. He has warm generous feelings, an enthusiastic admiration for the General, and a chivalrous adoration for his peerless wife. But he is too easy-going. He finds it hard to say No; and accordingly, though he is aware that he has a very weak head, and that the occasion is one on which he is bound to run no risk, he gets drunk—not disgustingly so, but ludicrously so. And, besides, he amuses himself without any scruple by frequenting the company of a woman of more than doubtful reputation, who has fallen in love with his good looks. Moralising critics point out that he pays for the first offence by losing his post, and for the second by nearly losing his life. They are quite entitled to do so, though the careful reader will not forget Iago's part in these transactions. But they ought also to point out that Cassio's looseness does not in the least disturb our confidence in him in his relations with Desdemona and Othello. He is loose . . . but we never doubt that there was 'a daily beauty in his life', or that his rapturous admiration of Desdemona was as wholly beautiful a thing as it appears, or that Othello was perfectly safe when in his courtship he employed Cassio to 'go between' Desdemona and himself. It is fortunately a fact in human nature that these aspects of Cassio's character are quite compatible. . . . There is something very loveable about Cassio, with his fresh, eager feelings; his distress at his disgrace and still more at having lost Othello's trust; his hero-worship; and at the end his sorrow and pity which are at first too acute for words.   BRADLEY, op. cit.

Emilia

[After citing III. iii. 290–9, G.B. goes on:] Since there is little subtlety about Emilia, the artlessness of the soliloquy pictures her the better.

> My wayward husband

—her incurious, tolerant, pedestrian mind finds this the aptest term for Iago's restless exigence and uncertain temper—

> hath a hundred times
> Woo'd me to steal it.

—to which point she would not go, and will not, as she answers him, admit to be going now:

> No, faith! she let it drop by negligence.
> And, to the advantage, I being there, took't up.

It is a nice distinction. But she that can make it will have the less difficulty in setting down her honest Iago's share in the business to 'fantasy'. Better to please him, too, and to find herself his 'good wench' for a change from his perpetual chiding (he greets her testily: her first words to him are 'Do not you chide': these jolly fellows, such good company abroad, are often less so at home); and better, by far, she must have found, not to cross him or question him if his 'wit' begins to turn 'the seamy side without,' as it does when, misgiving seizing her, she begs the handkerchief again. 'Tis proper I obey him' is her wifely code, and the mere tone of his present

> Be not acknown on't; I have use for it.
> Go, leave me

must warn her that she will be wise to obey him pretty promptly in this. Yet she must be conscious, too, that there is mischief in the matter. What licit use could he have for the handkerchief? But she chooses to shut her mouth and hold her tongue. . . .

She does not think very highly of the masculine nature, nor express herself very delicately about it [III. iv. 101–4 quoted]. But if lack of imagination leaves her blind to the heights, it lets her ignore the blacker depths about her, too. The Iago of the play's opening, envious and false beneath his honest surface, she will long enough have known for her husband; but of the demi-devil committed to Cassio's death and Desdemona's, and to Othello's ruin, how should she have an inkling?

H. GRANVILLE-BARKER, op. cit.

EMILIA's silence while her mistress lived is fully explicable in terms of her character. She shares with her husband the generalising trick, and is well used to domestic scenes. The jealous, she knows,

> are not ever jealous for the cause,
> But jealous for they are jealous.

If it was not the handkerchief, it would be something else. Why disobey her husband and risk his fury? It would not do any good. This is what men are like. But Desdemona dead sweeps away all such generalities and all caution. At this sight, Emilia, though 'the world is a huge thing', finds that there is a thing she will not do for it. By her heroic disregard for death she gives the only 'proof' there can be of Desdemona's innocence: the testimony of faith.   H. GARDNER, op. cit.

THE virtue of Emilia is such as we often find, worn loosely, but not cast off, easy to commit small crimes, but quickened and alarmed at atrocious villainies.

S. JOHNSON, edition of *Shakespeare*, 1765

EMILIA has won herself a place in the play's tragic heaven.

H. GRANVILLE-BARKER, op. cit.

The Othello Music

WHEN Othello is represented as enduring loss of control, he is, as Macbeth or Lear never is, ugly, idiotic; but, when he has full control, he attains an architectural stateliness of quarried speech, a silver rhetoric of a kind unique in Shakespeare [v. ii. 1–15 cited]. This is the noble Othello music: rich in sound and phrase, stately. Each word solidifies as it takes its place in the pattern. This speech well illustrates the Othello style: the visual or tactile suggestion—'whiter skin of hers than snow', 'smooth as monumental alabaster'; the slightly over-decorative phrase, 'flaming minister'; the momentary juxtaposition of humanity and the vast spaces of the night, the 'chaste stars'; the concrete imagery of 'thou cunning'st pattern of excelling nature', and the lengthy comparison of life with light; the presence of simple forward-flowing clarity of dignified statement and of simile in place of the superlogical welding of thought with molten thought in the more compressed, agile, and concentrated poetry of *Macbeth* and *King Lear*; and the fine outstanding single word, 'Promethean'.   G. WILSON KNIGHT, op. cit.

The Imagery

OTHELLO and Iago have entirely different attitudes towards their images. Iago is consciously looking for those which best suit his purpose. With Othello, however, the images rise naturally out of his emotions. They come to him easily and unconsciously whenever he is talking. He is a character endowed with a rich imagination; . . . Iago, on the contrary, is not a person with an imaginative mind; his attitude towards the world is rational and speculative. We find fewer images in his language than in Othello's. When he is alone, he uses scarcely any imagery, a fact which proves that the use of imagery is not natural to him, but rather a conscious and studied device by which he wishes to influence those to whom he is speaking. . . . Iago's images scarcely ever refer to himself, whereas Othello in his images constantly has himself in mind. Iago likes the form of general statement; he places a distance between himself and his images. He does not care to identify himself with what he says: he would rather have his utterances understood as being as objective, neutral and general as possible. In Othello's language, however, the personal pronoun 'I' is predominant; he is almost always talking of himself, his life, and his feelings. [Clemen cites II. i. 182–7 and III. iii. 454–61.] In these cases, as in others, with the innocence and frankness characteristic of strong natures who live within themselves, he always takes himself as the point of departure. . . .

[After citing I. iii. 328–334, I. iii. 349–51, and II. iii. 260–2, Clemen goes on:] Shakespeare lets Iago clothe his comparisons here in euphuistic style. This shows how conventional stylistic patterns are employed in the tragedies as a means of individual characterisation. For precisely this euphuistic parallelism corresponds to the cool, and, at the same time, hypocritical nature of Iago. It would be wholly foreign to the spontaneous and unconscious Othello to force imagery into such an artificial mould of parallelisms and symmetrically constructed periods. The euphuistic style is an intellectual, hyper-conscious child of the brain, combining skilful ingenuity with calculation. All these elements are characteristic of Iago himself.

The objects named by Iago belong to a lower and purely material world, whereas the things alive in Othello's imagination generally belong to a higher sphere. Iago's imagery teems with repulsive animals of a low order; with references to eating and drinking and bodily functions, and with technical and commercial terms. In Othello's language, however, the elements prevail—the heavens, the celestial bodies, the wind and the sea—the forces of nature, everything light and moving that corresponds best to his nature. At moments of intense emotion his imagery links heaven and hell together, bearing out his inner relation to the cosmic powers, and revealing the enormous dimensions and power of his imaginative conceptions. Hyperbole is therefore more often found in Othello's imagery than in that used by other Shakespearian heroes. [Clemen cites II. i. 185–7 as an example of 'the breadth of Othello's imaginative world'.]

It is . . . characteristic of the way in which the imagery portrays Othello's inner alteration, that from the third scene of the third act on, Othello's fantasy is filled with images of repulsive animals such as were up to that point peculiar to Iago. Iago's endeavour to undermine and poison Othello's imagination by his own gloomy and low conceptions has been successful. [This kind of imagery is, however, not present in v. ii. 'Editors']

W. H. CLEMEN, *The Development of Shakespeare's Imagery* (translated) 1951

IAGO has only his fair proportion of diabolic imagery, yet we undoubtedly gain the impression that in this play the theme of hell, as it were, originates with him and is passed to Othello later as Iago succeeds in dominating his mind. Statistics show this impression to be well founded. In Act I Iago has eight diabolic images and Othello none; in Act II he has six and Othello one. The change comes in Act III, where Iago drops to three and

Othello rises to nine. In Act IV Iago has only one while Othello has ten, and in Act V Iago has none and Othello six. It all begins then with Iago.

It appears that to Shakespeare Cinthio's ensign suggested (a) the contemporary atheist-Machiavel, and (b) the Devil himself. It seems to follow that Shakespeare thought of the 'new man' (with his contempt for traditional morality and religion) as a disintegrating force seeking to break down the social order that is a part of cosmic order—as, in fact, an instrument (no doubt unconscious) of the Devil in his constant efforts to reduce cosmos to chaos. This would be a very natural attitude for a conservative Elizabethan, and to express this attitude is one main function—a general function—of the diabolic imagery in *Othello*. Iago is a 'demi-devil' (v. ii. 300), worse than an ordinary devil, a bastard one, and his philosophy is a 'divinity of hell' (cf. *The Tempest*, v. i. 273).

s. l. bethell, 'The diabolic Images in *Othello*'
in *Shakespeare Survey*, vol. 5, 1952

The Prose of the Play

Iago dominates most of the prose in *Othello*, either speaking it himself, or causing others to speak it. It is one manifestation—and a very important one—of the character Iago has created as a disguise for himself: 'honest Iago', the blunt soldier, who speaks truth without counting the cost, and who cannot prevail on his conscience to let him remain silent. . . . But prose is not Iago's true language; whenever he is alone, he drops into the verse of the Machiavellian villain, the verse of Richard III or of Edmund. Iago's bluntness is the deceiving candour Cornwall pretends to find in Kent. . . .

Othello's mad prose and trance are the symbolic and literal manifestations of his breakdown. He is completely beside himself. When he recovers, he is made to watch (but not to hear) Iago's conversations with Cassio and with Bianca. All Othello's interjections are in prose; and one must consider the effect of hearing such prose from a man, who, until now, has spoken only verse of a remarkable brilliance and splendour.

m. crane, *Shakespeare's Prose*, 1951

APPENDIX

Shakespeare's Use of his Source

Othello is the only one of Shakespeare's four great tragedies to be based on a more or less contemporary story dealing with a more or less contemporary world. The source, except for a few details, is a tale in a collection of stories called *Hecatom-mithi* (A Hundred Tales) published in Venice in 1565, and written by Giraldo Cinthio. There is some reason to suppose that Shakespeare read this in the original.

In the Italian, none of the characters have names except Desdemona (Disdemona), whose name signifies 'misfortune'. Othello is simply 'il Moro', and Cassio (the Captain) and Iago (the Ensign) are described in terms of occupation. The blankly anonymous nature of the participants is only part and parcel of the unimaginative nature of the story.

Roderigo and Bianca are complete inventions by Shakespeare. Desdemona, who is rather insipid in the original, and Othello, who lacks dignity, are transformed. Cassio remains much as he was, though his actions are different, and he becomes human, not merely a Captain. The story makes no bones about Iago: he is introduced straight away as a scoundrel of very handsome appearance. His motives are not ambiguous: he is not concerned with promotion, but, having fallen deeply in love with Desdemona, and having had no success, conceives that Cassio is his rival, and henceforward hates both bitterly. Shakespeare has suppressed his three-year old daughter, who is the means whereby he gets hold of the handkerchief: as Desdemona dandles the child, he filches the handkerchief.

Emilia, in the story, is described as a beautiful and honourable young woman, who is greatly loved by Desdemona, so that they spend most of the day together. She is, however, aware of the plot to kill the lady, for Iago had wished to use her to further it. She is too afraid of him to warn Desdemona; and so, when Desdemona, troubled by her husband's changed demeanour, asks her to find out from Iago what the matter may be, she can only give her general good advice about her conduct. 'All these events' (i.e. Iago's plot), says Cinthio at the end, 'were related by the Ensign's wife, who knew about the whole thing.'

So much for the characters. As for the action, the transformation of story into play is a splendid illustration of Shakespeare's dramaturgy, as well as of his moral imagination. The whole of the First Act is his. In the tale, Othello and Desdemona marry against her parents' wishes, but live in happiness for some time. Shakespeare is responsible for making Desdemona motherless, for making her father love Othello and invite him to the house, for making Cassio a party to his wooing, and for the whole brutal arousing of Brabantio. The elopement, coinciding with the Turkish crisis, is not in Cinthio. There are no Turks, and no military urgency, and therefore no Council scene by night, in the story. Nor is there a storm on the way to Cyprus: all the characters travel in the same ship, and arrive without trouble.

From the landing in Cyprus to the plot to murder Desdemona, Shakespeare follows his source more closely, but there are still many differences. Cassio's degradation is not arranged by Iago: he is cashiered for striking a soldier in anger. Shakespeare's riskiest scene (IV. i), where Othello most obviously appears a gull, has only a slight basis in Cinthio. Since the story has no Bianca, her appearance in the play, flaunting the handkerchief, serves as apparently a crushing proof of Desdemona's lightness. As in the play, so in the story, the handkerchief is planted in Cassio's bedroom, but Cassio, having recognized it as Desdemona's, tries to return it to her by the back door of Othello's house when he knows him to be absent. Here the story makes reference to Iago's luck, which is so conspicuous in the play: at the very moment of Cassio's knock, Othello returns and hears it, looks out of the window, asks who is there, and runs downstairs. Cassio runs away, but Othello suspects that it is he, and that his wife knows about it. This episode, no doubt, is the source of Cassio's apparently furtive disappearance at the approach of Othello in the play (III. iii. 29–40), which gives Iago his first opportunity with Othello. Later on, in the story, Cassio gives the handkerchief to a fine sempstress, lodging in his house, to copy, and Iago leads Othello past the window where she is accustomed to do her delicate embroidery, when Othello sees it in her hand. Of the transformation that has been made here, there are several things to say: one is, that story-time has been made into drama-time; another, that the back door, the running downstairs, and the motiveless suburban suspicion are alien to the tone of the play; and that Shakespeare's invention, Bianca, brings to dramatic life what is flat in the story.

Since there is no Roderigo in the source, the attack on Cassio is much less exciting. Iago makes the attack alone, after being heavily bribed. This attempt on Cassio is not connected in time with Desdemona's murder. Shakespeare makes her mourning for Cassio's supposed fate occur on her own death-bed, when it is misunderstood by Othello as evidence of her guilty love. In Cinthio, her grief is one of the matters which anger Othello, and leads him to plot her death with Iago.

It is here that Shakespeare rejects his source most decisively. Iago devises a plot which involves neither knife nor poison, and which will leave both unsuspected. The plebeian tone of the source is worth some detail. Othello and Desdemona are in bed together. Iago, in his hiding-place near by, makes some pre-arranged noise. Othello tells her to get out of bed and see what it is. She does so, and is sandbagged by Iago. She does not die immediately, but calls to Othello, who gets out of bed to stand over her and tell her that this is what wives who cuckold their husbands deserve. While she prays, Iago finishes her off, Othello watching. They put her body on the bed, break her skull, and bring down a beam from the rotten timbers of the house upon her head. After this careful arrangement of innocence, Othello runs into the street, proclaiming the dreadful accident which has lost him his beloved wife.

The rest of the source is on the same level. Cinthio's Moor, for all his later barbarity and vulgarity, had loved Desdemona, and he now begins to hate Iago. He cannot have him done away with for fear of the inexorable justice of Venice, but he deprives him of his rank in the Army. Thereupon, Iago tells Cassio of such parts of the plot as exonerate himself, including the lie that it was Othello who wounded him. Cassio, now equipped with a wooden leg, as the result of Iago's bungled attack, brings a charge before the Signiory, Othello is arrested, and brought to Venice and tortured. He will not speak, is condemned to banishment, and is finally killed by Desdemona's relatives. Iago continues his contrivances in other directions, is eventually convicted of perjury, and dies after torture. The story ends 'Thus did God avenge the innocence of Desdemona.' It is out of this sordid and vulgar, though in some respects pathetic matter, that Shakespeare makes his last scene.

Nothing is more striking, among the differences between story and play, than the prudential and unheroic behaviour of the personages of the former. In Cinthio, Iago needs a good sum of money to be persuaded to kill Cassio; his pretence of virtuous indignation, and his assumption of indifference to all but justice for Othello, are Shakespeare's invention. He is vulgarized by the source, made more psychologically unusual and also intellectual by the play. The Emilia of the source, though she is loved by Desdemona, and apparently loves her, is aware of her husband's designs, but is afraid to betray him. It is all the more puzzling, therefore, that she is said to be honourable. In the play, Emilia's honour is of a different sort, though she pretends to nothing socially, and not much morally. Othello is the most vulgar of the lot: he takes good care to safeguard himself over Desdemona's murder, and is afraid, later on, when he has repented of his crime, to kill Iago.

All this is part of the transformation of melodrama and police-news into tragedy, and of the realistic into the heroic and noble. Othello in the play is not concerned with the consequence but with the 'cause'; and Emilia at the end becomes a figure of sacrificial love, a fitting companion of her mistress, whom she does not willingly betray.

Finally, Cinthio makes little of Othello's race and colour. He mentions his colour only once, and this is when Iago tells Othello that perhaps Desdemona wishes Cassio to be

reinstated because she is now bored with his own blackness.
Shakespeare makes more of the matter, but never through the
mouths of unprejudiced speakers, unless we may count
Roderigo's apparently casual exclamation

> What a full fortune doth the thick-lips owe!

(i. i. 66) as, in this case only, a neutral comment. Of more far-
reaching consequence are Brabantio's shock and anger at the
marriage, which eventually broke his heart. The question does
not arise for Othello until Iago has made it one ('Haply, for
I am black': iii. iii. 263). The only reference to race in Cinthio
is made by Desdemona herself, when she tells Othello, 'You
Moors are so hot, that the merest trifle excites you to anger and
revenge.' Shakespeare's Desdemona says almost the opposite
of this:

> I think the sun where he was born
> Drew all such humours from him.   (iii. iv. 30–1)

Nevertheless, Cinthio seems to have a moral to his story,
which he puts into Desdemona's mouth when she thinks she
has lost Othello's love, and tells Emilia that the ladies of Italy
will take her as an example not to marry a man whom Nature,
Heaven, and manner of life separate us from. These sentiments
are never part of Shakespeare's Desdemona, but are divided,
in effect, between Brabantio, where they are sincere, Iago, and
Othello, after Iago has contaminated him. Shakespeare and
Cinthio come closest together when Cinthio tells us that she
fell in love 'attracted not by feminine appetite, but by the
qualities of the Moor' (which he singularly fails to bring out).
This is Shakespeare's cue for Desdemona's 'I saw Othello's
visage in his mind'.